Classroom and Curriculum in Australia

A series edited by Malcolm Skilbeck which sets out to
remedy the lack of Australian material in an important
and fast-growing area—*Curriculum*. The intention is to
put the theory and the research on numerous aspects
of Curriculum firmly into the *classroom* setting, and to
provide teachers with material which will help them
understand a complex field.

The series will include books on:

Individual Differences (published)
Teachers as Curriculum Evaluators
Society and Curriculum in Australia
Curriculum Development and the School
Basic Curriculum

Classroom and Curriculum in Australia: No 1

Series Editor: Malcolm Skilbeck, Director,
Curriculum Development Centre

Individual Differences

Guidelines for Educational Practice

G.W. BASSETT
Professor of Education, University of Queensland

with
BETTY H. WATTS
Professor of Special Education, University of Queensland
and
BARRY NURCOMBE
Professor of Child and Adolescent Psychiatry, University of Vermont

SYDNEY
GEORGE ALLEN & UNWIN
LONDON   BOSTON

First published in 1978 by
George Allen & Unwin Australia Pty Ltd
Cnr Bridge Road and Jersey Street
Hornsby NSW 2077

National Library of Australia
Cataloguing-in-Publication entry:

Bassett, George William, 1910–.
  Individual differences.

  (Classroom and curriculum in Australia; 1).
  Index.
  Bibliography.
  ISBN 0 86861 120 4
  ISBN 0 86861 128 x Paperback.

  1. Educational sociology. 2. Educational
  psychology. I. Watts, Betty H., joint author.
  II. Nurcombe, Barry, joint author. III. Title.
  (Series).

370.193

Library of Congress Catalog Card Number: 78–55231

Set in 10.2 on 11 Times by Academy Press, Brisbane
Printed in Hong Kong

'A society which places such great value on education and schooling that it requires the individual to attend school for long periods of time must find the means to make education attractive and meaningful to the individual learner.'

Benjamin S. Bloom

Human Characteristics and School Learning

Thanks are expressed to Lloyd Logan who read the manuscript and made many helpful suggestions and to Melanie Young who prepared the index.

Contents

34.37 Motivation
53-57

Foreword

Professor Bassett is a writer whose work I have always enjoyed reading. I like his clarity—the direct style of a man who knows what he is writing about. I admire his humanity (that comes through so clearly from the printed word). I applaud his concern for the improvement of educational practice.

G.W. Bassett must be considered an Australian authority on the question of individual differences. *Each One Is Different*, a book arising from a conference that was convened by the Australian Council for Educational Research a decade and a half ago, and directed and reported by him, has surely assisted a generation of teachers and teacher educators to serve primary schoolchildren more sensitively and responsibly.

Headmasters For Better Schools, written in the same period, and at a time when I had assumed administrative control of teacher education in South Australia, influenced me greatly. Its simple statement of the characteristics of a good school, and its complementary message for the good administrator, taught me that an Education Department and all its trappings existed only to serve the welfare of each individual child in its care. It was one of the influences that moved me to issue the Freedom and Authority Memorandum—a charter for the operation of South Australian schools.

Most of the books in which Professor Bassett has been the senior author or contributing editor have centred on the primary school. This latest volume provides equally relevant guidelines over a wide spectrum from early childhood to adolescence. Yet its field is clearly defined. It does not deal with the specialised differences that occur among blind, deaf and spastic children; its concern is with 'ordinary' children in 'ordinary' schools—if we can ever again call children 'ordinary' after reading this book.

The introduction is a masterly summary of the complex issues that teachers and teacher educators must be aware of in the process of guiding human growth. To me it provides a complete justification in teacher education for studies in psychology, philosophy, sociology, logic, politics, biology and anthropology, as well as sheer pedagogy—but only if these can be related to classroom practices, school organisation, curriculum, and evaluation, in the way that the author does in Part Two of this book. Professor Bassett has examined the many-sided problems involved in catering for individual differences, and has related these to social, political and educational purposes, to values such as

ix

equality of opportunity, democracy, and a sense of community, to vocational planning, and to moral responsibility.

Part One is contributed entirely by co-authors. In three cohesive chapters they provide sociological and psychological perspectives of human growth and individual differences. They do so scientifically and in depth.

Betty Watts deals with personality differences from the viewpoint of the social psychologist. The factors that influence the personality of children—heredity, sex, social class, family, peer group, and self—are considered sensitively and sensibly, with teacher-child interaction and classroom conditions always in mind.

Barry Nurcombe discusses the relation between emotional disorder and learning. He sees the teacher as the key person in identifying children with emotional instability or learning handicap, or both. His chapter is helpful to the teacher in the difficult task of recognising and understanding such problems, and in arranging referral and treatment.

Betty Watts also contributes the final chapter in Part One, linking cognitive and linguistic considerations to the personality issues she has previously raised, and warning of the danger inherent in viewing one characteristic of a child in isolation.

Collectively, then, Part One is an up-to-date discussion of children's abilities—their functioning and significance for the classroom—not only in middle class mainstream culture, but in other groups such as Aboriginal children and the children of non-English-speaking parents.

Part Two epitomises Professor Bassett's fundamental approach. He does not write merely for the sake of publishing, but to contribute something of practical benefit to teachers. All that was discussed in the earlier part of the book is now drawn together to assist teachers in meeting the individual needs of children. Every facet of the school is touched upon—organisation, government, discipline, guidance, authority, curricula, human relationships, assessment, and evaluation. Who but Professor Bassett would have thought of using the Guba-Getzels human relations model to expound the classroom treatment of individual differences?

Yet this comprehensive advice from the scholarship, experience and wisdom of the authors is given modestly. There is no attempt to impose their findings upon teachers as prescribed principles, but rather as guidelines—simple, clear, and precise—for use by teachers who are still free to inject their own kind of genius into their tasks. For Professor Bassett sees each teacher as an individual, no less unique than each child.

All in all, this is a compelling book for anyone concerned with the general and educational welfare of the young. It is relevant to all who seek a deeper understanding of individual children—classroom teacher, counsellor, curriculum designer, even the administrator. For the good administrator of a school or of a system has the same goal in his administration as Professor Bassett has in his publications—the better development of each Australian child.

A.W. Jones
Director-General of Education
South Australia, 1970–77
University Fellow
University of New England
Armidale, N.S.W.

Introduction:
Individual Differences and Their
Significance for Education

Our concern in this book is with individual differences among school
children, and the significance of these differences for the way in which
schools are organised and conducted. An essential part of this task is
to determine the nature and extent of these differences that have a
bearing on education. This is dealt with in Chapters 1, 2 and 3, where
authoritative evidence is presented regarding the intellectual and social
differences and the personality traits of children. With this empirical
evidence as a basis, the task of drawing implications for educational
practice can be approached with more assurance. This is done in Part
Two.

A knowledge of the facts of individual differences, however, is not
enough in itself on which to base the educational judgements that need
to be made. Questions of value and purpose are also involved. The
teacher needs criteria by which to assess the significance of the different
abilities, attitudes, interests and actions of his pupils, and he needs an
educational philosophy to guide his handling of them. There is a world
of difference between a teacher whose purpose is to mould pupils,
whether in his own image or in conformity with some external standard,
and one who accepts the child as he is, and helps him to develop in
his own unique way. There is a world of difference between teachers
who see individual differences only in quantitative terms with pupils
as points on a frequency scale, and those who recognise also qualitative
differences.

The teacher must look to the philosopher as well as to the scientist,
and blend what is made valid by accepted values with what is justified
empirically and logically by a rational body of knowledge.

Three perspectives on individual differences thus become apparent
at the outset—that of the scientist who works to establish the facts
about pupils and their actions, that of the philosopher who looks
critically at the meanings that can be ascribed to personal and social
behaviour, and that of the educationist who attempts to establish a form
of intervention to guide human growth and development that is both
defensible and effective. These three perspectives are examined in

1

general terms as an introduction to the more detailed discussions of succeeding chapters.

The Scientific Perspective

Individual differences among children are studied in a number of disciplines: educational psychology, social psychology, psychological medicine, anthropology, sociology, medical sciences, physical education, and others. In this book the main evidence presented is drawn from psychological and sociological areas.

It must be stressed at the outset that there is no body of research-based theory dealing with the pedagogy of individual differences. How differences among students are handled depends on the judgement of the teacher, taking into account the diverse conditions regarding curriculum, facilities and organisation that apply. His knowledge of individual differences may be scientific; but the use he makes of them is practical. This point may be made clearer by a distinction between fundamental and operational research made by Hardie.[1] *Fundamental research*, as Hardie uses the term, yields knowledge that can explain and predict; *operational research* provides knowledge that can be used as a basis of judgement. For the psychologist, or other behavioural scientist, research on individual differences may be fundamental in the sense that its purpose is to predict or explain behaviour. For the teacher the same knowledge is operational, in being useful as a basis for action. It does not determine his behaviour, but it can guide it.

Because of this element of judgement in educational practice there is an obvious need for evaluation studies which test how well a particular plan has worked, and whether there are unintended outcomes. This is an important area of operational research in education, and has produced a great deal of research effort, particularly in the production of tests, questionnaires, rating scales, interview schedules, etc., and in the variety of devices for scoring them and analysing the results.

As has been stated, the evidence on the nature of individual differences in this book is drawn from psychological and sociological areas. The concern of these sciences is with the orderly description and explanation of human characteristics, and their treatment of individual differences is in line with this scientific spirit. They seek to identify differences, to trace their origin and development, to assess their strength, persistence, distribution and modifiability, and to clarify their relationship to such key processes as learning, creativity, and moral and social development.

The neutrality of the behavioural scientist and his striving for objectivity in research and theory should not be overstressed. Clearly he must observe the canons of science if he is to make any progress, nevertheless he works very close to normative concepts such as *physical health, mental health, adjustment, cognitive efficiency, normality* and *self-realisation*. It is important that the inherent normative nature of these concepts is explicitly recognised by both research worker and those who look to him for guidance so that a too facile relationship between the characteristics of children's behaviour and educational objectives is avoided. An example may make this point clearer. Observation and experiment may reveal that particular children show a strong need for social approval from their peers, and perhaps also from significant adults such as parents and teachers. However, to interpret this fact in itself as a basis for an educational programme to reinforce social approval may be dubious indeed. Child-rearing practices in a cultural group certainly create particular emotional needs among children, but the question of satisfying these needs (which is an educational question) may need to be assessed in terms of criteria different from those applied in the training experience. It may be, for example, that particular child-rearing practices create an undesirable degree of dependence, and that school influences should attempt rather to transform or counter this, than to reinforce it. The criterion *an undesirable degree of dependence* among children is not to be arrived at simply by observing them, but also by reference to social values about patterns of child behaviour. The converse of this comment is, of course, also true. An accurate knowledge of children's actual behaviour may with advantage temper a concept of discipline derived from traditional social values. However, if educational objectives are too readily identified with the scientist's findings about children—particularly those forms of behaviour that are suffused with cultural influences—the educationist may easily be caught in a circle of repetitive influence, conditions, as they are, dictating their own reinforcement and perpetuation.

A major question for the educationist is the degree to which differences are inborn or learned, and its implications for the complex interactional pattern of congenital and environmental influences in behaviour. If behaviour is fixed by congenital factors, the teacher's role, to that extent, is limited; if it can be modified by appropriate environmental influences, his role, correspondingly, is more influential. Are the scientist's findings optimistic in being compatible with a substantial modification of behaviour, or deterministic in setting definite limits to it? Do they suggest a fixed range of differences that the teacher must accept as determining what he can hope to achieve, or a range that can be enlarged or reduced by effective teaching? The answers to these questions, no doubt, depend to some extent on the particular differences being considered, be they physical skills, interests, intellectual abilities, physical characteristics, social behaviour and so on. All are necessary for an adequate coverage of educational practice.

Undoubtedly the major contribution to our understanding of individual differences has been made by the psychologist, and within psychological research on individual differences there has been a strong emphasis on psychometric methods. Broadly speaking, these methods have involved the identification of significant dimensions of behaviour, the quantitative assessment of them in selected samples by various instruments such as tests, questionnaires and rating scales, the statistical analysis of the results obtained to establish group norms and to derive other useful secondary data. The ingenuity shown in the development of evaluative instruments for measuring a wide range of variables has been impressive, as have been the statistical methods employed in the analysis of the data. Undoubtedly our knowledge of variability among children has benefited from the psychometric movement.

There are, however, inherent problems in measuring human behaviour which have not always been solved in a completely convincing way, and which should put the teacher on guard in interpreting quantitative data. First, there is the difficulty about the nature of the units and the scales used. Behaviour is quantified according to some arithmetical scheme, and the data obtained are manipulated by mathematical methods, addition, multiplication, etc. But it is doubtful if the numbers so obtained do have the same property as cardinal numbers. Almost certainly zero has no significance in a scale that measures human behaviour, and it is doubtful if the intervals along the scale measure equal increments. For example, in a percentage scale the measurement of difference between five points of the lower end of the scale cannot be assumed to be identical with a similar interval at the top part of the scale. It would be very easy unwittingly to construct a kind of behavioural ruler, calibrated in unequal intervals. Experts in psychological and educational measurement have grappled with this problem of scaling, and have invented ingenious remedies in particular cases, but the problem recurs.

There is also an inherent element of doubt regarding the validity of tests in relation to behaviour being investigated. Validity is established in various ways by careful workers in the field of test contruction, by securing agreement among competent people as to the correctness of the substance of the test, by correctly predicting a theoretical relationship involving the behaviour being tested, and by other methods; but the doubt remains.

Most serious of all, however, is the uncertainty about the identity and constancy of the behaviour elicited by tests for particular persons and at particular times. A person's performance in a test is part of a pattern of behaviour which is, to a significant degree, peculiar to him. The more complex the behaviour in question, the more likely it is that it mirrors personal experience. It is thus likely that the behaviour being measured in the case of one person is not the same as that in another, even though the test scores for each are the same. The mathematical identity may be no more than a chance phenomenon, the same test responses deriving from a pattern of different elements. Generalisations about the behaviour of different people thus need to be made with great caution. By the same token a person's test score may not have the same significance at different times because of the intervention of new experiences which affect it. This could be a simple matter of unreliability of the test, as, for example, when a person at one time performs better than another because he feels better, or because he just happens to have studied the right material. But it could also indicate a substantive change in the person from one time to another through experience. These features of test variability are of great importance for the educator.

The search for basic elements in terms of which differences among children may be expressed, and the derivation of appropriate units of measurement for them are obviously of major importance in the scientific study of children, but equally important and perplexing is an understanding of the process of development whereby these elements interact and combine to form the complex elements of behaviour actually encountered by teachers, such as reading achievement, written expression, accuracy and effectiveness of speech, good behaviour, reliability, industry, co-operation, creativity, etc. In speaking of personality, for example, we often resort to metaphors such as that of a *cable,* composed of strands that can be unravelled, or to which additional strands may be added. Another figure is of a *profile*, expressing in visual form the number and size of constituent elements. The cable figure conveys a longitudinal view, the profile, a cross-sectional one; but neither does full justice to the complexity of the growth process. This process is best described as one of integration, the formation of a unique product by the fusion of compatible elements. A child's progress in one activity is influenced by and influences his progress in another. His attitudes and values are interlocked with his skills and aptitudes. His drives to action are related to his ideas, his performances and judgements. To understand the person at any stage of development involves insight into an incredibly complex matrix of interwoven elements. Artists and writers attempt to capture it by intuitive acts of imagination which they express in their characterisations; scientists use descriptive and explanatory terms; and each must necessarily accept some limitation and approximation.

The contrast between the person as congeries of separate elements and as a unique coherent whole is expressed well by M.V.C. Jeffreys in the following quotation:

> We can 'know' a human being in what may be called 'dossier' terms; we can measure his I.Q. and record his height, weight, colour of hair and eyes and other particulars by which he could be identified. And we can 'know' our best friend in a different and intimate way, though we probably are ignorant of his I.Q., or even eye colour and such other data as the police would require if he were missing . . . the categories used to get 'objective' precision are such as to let the substance of the thing escape and leave us with an empty formula . . .[2]

The claim that the educationist makes on the scientist is to secure some precision in his understanding of the differences that distinguish his pupils, without letting the 'substance of the thing' escape.

The approach made in Chapters 1, 2 and 3, which deal with psychological aspects of individual differences, is intended to meet this claim. These chapters are quantitative where this is necessary, but predominantly are descriptive, explanatory and analytic, with the individual as a whole at the focus of attention.

The Philosophical-Political Perspective

According to Kneller,[3] philosophy as an activity has three modes or styles: the speculative, the prescriptive and the analytic. The speculative mode stresses the synthesis of ideas; it is a search for order, wholeness, coherence. The prescriptive mode seeks standards and criteria of judgement. It is concerned with questions of value, preference, objectivity and priority. Analytic philosophy concentrates on the elucidation of words and concepts, exposing inadequacies, inaccuracies and inconsistencies of thought. It is concerned more with criticism than with formulation of theories and systems of thought. The three approaches need not be exclusive, but rather express a particular emphasis. All three are clearly relevant in considering the question of individual differences in school or in society, because social and political philosophies, value judgements and logical analysis are all involved.

Equally clearly the facts of human variability are of profound significance to political philosophy both for their relevance to the personal life of individuals and to their part as citizens. The questions that arise are legion, and only some can be referred to here.

A problem of perennial interest has been the role of the citizen and its compatibility with individuality. Clearly, if there is to be an associated life, it must be regulated in various ways which require some limitation on individual autonomy. Some social controls are formalised in the legal-political system; others derive from social processes such as economic needs, social-class expectations, religious obligations, and conventional manners.

Modern societies seem able to offer some scope for the exercise of human differences through the multiplicity of work opportunities, leisure, travel, entertainment, political activity, sophisticated mass-communication media, and the like. But it is the negative aspects of modern society that obtrude: the frequent breakdown of community life in urban centres and the inadequate substitute for it in the suburbs, the sense of political impotence of the ordinary person with regard to government at all levels, the pervasiveness of materialistic values in business and industry, and increasingly in the professions as well, the lack of satisfaction in work and leisure, and the widespread unconcern about suffering and poverty abroad.

This theme of man-in-society in some form or other has occupied the attention of Western philosophers from Plato to the present day, and has produced a host of analytical studies as well as speculative utopian designs for the proper nurture of mankind—those of Plato, More, Butler, Hegel, Rousseau, and Marx, to name a few.

The emphasis in these ideal societies is on forms of social control particularly on government. A recent philosophical movement, existentialism, expresses, rather, the central importance of the individual. It is, in a sense, a philosophy of protest against the domination of the State. Although it generally recognises the nineteenth century Danish philosopher Kirkegaard as its founder, it embraces a wide range of views, including theological (both Christian and Jewish), atheistic, literary, and philosophic. Perhaps best known of the existentialists, at least to educators, are Sartre, the French man of letters, and Buber, the Jewish theologian. What unites existentialists is their concern with man as man. In different ways they stress his need for freedom as a basis for development, the necessity for responsible choice in matters of morality, free from arbitrary constraints. They stress also existentialism as a special form of knowledge, different from the abstract concepts and models of scientific thought, and deriving from direct experience with its sensory and affective qualities. They do not, of course, reject scientific knowledge, but they believe that it needs to be balanced with a subjective, private view of phenomena and people.

Existentialism clearly has an important message for the teacher concerned with individual differences, and we shall return later to consider its educational implications in more detail.

Few societies are free in the sense in which existentialists crave for freedom. Most democracies, however, plan for freedom in various ways. Politicians, as well as political theorists, do not always agree on measures likely to promote the welfare of citizens. They do, however, base their programmes on the fact that people differ, even though they do not always appreciate the subtlety and magnitude of the differences. Among many issues relevant to social planning three are singled out for comment here as having a crucial bearing on education. These are (1) the problem of making opportunity equal, (2) the need for vocational planning, and (3) educating citizens for effective participation in democratic government.

Equality of Opportunity

Equal opportunity for all citizens is a cardinal principle of social justice in a democratic society. Making it a reality, however, is a hydra-headed problem, and few societies can claim complete success. Equality of the sexes, of ethnic groups (particularly where minorities are involved), of wealth and material possessions among the people, and between labour and management, are some of the recurrent themes of this social drama. Each has its special problems and needs its special remedies, but underlying all is the problem of effectively relating the concepts of equality to that of individual differences. An instructive example is afforded by the legal approach to racial segregation in schools in the United States. Prior to 1954 racially segregated schools were legal under federal law, provided that educational facilities (teachers, buildings, etc.) were equal. In the Supreme Court judgement of 1954 this doctrine of 'separate but equal' was rejected. Segregation in itself was pronounced to be a form of inequality, and became illegal. The problem of Negro education in the United States is, of course, a particular one, and may not be relevant to others elsewhere. Can the rights of ethnic minorities in Australia be guaranteed effectively by a policy of assimilation, or is it necessary to preserve their cultural identity? The current concern about the need to assimilate migrants culturally, particularly by facilitating their adoption of English as a language, and the move to help Aborigines to preserve their cultural identity, including the use of their own language, are striking examples of our ambivalence in answering this question. Can equality of opportunity for men and women in our society be achieved without requiring identity of behaviour? Can poverty be eliminated without adversely affecting incentive and industry? Can differences between management and labour be reconciled other than by use of socialistic models?

Most areas of inequality in social life are entrenched. People are born into poverty, and their lack of stimulation compounds their deficiencies. Poor cultural standards in the home, and low levels of aspiration for work and education, tend to reproduce themselves in families and social groups. Similarly with sex differences: social custom dictates conventional roles from childhood and these become self-perpetuating.

There is much that can be done politically to increase equality of opportunity, but it is generally accepted that an essential key is the process of education. It is by education—both formal and informal—that knowledge and skill are more widely spread and attitudes changed, thus increasing the possibility of social mobility.

Equalising educational opportunity has two phases, the political and the educational. The political role is an enabling one. It authorises action and provides facilities. These are essential, but not in themselves sufficient without the professional contribution of teachers and educational administrators. Political action varies, of course, from country to country according to circumstances. Factors such as political ideology, and social, economic, geographic, demographic and historical factors all play a part.

We can conveniently conclude this section by listing the main political steps taken in Australia to facilitate equality of opportunity in education:

1. The creation of public systems of education in all States in the latter part of the nineteenth century. These provided elementary education free, compulsory and secular for all.
2. The extension of popular education to the secondary level by stages throughout the first half of the twentieth century. This movement expressed the growing acceptance of the idea of secondary education as a stage of education for all adolescents rather than, as formerly, a special training for intellectually able children to enter university.
3. The use of scholarships by both Federal and State Governments to assist needy students to remain at school, and to go on to higher education.
4. The provision of special facilities for pupils in isolated areas. These include correspondence tuition, schools of the air using radio networks, one-teacher schools, and subsidised bus travel. Although the proportion of schoolchildren in isolated areas is not high, the problem of providing schooling for them on an equitable basis with children in the towns and cities has received close attention.
5. The setting up of schools for handicapped pupils (the blind, deaf, spastic, etc.) and the provision of special facilities for disadvantaged groups such as Aborigines and migrants.

6. The subsidising of independent schools to ensure that they are able to cater for their pupils on equal terms with those in government schools. This is a recent policy, replacing that of withholding financial support enunciated when the public systems of education were established.

7. The setting up of additional facilities for higher education to cope with the expansion of secondary education. This is a contemporary movement, and has been achieved by increasing the number of universities, and establishing colleges of advanced education as alternative tertiary institutions. New arrangements for training teachers have also been introduced, involving greater autonomy in the administration of colleges, upgraded courses and improved facilities.

8. Preferential treatment for disadvantaged groups in the community. This is a major theme of the report of the Interim Committee for the Australian Schools Commission, *Schools in Australia* (1973, commonly known as the *Karmel Report*), and of the first report of the Schools Commission (1975). Both these influential reports recognise that the policy of equal right of all children to education has not proved to be the same as their right to equal education, and they draw attention to the need to equalise the outcomes of schooling, as well as providing equal access to it.

In stating the problem in this way emphasis is shifted from the main political interpretation of equal opportunity, namely getting children into educational institutions and helping them to stay there, to the educational processes that are followed in the educational institutions which determine how well the opportunity is used. Reforms in these processes may also need political support, since additional financial assistance for equipment, teacher development, ancillary services, and other facilities may be needed, but the central task is an educational one, and can be solved only by teachers in the way in which they interpret and discharge their task.

The concept of equal outcomes is an appealing one, but can easily be oversimplified. It can scarcely be construed as identity of outcomes. On philosophical grounds it would be difficult to justify an objective of producing like-mindedness in children in values, tastes and beliefs, or even in the same knowledge and interest in all areas of the school curriculum. The interpretation of equal outcomes made in the *Karmel Report* is realistic, namely equal mastery of the basic skills needed by children to participate in society as valued and respected members. Beyond that it favours a wide diversity of schooling and opportunity for further education. The Schools Commission puts the same idea in this way:

A basic plateau of competence is needed by all children if they are to become full citizens able to exercise options. Some children and young people need more assistance and time to reach this plateau than others, and resources should be distributed and approaches varied in an effort to meet this need.[4]

The different-but-equal concept of the *Karmel Report* as applied to outcomes of schooling brings us to the limit of present thinking about this matter. It is clear that the 'equal mastery of basic skills' that the report refers to, enabling everyone to participate in society as 'valued and respected members', is pitched at a fairly high level. It is nothing less than 'to be able to relate to others, to enjoy the arts both as a participant and as a patron, to acquire physical grace and to exercise developed mental powers in all aspects of living'[5]. Whether such an egalitarian view commands substantial public support is doubtful; but it is an attractive view to teachers, although acknowledged as difficult in making it a reality.

Vocational Planning

A modern society needs a wide range of vocational skills, and it is obvious that it must provide facilities for their development if the society is to be progressive. Matching the patterns of these skills to the variety of talents and tastes of employees is a complex equation. Two broad approaches to it are to be found, each expressing a distinctive social philosophy.

One approach emphasises economic analysis and manpower planning. Targets are set for different types of employment, and training facilities are geared to these. Entry to specific vocational courses, and to the programmes of general education that lead to them, are regulated in various ways by the use of quotas and selection procedures. Developing nations, which suffer from shortages of particular types of specialists and also from limited economic capacity, tend to adopt a manpower approach to social planning, and to view education principally as an instrument for assisting social progress. In these countries manpower needs are likely to weigh more heavily than the aspirations of individual citizens.

The other approach is to accommodate educational and vocational opportunities to the demand for them, demand being assessed in terms of such factors as the individual's perception of his own capacities and interests, his parent's aspirations for him, and community expressions of desirable educational standards and facilities. Increased demand is met by an expansion of the educational system (or at least by the recognition of the need for it), and greater emphasis is put on schemes of vocational and educational guidance to moderate unsuitable choices than on prescription and selection. Educational systems in Australia, as in other well-developed countries, have followed an expansionist policy, accepting the accelerating demand for education, and an open door policy to vocational opportunity. That until recently this has not led to serious maladjustment in the economy is due to a number of factors. Probably most important has been the generally consistent expansion in the economy, sustaining a need for most types and levels of employment. A further factor has been the progressive upgrading in qualifications set for particular types of work. This upgrading may, in part, have been due to the changed nature of many types of work, necessitating higher qualifications. It is likely, however, that a significant influence has been a small but progressive upward adjustment by employers of the basic qualifications to match the greater availability of better educated recruits. It is also likely that some students have been prevented from taking advantage of the opportunities that did exist, thus keeping in check the inflationary forces of education-on-demand.

At the present time, in well-developed democratic countries a greater need for social planning is evident, and it is likely that a mixed system will emerge as a compromise between conservative and socialist political views. In this there will be greater use of national planning, but a significant reliance also on a process of self-selection whereby social mobility is kept open to individual choice and achievement.

Democratic Citizenship

In a democracy effective citizenship involves more than an efficient division of labour. A free society is necessarily pluralistic, and needs to encourage the interplay of ideas and opinions that leads to a critical and well-informed approach to social and political issues. Indeed the most significant characteristic of a democracy is its reliance on the participation of its citizens in government. If this is taken seriously and done well, other concomitant features of a free society such as its sense of community and its innovative character may occur as well. Democratic institutions and practices can be promoted and protected to a degree by political action, for example, by legally protecting freedom of speech, and by open planning and government. But they rely heavily on educational processes to make them a reality. It is only education that can hope to produce the behavioural changes that underlie free and responsible citizenship. This educational task is very difficult, and few societies can claim more than limited success. What it involves is more appropriately dealt with in the next section.

The Educational Perspective

We come now to the educationalist's perspective on individual differences, which, of course, is the main concern of this book. This perspective is bifocal. It recognises individual differences and the need to relate educational practices to them whatever the philosophy of education may be. In accordance with this view the proper handling of differences is essentially a matter of efficiency. It recognises also the need to relate educational practices to a philosophy of education in which the particular needs of the individual are defined. The second view embraces the first, but it will be convenient to comment on each separately.

Making Education Efficient

Efficiency, as a concept in mechanics, is a measure of output in relation to input. It may be applied to education, even though appropriate assessments of input and output are harder to make than in the case of mechanical systems.

The need for efficiency in educational practice is obvious when the enormous cost and value of it to the individual and to society are considered. The suspicion that a great deal of this investment yields a poor return is a matter of great concern, as frequent public criticism by both employers and educationists amply testifies.

The efficient handling of individual differences in teaching is usually associated with objectives which stress the value of individuality, but whatever the objective may be, education is made more effective by making it more individual. If the aim is to secure greater uniformity among pupils, thus increasing like-mindedness in beliefs, values, attitudes and tastes, ensuring an understanding of common bodies of knowledge believed to be essential, or cultivating the same kinds of skills, a knowledge of individual differences is needed to reduce or eliminate them. If uniformity is the objective, differences among children may be regarded as an inconvenience in what otherwise would be a straightforward pedagogical task, or even as a threat to its success; but they cannot be disregarded. If the aim is to maintain or increase heterogeneity among pupils in their outlook, intellectual grasp, and repertoire of skills, the starting point also should obviously be a knowledge of actual and potential differences, and the methods used should accord with this knowledge.

An analysis of the conditions for improving efficiency in teaching is undertaken at some length in Part Two, after the nature of these differences is clarified in the intervening chapters. Here it is only necessary to indicate in a general way the kinds of action that are needed. These are summarised and commented on in the section immediately following. It is hoped that the points made will be for the reader what Ausubel calls 'advance organisers',[6] providing a structure into which succeeding material may be appropriately placed:

1. Establishing a supportive relationship between home and school
2. Creating conditions in which children are adjusted to school and receptive to its influence
3. Establishing a form of class and school organisation that allows proper recognition of children's individuality
4. Using methods of teaching that most effectively take account of individual differences
5. Relating evaluation appropriately to individual differences.

The School as a Social Institution

The school is a social institution, and its effectiveness must depend to a substantial degree on the kind of social climate that it creates. Achieving an effective climate in a school is a rather special task. There are few, if any, comparable institutions, except perhaps the family, and there is such a large disparity of scale in this comparison that it cannot be followed too closely. Certainly a business or industrial organisation is not a suitable parallel. In such organisations human relations in management do play a part, but their primary objective is expressed in terms of output of goods or services, and the social aspects of the management are a means to this end. In a school the child's personal and social development is the end. A school, like a good family, creates an environment that both stimulates and protects. It encourages children to attempt new tasks and to experiment with human relations without the threat of punitive measures in the event of failure. If the school is perceived by children as relevant and satisfying in this way, it is to this extent likely to be efficient. When it creates a fear of failure and a threatening atmosphere, and its curriculum is not aligned with the needs and interests of children, it fails to interest them, and must be deemed inefficient, no matter what other favouring conditions exist, such as modern buildings, well-qualified teachers and interested parents.

School and Class Organisation

If a school is to be efficient, its organisation must be functionally related to its objectives. This applies to the way in which classes or teaching groups are managed, as well as to the way they are formed as part of the whole school organisation. How teachers conduct their classes usually has implications beyond their own class, and in turn it is affected by what is done by the principal and other teachers. A responsive and flexible scheme of organisation in a particular school is most likely to emerge if all concerned participate in its planning, working, of course, within the external constraints that may be imposed on the school. The idea of an individual school as a significant unit of planning is rapidly gaining ground in response to the present strong pressures towards change. New objectives, although directed to all schools, need to be interpreted by each school according to its particular character, the community in which it is set, the nature of its children, and the special interests and skills of its principal and staff. School and class organisation thus are likely to take different forms, although guided by the same general objectives, the same general understanding of the nature of children, and of organisation theory. Understanding this is likely to increase the prospect of efficiency in schools.

The traditional principle of organisation employed to cater for individual differences among pupils is homogeneous grouping. Within classes this may take the form of grouping by ability, by standard of achievement, by sex (in classes with both boys and girls), and less commonly, by community of interest. Within schools it usually takes the form of grades, streams (as in multilateral high schools with academic studies and various vocationally oriented courses such as technical, commercial, and home science), special groups (for example, for remedial work), and special schools (for example, for handicapped pupils). This method of handling pupil variability has come under criticism on a number of counts.

First, it is clear that homogeneity among a group of pupils cannot be achieved in all respects because of the unique pattern of traits, aptitudes and interests of each pupil. A group that is homogeneous in one respect is likely to be heterogenous in others. Hence at best only a partial solution is achieved. This criticism may be countered to some degree by the argument that not all individual differences are equally significant, and that heterogeneity among less important characteristics need not detract from the value of homogeneity based on more important ones such as intelligence, special aptitude or defect, and vocational ambition. It could be countered also by the proposition that a homogeneous grouping plan could be flexible, allowing the same pupils to be members of different groups for special purposes. The latter interpretation of homogeneous grouping is much more acceptable to critics of the fixed grade and streaming system.

Second, as has been already raised in discussing psychological perspectives, a belief in determinate aptitudes, skills, interests and other qualities that type children, as a basis for segregated teaching, is suspect. Undoubtedly there are genetic factors that set limits to achievement, and there are qualities that make behaviour consistent and predictable, but it is also true that most forms of behaviour can be modified by environmental changes. What are assumed to be fixed modes of behaviour and predictable levels of performance are usually the uncritically examined products of particular environments and beliefs, and, in fact, may change as these environments and beliefs change. This is most obvious in the case of disadvantaged groups such as Aborigines and migrants, but it is also true for the advantaged groups. Fixed homogeneous groupings tend, rather, to reflect present circumstances than future possibilities, and hence reinforce the *status quo*.

Third, it is abundantly clear that segregated schemes of organisation, whether correctly based on significant individual differences or not, have unfortunate by-products serious enough to call them into question. For example, schools segregated by sex to facilitate certain academic aims may have undesirable and unintended outcomes in regard to social adjustment as it is related to sex; some classes streamed by ability may develop an unsatisfactory attitude to schoolwork, gaining a self-image of low achievement in line with teachers' low expectations for them.

Fourth, it must be admitted that any scheme of classification of pupils can be based only on features of their behaviour that are open to testing and observation. Yet much of their behaviour is as yet undetermined. This is particularly the case with affective trends such as interests and tastes which in the long run are going to play a highly significant role in the pupils' future life. Classifying children, and teaching them according to what is assumed to be their needs, tend to intensify existing features and limit the possibility of their acquiring new ones. The case of academically able students in secondary school, solemnly directed towards matriculation, and cut off from a whole range of potentially rewarding experiences in art, music, manual arts and the like is not uncommon, as is the case of many students who, because they are good at science, have only limited prospects of contact with the humanities and the arts. Many students discover the possibility of new interests only after they have left school.

Fifth, most forms of classification are based on cognitive and psychomotor factors and take less account of affective factors. It is thus only fortuitous if academic groupings make any significant contribution towards the social cohesion desirable in a school community. In fact they may easily have a divisive effect, and on this score detract from efficiency.

It is for reasons such as these that modern schools are searching for methods of school and class organisation that will cater more sensitively for the almost infinite variety among pupils. Schemes based on classifying and typing pupils are giving way to more open arrangements, allowing children greater scope to explore new activities and widen their range of interests both in school and in the community. New objectives, or new versions of old ones, are placing more positive value on heterogeneity, whether it be in age, ability, interest or economic and cultural background. The challenge to efficiency in school organisation today is to plan for this more expansive approach, without allowing it to degenerate into mere permissiveness, expressing rather a rejection or neglect of the old objectives than a positive pursuit of the new.

Teaching Methods

Teaching methods may be broadly classified into two groups, one relying mainly on a controlled presentation to pupils by the teacher, the other on stimulating pupil activity. The first may be regarded as the traditional role of the teacher as one who explains, describes and narrates. Presentations of this kind often use questioning to check whether what is said is being understood, and they may be supported by audio-visual aids which help to clarify the points being made. Lectures or lessons of this type, being mainly monologues, can be and often are presented by means of books, radio, television, film, and other media. In this form they are used by individual pupils, or broadcast to all who wish to listen.

The second group includes methods in which the teacher acts as a catalyst and guide, creating situations which stimulate pupils to engage in learning activities, and assisting them to pursue them effectively. We could say that these situations require the pupils to undertake research. The term is not used in quite the same sense as when applied to the mature scholar's work at the boundaries of knowledge, but it is a valid use. It implies a personal identification of the learner with the problem in question and a desire to explore it, the use of resources for a particular purpose, an independent approach by the pupil, and an exploratory and creative character to his learning contrasted with the orderly, structured account prepared by a teacher. The contrast is akin to that between painting a picture and listening to a lecture on art, or between building a piece of apparatus in physics rather than watching a demonstration dealing with its construction. The teacher's role in this approach through pupil activity is much less didactic and more managerial. He contrives situations, provokes curiosity, provides resources, asks and answers questions, encourages and supervises.

Each of these broad types of teaching strategy is designed to achieve the same general result, namely learning by the pupil, and without doubt each is valuable in its proper place, The first, however, is less adaptable to the differences among pupils, and although it has been widely used and appears to be the shortest cut to learning, it is certainly inefficient in many situations of class teaching in which it has been used. When the acid test—of the pupil's understanding, retention and interest—is applied, the apparent efficiency of this method is dubious. Indeed it is quite astonishing how many lectures, lessons, TV programmes and the like that a person experiences have only minimal behavioural effects. It is not just that well-prepared lessons fall on deaf ears. The listener hears, and he believes he understands. But he finds that to follow the thought of another is a different process from initiating or reconstructing the same ideas himself. It is in this positive creative phase of the process of understanding that pupils so often fail, and in which the weakness of the didactic method become apparent.

But whatever value mass instructional methods may have, it must be accepted that in most situations in schools the heterogeneity of the pupils makes them inefficient. All learning is individual; no one can learn for another. Individualised teaching methods recognise this commonplace fact better than do massed instructional methods, and because of this are more likely to be efficient.

Evaluating Educational Objectives

A highly significant factor in any plan to maintain efficiency is provision for progressive evaluation to check whether stated objectives are, in fact, being met. The criteria of assessment must be compatible with the nature of the task. The following account of a review of a symphony concert at the Royal Festival Hall in London by a work-study engineer is almost certainly apocryphal, but it is a good example of unsatisfactory evaluation because of the incompatibility of criteria and task:

> For considerable periods the four oboe players had nothing to do. The number should be reduced and the work spread more evenly over the whole of the concert, thus eliminating peaks of activity. All the twelve violins were playing identical notes; this seems unnecessary duplication. The staff of this section should be drastically cut. If a larger volume of sound is required, it could be obtained by electronic apparatus.
>
> Much effort was absorbed in the playing of demi-semi-quavers: this seems to be unnecessary refinement. It is recommended that all notes should be rounded up to the nearest semi-quaver. If this were done it would be possible to use trainees and lower-grade operatives more extensively.
>
> No useful purpose is served by repeating on the horns a passage

which has already been handled by the strings. It is estimated that if all redundant passages were eliminated the whole concert-time of two hours could be reduced to twenty minutes and there would be no need for an intermission.[7]

Testing is, of course, a commonplace in educational practice. Many think it plays too prominent a part, and by a curious reversal of roles, determines the objectives, rather than keeps a proper audit of their realisation. It is obviously important, in measuring scholastic results, to measure those that reflect objectives. However, it is not uncommon to find that this is not observed. Schools profess a wide range of objectives, embracing personal and social changes as well as those involving cognition and skills, but do not always use them all as tests of success. Even within the cognitive domain the range of professed objectives is not always matched in evaluation, tests of memorised knowledge predominating in spite of claims to deal with higher mental processes as well.

The evaluation of the activities of children is essential, but it is not sufficient as a guarantee of efficiency in education, even when appropriately matched with a broad range of teaching objectives. Critical appraisal must be directed also to the organisation and administration that support the teacher's work. If this is taken for granted, as it often is, it is likely that sources of inefficiency will go unnoticed. Appropriate indices of efficiency in organising and administering education are not readily apparent. This is due, in part, to the inadequate formulation of explicit organisational and administrative policies and procedures, and also to the lack of theoretical knowledge about these processes. The clarification of objectives for the institutions and for the system as a whole is an essential task in making education more efficient, as is the development of appropriate executive procedures.

The increasing acceptance by governments of expenditure on education as an investment has intensified the need for devising ways of assessing the benefits gained. This cost-benefit approach is salutary in its emphasis on a realistic approach to the assessment of accountability, but it has its dangers also. The framework for the study of this relationship has tended to be mainly economic. Important outcomes, that by their very nature cannot be costed in this way, are thus likely to be overlooked, or put aside.

A further cautionary note needs to be sounded. While it is necessary to stress the need for correspondence between objectives and evaluation, it must not be allowed to exclude the possibility of outcomes which differ from the original objectives. There is a creative element in education and hence a degree of indeterminacy of action. The unintended outcomes that result may be valuable and must somehow be brought into the input/output efficiency ratio.

Also it must be noted that some educational processes are their own end. The satisfaction derives from the process itself, and does not necessarily need a terminal result in the ordinary sense. Indeed, in some cases the end result is an anticlimax. In this respect human development is different from a manufacturing process. An incomplete car is of little use, but in an organic process such as human growth and development the process is continuous, and no stage of development can be regarded as the final product, or be justified only for its tributary or preparatory role to a later stage. Peters expressed this point effectively in the following statement, and with it we will conclude this preliminary discussion of evaluation—

> To be educated is not to have arrived at a destination; it is to travel with a different view. What is required is not feverish preparation for something that lies ahead, but to work with a precision, passion and taste at worthwhile things that lie to hand.[8]

The School and the Community

A somewhat neglected factor in considering the school's effectiveness is its relationship with the community, and particularly with the parents. Yet it is very important, particularly when the school is embarking on programmes that are new, and its life and work are increasingly unfamiliar to those outside. Each child has his own background, and for good or ill the house and street transmit their own patterns and codes of behaviour. If these are incompatible with those underlying the school's programmes, the maladjustment at least results in a failure to reinforce the work of the school, and at worst produces open conflict.

An effective programme of liaison between school and home would greatly increase the teacher's insight into children's patterns of conduct at school, and the parents' familiarity with new curricula and new methods. The greater co-operation made possible could significantly improve the efficiency of the school. How this might be achieved is discussed in later chapters.

In concluding this review of the elements involved in achieving efficiency in schools, it should be made clear that it is by such methods that the teacher is able to make equality of opportunity a reality. The political and administrative measures discussed earlier are essential, but they can do little more than ensure that children are brought into schools and assisted financially to stay there. This is only the starting point. Whether equal opportunity occurs depends on the effectiveness with which the potentialities of the children are recognised and cultivated. It might appear that equality of opportunity is achieved when all are treated alike. But this interpretation of equality is superficial. In fact identity of treatment disregards individual needs, and in so doing makes opportunity unequal.

Individual Differences and Educational Philosophy

The case for close attention to individual differences based on efficiency is a strong one, but it is greatly reinforced if the philosophy that guides educational practice supports the development of individuality as an intrinsic objective.

Educational philosophy is often a blend of local influence and a wider educational tradition deriving from a more universal culture. In Australia this local culture is not very vocal or well articulated. It is usually expressed in a minor key, becoming explicit when controversies occur on questions such as religious education, sex education, and equality of opportunity, or when the need for planning in various sectors of society forces a discussion of objectives into prominence. Margaret Mackie expresses this thought in these words:

> Democracy, whether it fulfils potentialities better than other systems or not, is a system of government in which political power is diffused throughout the community. There is no group distinguishable as the ruling class, though it is not true that everyone is politically active all the time. Different groups become active when their interests are involved. The people who become vocal, for instance, when toll roads are proposed, may be people who have never before come forward in any matter of public policy. In democracy the framework in which they can become active exists.[9]

To be able to take advantage of the freedom that democracy offers, each person needs to be educated, and it is to be expected that the quality of democratic society improves with the spread of education. Not all social observers, however, accept this optimistic view. Mencken, for example, is contemptuous of what he calls the 'eternal mob' and of the common man's prospects of becoming democratic man—

> Human progress passes him by. Its aims are unintelligible to him and its finest fruits are beyond his reach. What reaches him is what falls from the tree, and is shared with his four-footed brothers . . . All the durable values of the world, though his labour has entered into them, have been created against his opposition. He can imagine

nothing beautiful and he can grasp nothing true. Whenever he is confronted by a choice between two ideas, the one sound and the other not, he chooses almost infallibly, and by a sort of pathological compulsion, that one that is not.[10]

Even if it is true that the common man has changed but little since the 'earliest recorded time', as Mencken claims, it may still be possible that he has made some progress towards free and responsible citizenship in the half-century since Mencken wrote. For it must be remembered that this half-century represents about half the time in which education has been available to him. Universal popular education is a newcomer in history, and its effects in helping to create democratic man would, at best, be just beginning to show. Whatever disillusionment there may be about the outcome of a century of education for all in the more advanced nations, it does seem fair to claim that the diffusion of knowledge, skill and culture has had observable effects. It is true that these effects seem to be more marked in the improvement of each person's capacity for self-advancement and material success (resulting in a more mobile and more acquisitive society) rather than in the refinement of his artistic and spiritual appreciation and the general quality of community life. An educational philosophy that is able to interpret its role in promoting social improvement in much more generous terms than merely the creation of universal literacy, the inculcation of a stereotyped social and moral code, and training in marketable skills, could conceivably make a big impact on the development of culture. The cultural diversity that a democracy in theory allows could become a reality, and by so occurring, become self-reinforcing. The prospect is perhaps somewhat idealistic and, of course, requires the support of other agencies, but it is a worthy aim for modern education, and at the heart of it is respect for individuality and skill in recognising its nature and nurturing it.

A major objective in fostering individuality is the freeing of intelligence. For Margaret Mackie, this is synonymous with the educative process. She writes, 'When I use the word "education" I mean inquiry, investigation, discovery, invention, creative thinking (whether in literature, the arts, mathematics, or work or anything else).'[11]

Gardner Murphy, too, stresses the creative aspect of the student's thought, and the need for a relationship between teacher and taught in which the teacher's mind evokes a resonance in the outreaching mind of the learner—

The teacher who can embody and implement such a relationship can teach more than skills, can teach a certain readiness for life. A teacher who knows the individual richness of the resonance patterns

of mankind will not try to mold a pupil into his or her own image
—he will know, deep in his bones, that the pupil must be himself.[12]

Ideally a democracy should be in close harmony with an educational
system that expresses this spirit, but all too commonly in practice,
political, industrial, commercial and other needs of a modern state cut
across it, and it is to the educational tradition that the teacher must
look for support. This is the wider tradition with which education is
linked historically—particulary the civilisation of the Western world.
Allegiance to the tradition gives the teacher an element of independence
from local social and political influences. The distinctive intellectual and
moral qualities of this tradition, which have been shaped by two
thousand years of Judaic-Hellenic-Christian thought, are strongly
individualistic, stressing personal integrity of thought in inquiry, a
concept of justice which recognises individual rights, and an element
of compassion for others.

The balance of these elements has varied at different times and in
the hands of different interpreters, the intellectual tradition probably
being dominant. Whitehead expresses this sense of balance in his
definition of culture: 'activity of thought and receptiveness to beauty
and humane feeling'.[13] Matthew Arnold's famous treatise on culture also
argues strongly for a balance between the intellectual and the humane.[14]
He quotes approvingly Montesquieu's view that the first motive that
ought to impel us to study is the desire to augment the excellence of
our nature and to render an intelligent being yet more intelligent; but
he goes beyond this—

> But there is of culture another view, in which not solely the scientific
> passion, the sheer desire to see things as they are, natural and proper
> in an intelligent being, appears as the ground of it. There is a view
> in which all the love of our neighbour, the impulses towards action,
> help, and beneficence, the desire for removing human error, clearing
> human confusion, and diminishing human misery, the noble aspira-
> tion to leave the world better and happier than we found it—motives
> eminently such as are called social—come in as part of the grounds
> of culture, and the main and pre-eminent part. Culture is then
> properly described not as having its origin in curiosity, but as having
> its origin in the love of perfection; it is *a study of perfection*. It moves
> by the force, not merely or primarily of the scientific passion for pure
> knowledge, but also of the moral and social passion for doing good.[15]

Arnold's plea for a balance between humane and scientific culture,
made over a century ago, is highly relevant today when the success
of scientific thought has been so dramatic. The individual's capacity
to inquire has clearly outrun his capacity and opportunity for the

enjoyment of life, and for ensuring equal satisfaction to others. There is now a mounting concern for the preservation of the environment, for improving the quality of life—particularly in the cities—, for the enjoyment of the simpler pleasures of nature, and for the amelioration of poverty and cultural deprivation.

The cultivation of individuality, as an educational aim today, is strongly influenced by this existential element. A spiritual interpretation to it is given by Martin Buber, and although his expression is distinctive, we may regard his outlook as representative of a significant religious-humanistic view important to the teacher today. He writes as follows:

> I would say that every true existential relationship between two persons begins with acceptance. By acceptance I mean being able to tell, or rather not to tell, but only to make it felt to the other person, that I accept him just as he is . . . I can recognize in him, know in him, more or less, the person he has been created to become . . .[16]

Dealing more specifically with acceptance in the teacher-pupil relationship, he writes,

> If education means to let a selection of the world affect a person through the medium of another person, then the one through whom this takes place, rather, who makes it take place through himself, is caught in a strange paradox. What is otherwise found only as a grace, inlaid in the folds of life—the influencing of the lives of others with one's own life—becomes here a function and a law. But since the educator has to such an extent replaced the master, the danger has arisen that the new phenomenon, the will to educate, may degenerate into arbitrariness, and that the educator may carry out his selection and his influence from himself and his idea of the pupil, not from the pupil's own reality.[17]

This concern for the pupil's 'own reality', as distinct from the teacher's or parent's determination of it, is interpreted by some as an undesirable permissiveness, and they react with suspicion to a view of education that stresses individual differences. But there need be no anomaly here. Permissiveness is not itself a positive code of behaviour, but the negation of it. It is simply nonconformity, which is a useless guide to teachers and parents. But on the contrary, the injunction laid on the young to inquire and to deal critically and creatively with ideas is a strict form of discipline. Certainly it may lead to the denial of some accepted beliefs, but not in a *laissez-faire* spirit. Receptiveness to humane feeling likewise invokes a positive and difficult code. Permissiveness, by contrast, is insensitive to the well-being of others.

It is essentially egocentric in orientation, following the line of least resistance, hedonistic rather than responsible. The cultivation of individuality in pursuance of the ideal of the free and responsible person is thus the antithesis of permissiveness.

The educational tradition, then, to which a teacher should be attuned, and to which he must induct his pupils, is liberating but exacting. At the heart of it is the freedom and responsibility of individuals, whether this is expressed in the form of intellectual investigation, in creative expression, in the enjoyment of nature, or in humane feeling.

The claims on a teacher to serve a community, and at the same time to make a particular view of culture more widely prevail, may produce a situation of stress. In a society which regards education merely as an instrument of commercial, industrial or military efficiency, or of socialisation in particular political beliefs, divergence among pupils may be considered irrelevant or even subversive.

K.D. Benne expresses this disregard for individuality in the following pessimistic passage:

> Personal autonomy is widely giving way to compliance. The aim of development is not personal integrity but consensus, not rectitude but adjustment. Morality is becoming a statistical not an ethical concept. That is, we are widely confusing statistical norms with moral norms. To get a statistical norm is to take a collection of responses to some situation and find a central tendency. If you then go along with the central tendency in your responses, you are moral, since the moral response is what the others think is moral.[18]

In such a social setting the teacher's view of the importance of individuality is likely to collide with influential values, creating severe problems of adjustment for himself, the pupils, and their families. Some conflict between exploitive forces and educational ones in a modern state is probably inevitable. Is it possible for desperate questions such as the following to be answered with some element of optimism? 'Can a teacher teach rationality in such massive unreason as flourishes in our time and the panic which often halts the efforts to rethink our twentieth-century predicaments?'[19] Can we release pupils from demoralising fear and teach them a love of knowledge, an acceptance of others, a sense of inner direction, an awareness of self? Can we teach the child to think effectively, to be moral in his relationships with others, and to discover for himself an existential reality which he 'bumps into, hears, smells, fingers, looks at, manipulates, enjoys'?[20] The faith the teacher lives by is that he must try.

In concluding this introduction it may be helpful briefly to draw together in summary the main points expressed.

The educationist in his approach to individual differences embraces the contribution of both the scientist and the philosopher. Scientific insight gives him understanding and control, and makes methodology possible; philosophy gives him interpretation and direction. Both are essential. Constant expansion in research effort is needed to clarify the nature of these differences, and to suggest effective ways of handling them. Constant engagement with philosophical issues is needed to define purposes, and to prevent action from becoming routine.

A strong case can be made out for greater attention to individual differences in objectives, methods and programmes to increase efficiency in education. The enormous investment that a modern state makes in its educational system sharpens the need for care in accounting for it. Treating pupils who are different as though they are alike, even if the objective is to make them alike, is inefficient. If the aim is to help them to realise a unique quality, it is perverse as well.

An even stronger case exists when the cultivation of individuality is held to be an end in itself. The main sanction for this view derives from the nature of civilised culture with which the educational tradition is indissolubly linked. Central to this is the person's integrity in critical inquiry, his freedom to create, and his moral sense in relation with others. Educational programmes must be geared to these objectives if they are to be in harmony with this tradition.

The teacher's freedom to pursue these objectives may be somewhat constrained by competing objectives which a society may impose, and the teacher may be placed in an ambiguous position. This interactional relation between a school system and its environment is inherent. How fruitful or maladjustive it may be is obviously relative, and must be worked out by particular communities in their own way. In a democracy such as ours, there is an obvious need for individual differences to be used to promote efficiency in learning, and because of the particular quality of social life which a democracy seeks to establish, there is a need also for active programmes which promote responsible citizenship, which encourage the capacity for disciplined criticism and innovation, and strengthen the individual's resources of inner direction as a hedge against the dangers of alienation in a mass society.

What the school might do in a detailed way is taken up in Part Two. But first, what, in fact, do the scientists say about the nature of individual differences?

References

1. Hardie, C.D., 1965. 'Research and Progress in Education'. *Australian Journal of Education* 9, 3.
2. Jeffreys, M.V.C., 1957. 'Existentialism', in Judges, A.V. (ed.), *Education and the Philosophic Mind*. George G. Harrap and Co: London, pp. 66–68.
3. Kneller, G.F., 1971. *Introduction to the Philosophy of Education*, 2nd edn. John Wiley & Sons: New York.
4. *Schools Commission*, 1975. *Report for the Triennium 1976–78*, p.7.
5. Report of the Interim Committee for the Australian Schools Commission, 1973, *Schools in Australia*, Canberra (Karmel Report), p. 27.
6. Ausubel, D.P., 1963. *The Psychology of Meaningful Verbal Learning*. Grune & Stratton: New York.
7. *Argosy*, December 1959.
8. Peters, R.S., 1965. 'Education as Initiation', in Archambault, R.D. (ed.) *Philosophical Analysis and Education*. Humanities Press: New York, p. 167.
9. Mackie, Margaret, 1966. *Education in the Enquiring Society*. Australian Council for Educational Research: Melbourne, p. 62.
10. Mencken, H.L., 1927. *Notes on Democracy*. Jonathan Cape: London, p. 72.
11. Mackie, 1966. *Op. cit.*, p. 2.
12. Murphy, Gardner, 1961. *Freeing Intelligence Through Teaching*. Harper & Bros: New York, p. 57.
13. Whitehead, A.N., 1932. *The Aims of Education*. Williams & Northgate: London, p. 1.
14. Arnold, Matthew, 1932. *Culture and Anarchy*. Cambridge University press: Cambridge.
15. Ibid., pp. 44–45.
16. Martin Buber speaking in a dialogue with Carl Rogers in 1957, and reproduced in Friedman, Maurice (ed.), 1965, *Martin Buber, The Knowledge of Man*. Harper & Row: New York, pp. 181–2.
17. Buber, Martin, 1955. *Between Man and Man*, trans. Ronald Grefor Smith. Beacon Press: Boston, Mass., p. 98.
18. Benne, Kenneth D., 1961. *Education in the Quest for Identity and Community*. College of Education, Ohio State University: Ohio, p. 11.
19. Murphy, 1961. *Op. cit.*, p. 58.
20. Ibid., p. 24.

Part One

PSYCHOLOGICAL AND SOCIOLOGICAL PERSPECTIVES ON INDIVIDUAL DIFFERENCES

1. *Individual Differences in Personality Characteristics: Psychological and Sociological Perspectives*

Introduction

The disciplines of psychology and sociology offer the teacher a wealth of knowledge about the individual. They provide theoretical frameworks for understanding the person, both as an individual and as a social member, and, in addition, yield data on the nature, degree and sources of variation of children's behaviour and characteristics.

Not all of the individual's characteristics can be discussed in two chapters. Characteristics of particular significance for the educational process have been selected. Chapter 1 examines various personality characteristics: motives, values and attitudes, aspirations and expectations, and self-concept. In Chapter 3, cognitive and linguistic development are discussed.

This partition of the child—into personality characteristics and cognitive and linguistic characteristics—is, of course, artificial. The child functions in all his settings as a total being. Moreover, there is, to some extent, an interrelatedness between various aspects of his development. For example, his level of cognitive development helps to shape his moral behaviour; his linguistic development helps to govern the nature of his social interaction; his self-concept in part determines his approach to, and success in, learning tasks.

But we cannot speak of the whole child at once. The very complexity of his nature requires us, at least initially, to make a separate study of the nature and determinants of each of his characteristics. On the basis of this understanding, we can then perhaps achieve an insight into the functioning of the total child.

A child achieves his uniqueness as the result of a complex interplay between genetic and environmental influences. The mechanisms of heredity ensure (except in the case of identical twins) a unique genetic blueprint for his development. The environments in which he grows to maturity further ensure his uniqueness. He is not a passive recipient of environmental forces. Rather he responds selectively to these forces, the nature of his response being a function of the characteristics he has already developed. Thus, to a degree, he creates his own environments, and helps determine the influence they will have upon his further development. Rogers is one of the many theorists who emphasise the active role of the individual in his own development—

> I am not compelled to be simply the creation of others, moulded by their expectancies, shaped by their demands. I am not compelled to be a victim of unknown forces in myself . . . I am increasingly the architect of self. I am free to will and choose. I can, through accepting my individuality, my 'isness', become more of my uniqueness, more of my potentiality.[1]

Havighurst,[2] too, emphasises the role of the individual. He believes that as the self evolves, by the age of three or four, it becomes increasingly a force in its own right in the defining and accomplishing of developmental tasks. Thus the uniqueness of the individual, with its origin in his genes, is further fostered by his interactions with the environment, and is finally guaranteed by his choices.

As we shall see, environments do exert pressure on the growing child; they are a source of restriction and of opportunity. Certain environments favour the development of some of the child's potentials and the suppression of others.

Chapters 1 and 3 present a brief examination of selected personality and cognitive characteristics in which a range of variability is likely to be encountered within a single classroom or school. Sources of this variability are analysed in some depth.

The Nature of Personality Characteristics

1. Motives

The Concept of Motives

Motives can perhaps most simply be described as internal forces to action. They are internal factors which arouse, direct and sustain a person's behaviour in a given situation.

Psychologists have offered a number of classifications of motives, frequently conceptualising these motives as needs. Here, those of particular significance in the classroom will be outlined. Maslow,[3] for example, postulates a hierarchy of needs: the most basic or lowest needs are physiological needs—needs for food, rest, sex, etc. In an ascending hierarchy are the needs for safety, love and belongingness, esteem, and finally for self-actualisation (the need to become what one is capable of becoming, the need to develop one's potential). Maslow believes that only as the lower needs are satisfied, at least to a reasonable degree, can the higher needs emerge as motivators of action.

Murray also proposed a classification of needs.[4] His list of human needs is extensive, including, for example, achievement, affiliation, aggression, autonomy, 'nurturance', order and 'succourance'. Two of these needs—the need for achievement (summarily referred to as n. Ach.) and the need for affiliation (n. Aff.)—have been intensely interesting to psychologists, and seem particularly relevant to the educator.

Need for Achievement. McClelland and his colleagues at Wesleyan University during the later 1940s and early 1950s made a detailed study of this motive.[5]

The essential characteristic of n. Ach. was defined by them as *affect in connection with evaluated performance*. The achievement goal was seen to be success in competition with some standard of excellence. Heckhausen, adopting essentially the same approach as McClelland, describes n. Ach. thus:

> Achievement motivation can . . . be defined as the striving to increase, or keep as high as possible, one's own capability in all activities in which a standard of excellence is thought to apply and where the execution of such activities can, therefore, either succeed or fail.[6]

Atkinson,[7] further exploring this motive, was interested to discover what factors would arouse n. Ach. and cause it to manifest itself in overt goal striving. As a result, he concerned himself not only with the strength of the motive in a particular individual, but also with his expectancy of success in a given task and with the incentive value of the success in attaining this given task. He believed that a person's motivation in a given situation is a function of all three of these variables.

He and his associates believed that a history of success increases a person's expectancy of success in the same or similar activities, while failure leads to a decrease in the expectancy of success. In seeking to define the incentive value of success, Atkinson worked from the basic fact that mastery of a difficult task is usually more attractive than mastery of an easy task and that the former leads to a greater pride in accomplishment than does the latter.

Thus, Atkinson sees the highest degree of achievement motivation exhibited in an individual with strong n. Ach., engaged in a task of challenging difficulty in which he has some expectancy of success; such an individual is not tempted to exert himself in a task which he perceives as either too difficult or too easy.

Later research showed that the need for achievement was composed of two separate and opposed tendencies—the tendency to achieve success and the tendency to avoid failure. Individuals differ in the relative strength of these two tendencies—

> Where the motive to achieve might be characterized as a capacity for reacting with pride in accomplishment, the motive to avoid failure can be conceived as a capacity for reacting with shame and embarrassment when the outcome of performance is failure. When this disposition is aroused within a person . . . the result is anxiety and a tendency to withdraw from the situation.[8]

Need for Affiliation. McClelland and his associates defined n. Aff. in terms of concern for establishing, maintaining or restoring positive affective relationships with others; the term 'friendship' comes close to describing the relationship.

This need is similar to, though not identical with, other needs which have been extensively investigated: the need for nurturance, the need for approval, that is, the desire to win the approval of significant others, and dependency needs.

Zigler and Child,[9] in their extensive review of variables in social-isation, show the overlap between these needs, and the difficulty of discussing them as quite separate needs. Students in whom the need for affiliation or the need for approval is marked, will be motivated in their endeavours by a desire for pleasant interpersonal relationships with both their teachers and peers. They are likely to strive for success, not as an end in itself, but rather because they believe that such success will please people who are important to them.

Locus of Control. During the last decade an increasing interest has been shown by researchers in what Rotter termed 'sense of personal or internal control of the environment'.[10] We can distinguish between those who have an external locus of control (i.e. believe that fate or luck or some external force determines what happens to them) and those with an internal locus of control (i.e. believe that what happens to them is a function of their own actions and hence within their own control).

Kelley and Thibaut distinguish between the orientations to tasks exhibited by individuals with internal and external locus of control;[11] the former adopts an information orientation, is highly responsive to task cues, and engages in information-seeking behaviour; the latter has, in contrast, a hedonistic orientation—he reacts rather to the pleasurable and painful aspects of a situation.

Significance of Motives in the Classroom

Some psychologists would argue that motivation is not an indispensible condition for learning—at least for short-term and limited-quantity learning. Most, however, maintain that motivation is an essential prerequisite for significant long-term learnings.

An aroused motive mobilises the child's energy, effort and striving. Under its influence, he directs his efforts towards goals which he believes will satisfy that motive. If, for example, he has a strong felt need for teacher approval, he will strive with tasks where success will, in his view, bring praise and approval from the teacher.

Motives play a further role in learning: only under the influence of an aroused motive will a child use his abilities fully to deal with a given situation.

The child in the classroom who is not motivated towards school goals is likely to be unsuccessful. His poor performance may lead his teacher to conclude that he lacks ability. While this will sometimes be true, often his performance reflects a lack of motivation, a lack of involvement, rather than a lack of ability.

Individual Differences in Motivation

Children differ markedly in their motivations for learning as well as in their motivation for their general behaviour. Individual differences in motivational patterns have as much significance for the educational process as do individual differences in the cognitive domain. The latter have, however, been the major focus of concern for innovators. Justification for organisational plans, instructional materials and procedures has, to a large extent, rested on their claims for efficiency in catering for a range of cognitive skills and abilities. Motivational differences, too, call for differential treatment. If teachers know the dominant motives of each pupil, teaching procedures appropriate to the arousal of these motives can be developed and implemented.

Using Maslow's classification, we can think readily of children whose major concern is the need for love and belonging. An insecure, unloved child is likely to be so preoccupied with these lacks that he has little energy for higher needs, such as the need for self-actualisation or the needs to explore or know.   ·

There are differences among children in the same classroom in the strength of their need for achievement. Some children display high levels of this motive while others, characteristically, do not strive for excellence. They may, on the contrary, be motivated by n. Aff. or the desire for approval.

Even the first group (with high n. Ach.) do not constitute a homogeneous group. Some are striving to succeed; others are motivated by a fear of failure. Furthermore, not all children with high n. Ach. see the classroom as a setting for achievement; not all feel a personal challenge; not all place a high premium on school success. In such cases, school learnings will not be energised and directed by this motive.

In some, but not in all cases, children's latent achievement dispositions will become aroused and motivate their school learning. Campbell suggests that situational factors in the classroom will arouse or suppress the motive.[12] He includes as important situational elements: prior satisfaction of more demanding needs, size of group, the degree of emphasis on problem-solving methods, guidance towards and recognition of success, and the value placed on success. The attitude of the teacher is an important situational factor in the classroom which helps to determine whether a child's dominant motive is called into play in the service of school learning.

Some children strive in the classroom to satisfy their needs for affiliation and/or approval. If they desire approval from the teacher and feel that school success will bring this approval, it is highly likely that this motive will be called into play. If, however, they can satisfy their affiliative and approval needs from significant sources outside the classroom, they may well judge school activities as of little personal importance and so strive only minimally towards classroom goals.

The children in one classroom are, again, likely to differ in respect to their locus of control. Some will feel their own actions are responsible for their successes and failures, and, if success in this area is of personal importance, will devote energy and attention to the learning task. Others will believe that they are predoomed to failure or that they will succeed only if luck is on their side; such students are most unlikely to exert themselves in the classroom activities.

Rewards and reinforcements for learning are an accepted element of most teaching strategies. However, reward-punishment systems are learned by children and thus for this reason also there will be differences among children; what is viewed by one as a reward might be to another something of no consequence or attractiveness.

2. Values and Attitudes

The Concept of Values and Attitudes

The values we hold determine the goals towards which we strive; we devote our energies to areas which we hold to be personally important to us. A psychological view of values is offered by Ausubel and Sullivan—

Values refer to ways of striving, behaving and doing whenever purpose and direction are involved or choice and judgment are exercised. Values are implied in the relative importance an individual attaches to different objectives and activities, in his moral, social and religious beliefs and in his aesthetic preferences. They underlie sanctioned ways of behaving and interacting with people in a given culture and the kinds of personality traits that are idealised.[13]

Attitudes are related to values, and probably more research attention has been concentrated on attitudes than on values. Some psychologists take the view, however, that values are more fundamental than attitudes. Rokeach,[14] for example, argues this view. He believes that values become our standard for guiding behaviour, and for developing attitudes towards relevant objects and situations. He sees three main differences between values and attitudes: an attitude represents several beliefs focused on a specific object or situation, while a value is a single belief, guiding actions and judgements across specific objects and situations and beyond immediate goals to more ultimate end-states of existence; a value, unlike an attitude, is an imperative to action and, again unlike an attitude, is a standard or yardstick. Furthermore, he draws a distinction between terminal and instrumental values. This is a distinction between values representing ends and those representing means. Terminal values include a comfortable life, an exciting life, inner harmony, self-respect; in contrast to these are the instrumental values such as being ambitious, helpful, imaginative, independent.

Havighurst sees one of the developmental tasks of adolescents as acquiring a philosophy of life:[15] such a philosophy embodies the values which the individual holds to be of central importance to himself. This philosophy, organised around a hierarchy of values, serves as a reference point for the individual's behaviour.

Whereas Rokeach has proposed a relatively large number of values, both instrumental and terminal, many other theorists have sought to find a smaller core of central values. Allport, Vernon and Lindzey see six major value orientations:

1. *Theoretical* (dominant interest: the discovery of truth, interests are empirical, critical and rational)
2. *Aesthetic* (sees the highest value in form and harmony: chief interest is in the artistic episodes of life)
3. *Political* (primary interest is in power; seeks above all else, personal power, influence and renown)
4. *Religious* (the highest value is unity; seeks to comprehend the cosmos as a whole, to relate to its embracing totality)

5. *Social* (the highest value is love of people; prizes other persons as ends, and seeks to be kind, sympathetic and unselfish)
6. *Economic* (characteristically interested in what is useful, what is practicable)[16]

They believe that a profile of the individual's position on each of those six values indicates the relative importance of each of the values as guides to his behaviour. One would expect quite different life choices and day-to-day behaviours from two individuals—one who is characterised by comparatively strong theoretical and aesthetic values and the other who places greater emphasis on political and economic behaviours.

Florence Kluckhohn has also emphasised a small core of central values:[17] man's nature, his relationship with nature, his motives, his relationship with others, his time orientation and his activity orientation.

Attitudes consist of three components: a cognitive component (the beliefs of the individual about the object—particularly his evaluative beliefs), a feeling component (the emotions concerned with the object, positive or negative) and an action component (the behavioural readiness associated with the object).[18]

Each individual holds many attitudes towards objects and situations, and for any given individual these attitudes vary in strength, in direction (positive and negative) and in salience (importance for the individual).

Among the attitudes most important for the educator are the child's attitude towards himself,* towards education, towards peers, towards groups other than his own, and towards authority.

Significance of Values and Attitudes in the Classroom

Children's values and attitudes are of concern to the teacher for two quite different reasons. First, the development of values and attitudes is seen as one of the objectives of the school curriculum. In this, as in all other areas of learning, teachers will be successful only if they work on known foundations.

Second, students' values and attitudes determine the goals towards which they strive. It is highly likely that a child's lack of striving in the classroom will be a function of his values and attitudes rather than of his motive strength. Only if classroom goals are consonant with his values (that is with his desired ends or means) and only if he holds positive attitudes towards education and/or the teacher and/or classroom activities, will the child strive to achieve success.

Some groups of adolescents, particularly during the last decade, have expressed protest against the irrelevance of the school curriculum and

*This is discussed in detail in a later section of this chapter.

have become alienated, to varying degrees, from the school. This perceived irrelevance can perhaps best be understood in the light of a mismatch between the students' values and school activities and emphases.

Individual Differences In Values and Attitudes

Students in the one classroom differ widely in their values and attitudes. If we consider each of Rokeach's instrumental values, it is immediately obvious that various children occupy all points on a continuum, for example, between unambitious and ambitious; among the ambitious, some direct their energies towards the terminal value of a comfortable life, while others strive towards goals such as a sense of accomplishment or social recognition. Again, children vary in their valuation of independence; some seek independence in pursuit of inner harmony while for others the ultimate goal is an exciting life.

Achievement-related values among the adolescent age group have been the focus of a number of studies. Coleman,[19] for example, on the basis of empirical data, has written of the adolescent subculture, with values and activities quite distinct from those of adult society. Spindler has examined the value system of youth in the light of what he has called emergent values as contrasted with traditional values.[20] These are summarised as follows:[21]

Traditional	Emergent
1. *Puritan Morality*, consisting of the marks of 'common decency', such as: thrift, self-denial, sexual restraint; commitment to unchanging moral or ethical standards.	1. *Moral Relativism.* Absoluteness in right and wrong is not acceptable as a principle of conduct; the group sets the standard of morality; emphasis on *shame* rather than guilt; lack of commitment to standards; values are in a state of flux.
2. *Work-Success Ethic*, which endorses the value of hard work as the key to success ('work is good'); everyone has an obligation to strive for success and to value achievement and self-improvement.	2. *Sociability*, which entails getting along well with others. Affability and successful interpersonal relations are more important than hard work.

Continued next page.

Traditional

3. *Independence* (The Autonomous Self). The self is sacred and is of more consequence than the group. Self-activity and originality are sanctioned; self-determination and self-perfection are the criteria of personal worth.

Emergent

3. *Conformity.* The antithesis of the autonomous self. Everything is relative to the group goals; compliance to group wishes and demands is to be sought after.

4. *Future-Time Orientation.* The future is more important than the present or the past; present gratifications should be deferred in favour of future rewards.

4. *Present-Time Orientation.* Instead of looking to and providing for the future, we should live for the 'here and now'. As the future cannot be predicted, a hedonistic outlook is sanctioned.

Research results suggest that young people are more likely than adults to hold emergent values, and, as a consequence, to place a low value on school achievement relative to personality, reputation, athletic ability (boys), and friendliness (girls).

It would seem that students holding traditional values are likely to perform rather better in school work than are their peers who hold emergent values.[22] McSweeney,[23] in a Queensland study, found no difference between his high-achieving and low-achieving adolescents in respect to values associated with morality or autonomy, but found significant differences, in the predicted direction, in relation to work success *v.* sociability and future *v.* present time orientation.

Contemporary writers paint somewhat different pictures of the values of youth in the 1970s. Some see youth as holding values reasonably sharply divergent from those of the older generation, that is from the white Anglo-Saxon Protestant ethic.[24] Others, such as Mussen, Conger and Kagan, take a more conservative view. For example, after reviewing research evidence, these authors conclude that although some youth have become social or political activists, and some have become dropouts—

The majority of adolescents have remained, and intend to continue to remain, in the mainstream of society and its overall evolution, and they are interested in success as conventionally defined. They are aware of the pressures and the accelerated, often hectic pace of modern life, but for the most part they feel they can cope. They are learning to live with uncertainty and ambiguity in many spheres and they are neither activists nor drop-outs. Despite the pressures and contradictions of their era, most find more satisfaction than dissatisfaction in their daily lives. They appear at least as happy as earlier generations, and possibly more so than many. If anything, they appear less anxious than their parents were at the same age.[25]

Students vary, furthermore, in their attitudes to education. Some are positively oriented towards education, seeing it either as a means of achieving some of their life goals or enjoying it as a process—a process which challenges and allows rewarding achievements. Others have a negative orientation; this group includes at least two subgroups—those who perceive education (or what the school offers) as personally irrelevant, and who suffer it as they must, some docilely, some militantly; and those who find school a series of unpleasant, failing experiences.

Some students display a positive attitude towards school, but this attitude is unrelated to the academic programme of school. Rather, the attractiveness of the school lies in the opportunity it provides for social contacts and friendship.

Again there are differences in their attitudes towards authority, ranging from passive, conformist acceptance of authority (whatever the guise of authority—the teacher, the system, the textbook), through to active opposition towards authority in any form. Some students feel at ease and function adequately in authoritarian classrooms, while others, to maintain positive attitudes, need to feel themselves as fully participating members in a democratic institution.

Attitudes to peers vary. Some find security in the group, drawing derived status from their membership; some are leaders, at least some of the time, while others, in the main, are followers, but contented in their role because of their acceptance by the group. Another group includes the isolates—those who find no friendship, recognition or acceptance by their peers. Yet another group needs special mention: these are the students who prefer a somewhat solitary path, who would rather pursue their own independent goals than be caught up in a maelstrom of peer group activities. The school system can make life difficult for these youngsters if it brings pressure upon them continually to participate in group activities.

Finally, there are differences among students in regard to their attitudes to groups other than their own. The continuum here ranges from the high ethnocentric individual who views those different from himself (in race, colour, socio-economic status, religion, values) as necessarily inferior, through to the individual who values other people as ends, who perceives some similarities between himself and all others and who welcomes, enjoys and appreciates difference.

3. Aspirations and Expectations

The Concepts of Aspirations and Expectations

Rosen, in his studies of differential rates of social mobility among various ethnic groups in the United States, postulated the significance of what he termed an *achievement syndrome*, composed of achievement motivation, value orientations and educational-vocational aspiration levels. He emphasised the critical importance of these aspirations.

The third of the three components of the achievement syndrome postulated by Rosen relates to culturally determined educational and vocational aspirations. Thus he believes that

> unless the individual aims for high vocational goals and prepares himself appropriately, his achievement motivation and values will not pull him up the social ladder . . . An educational aspiration level which precludes college training may seriously affect the individual's chances for social mobility.[26]

Children's particular aspirations obviously reflect the values they hold. The ambitious child, prizing the ultimate goal of personal achievement, develops far higher aspirations than does the unambitious child. The aspirations of youth concerned with social recognition are basically different from those of youth concerned with such issues as social justice and equality.

Children's expectations, as well as their aspirations, are of importance; in fact, the former may be more significant than the latter. Aspirations may have a fantasy element; they are what one might like to happen, without regard to circumstances. Expectations, on the other hand, acknowledge the surrounding realities; they are what one expects to happen and are bound by circumstances.

As we shall see later, certain groups in the community may have high aspirations but somewhat lower expectations of what they will, in fact, achieve. In such cases, their expectations rather than their aspirations will determine their efforts.

Significance of Aspirations and Expectations in the Classroom

The level of the student's educational and vocational aspirations helps to determine the goals he sets for himself in the classroom and the energies he devotes to the pursuit of these goals.

Furthermore, his educational performance is adversely affected if, in terms of his own abilities and other constraining forces, his aspirations are unrealistically high or low. In the former case, disillusionment, failure and ultimately alienation from the school are likely consequences. In the latter case—unrealistically low aspirations— wastage of talent and narrowed horizons are likely to result.

Individual Differences in Aspirations and Expectations

The school and its programme will be perceived by only a proportion of students as consonant with their aspirations. This group is itself a heterogeneous one: some aspire to intellectual excellence and find the school offers scope for these aspirations; others aspire to a school certificate which will open preferred occupational doors. Yet others aspire to goals which seem remote from school and school endeavours. These are the reluctant stayers-on, students who in some cases are anxious to complete their compulsory attendance and then be free to pursue matters and issues that are more real to them than what the school offers.

4. The Self-Concept

Nature of the Concept of Self

This concept is variously defined by different writers. In this chapter, a wide connotation is given to the term—a connotation as wide as that of Allport, who uses the term *proprium*—

> Personality includes these habits and skills, frames of reference, matters of fact and cultural values, that seldom or never seem warm and important; also all the regions of our life that we regard as peculiarly ours, and which for the time being I suggest we call the *proprium*, include all aspects of personality that make inward unity.[27]

Personality theorists, in particular Ausubel and Sullivan,[28] and Erikson, have conceptualised these warm regions of our life—the central core of our personality—in ways which have much to offer to the teacher.

The former view ego, an organised system of interrelated self-attitudes, self-motives and self-values, as a product of interaction between current social experience and existing personality structure, the interaction being mediated by perceptual variables. Characteristics of the social environment determine the direction of development and contribute to the growing structure of personality. Endogenous (or internal) variables, the product of previous interactions between the individual and his environment, determine the direction of change in response to current experience. Perceptual variables play a mediating role in this interactional process.

Ausubel and Sullivan see the very young child (two–three years) as facing a development crisis: whereas in infancy he was nurtured and few demands made on him, he is now expected to fit in with the family, to subject himself to the guidance and decision-making powers of his parents and to begin to do such things for himself as his growing maturity makes possible.

This crisis can be solved in one of two ways: the child can adopt a 'satellising' orientation to his parents or he can become a 'non-satelliser'. In the former case, he develops feelings of intrinsic security and adequacy (derived status). He is secure and adequate because he is loved and accepted as himself; he internalises parental attitudes and values. Throughout the years of primary school, he continues to depend, in the main, on the derived status, working gradually and relatively calmly towards ego-maturity goals: a lessening of hedonistic motivation, the acquiring of increasing executive independence and more self-critical ability, and the abandonment of special claims on others' indulgence.

The non-satelliser presents a very different developmental picture. While he, too, works towards the ego-maturity goals, he does not have the satelliser's inner sense of security. This may arise because he is unwilling to undergo the ego-devaluation process and adopt an uncritical subordinate role to his parents and/or because his parents may not unconditionally accept him; he may be rejected or overvalued, seen as a means to an end, not an end himself. He must seek primary status —feelings of adequacy and security through his own achievements.

At adolescence, Ausubel and Sullivan see a further crisis. If the adolescent is to achieve the task of growing up, he must not only continue the pursuit of the ego-maturity goals, but he must also seek ego-status goals: greater volitional independence, a greater emphasis on primary than on derived status, heightened levels of ego aspiration, placement of moral responsibility on a societal basis, and the assimilation of values on the basis of their judged validity or consonance with his major life goals.

The satellising child is likely to be less anxious in his pursuit of these goals than the non-satelliser, because of the intrinsic feelings of security and adequacy he enjoys. The adolescent who makes steady progress towards ego-status goals is likely, too, to have inner feelings of confidence as approaching adulthood comes into discernible reach.

Erikson conceptualises personality development somewhat differently,[29] although he, too, adopts an interactionist stance. He sees the developing individual overcoming a series of crises; his personality health at any point is a function of the solution he finds to each crisis, each solution occupying a position on a favourable-unfavourable continuum. There are eight psycho-social life crises as life unfolds. The successful solutions to these crises are a sense of trust, of initiative, of autonomy, of industry, of identity, of intimacy, of generativity and of ego integrity.

The school entrant has encountered the first three crises. The emotionally healthy five-year-old has feelings of trust in the world and himself, feels that he is a autonomous person with a mind and will of his own, and has begun to develop a conscience that is not too constricting, that allows him to will without too great a sense of guilt. As he grows he meets later challenges to these earlier senses, but if he has solved his earlier developmental crises he is likely to cope well with these later challenges.

Erikson sees the child in the years of primary school as concerned primarily with the industry or achievement crises—

The chief danger of this period is the presence of conditions that may lead to the development of a sense of inadequacy and inferiority. This may be the outcome if the child has not yet achieved a sense of initiative, or if his experiences at home have not prepared him for entering school happily, or if he finds school a place where his previous accomplishments are disregarded or his latent abilities are not challenged. Even with a good start the child may later lapse into discouragement and lack of interest if at home or school his individual needs are overlooked—if too much is expected of him, or if he is made to feel that achievement is beyond his ability.[30]

He sees the critical problem of adolescence as concerned with identity —the youth must, during this moratorium permitted by the society, find himself, define his identity—

The childhood self is largely defined by parents and a few other key persons . . . The adolescent self must be re-examined and re-integrated. On the one hand it must be consistent with the adolescent's new capacity for rationality, the humanization of his conscience, and the integration of his impulses. On the other hand, it must be reconciled with the socially available possibilities for work, love and play in modern society.[31]

Both Ausubel and Erikson offer frameworks which allow us to see the importance of the child's orientation to his world, of his degree of exploratory or inhibited behaviour, of his response to challenges, of his level of dependence/independence, and, perhaps most importantly, of his attitude to and evaluation of himself.

Significance of the Self-Concept in the Classroom

The child's self-concept is one of his most significant personality traits. How he views himself and his role in his immediate social setting, and what characteristics compose his picture of his actual self and of his ideal self, will determine, in large measure, his strivings and achievements.

The child asks himself: 'Who am I?', 'Of what worth am I?'. 'How competent am I?', 'What are my strengths and weaknesses?', 'Can I do the things which matter to me as well as other people can?', 'Do other people like me? Do they value me?', 'Am I like other people? Am I like successful people.'? 'What does the future hold for me?'

On his answers to questions such as these depends his striving in the classroom; the degree of his educational success—or failure—is in part a function of his level of striving.

The consequences of a positive feeling of identity and of a favourable self-concept include: an expectation of success and a mobilisation of effort to turn the expectation into reality; a desire to meet challenges; a feeling of competence that allows him to bear occasional failures and not to be defeated or engulfed by them; an expectation that others will like him and think well of him. Such a child is likely, other things being equal, to meet success in the school situation; this success will reinforce his feelings of self-esteem.

The consequences of negative feelings of identity and of unfavourable self-concept are all-embracing and far-reaching. Jessor and Richardson,[32] reviewing the available research evidence, have summed up these consequences: feelings of helplessness and inferiority, passivity and defeat, an effacing self-image, expectations of failure, and belief in negative expectations of themselves by teachers.

The child with a personality pattern such as that described by Jessor and Richardson is highly unlikely to achieve either success or satisfaction in the classroom.

The child's basic orientations to himself and to his social world also help determine the nature of his teachers' responses to him in the learning situation. For example, the following types of students attract quite different responses from teachers: the insecure, highly anxious child; the outgoing confident, exploring child; the mistrustful child; the child making only slow progress towards ego-maturity goals. Teacher responses, in their turn, are an important determinant of the child's success in the learning situation and also of his further personality development.

Individual Differences in Self-Concept

Because of their prior experiences, and adjustment to these experiences, children in the one classroom present a variety of personality profiles.

Some enter the classroom, having satellised to their parents; they are likely (depending on the teacher's personality) to have easy, conforming attitudes, anxious to learn to please significant others. Because of their feelings of inner security, they are likely to form good peer-relationships and, out of a sense of confidence, are likely to enjoy being challenged by classroom tasks, provided the difficulty level of these is appropriate to their levels of ability. Others, the non-satellisers, are likely to be less easy in themselves, striving, as they must, for status through their own achievement. Their earlier developed attitudes to non-accepting parents are likely to be transferred to teachers. Those among them who are overvalued at home will meet the school's attempts to show them reality with differing degrees of anxiety and hostility.

As they grow and develop, some children take pride in assuming an ever more mature role, while others seek to cling to the certainty of earlier less mature relationships.

In Erikson's terms, some enter the classroom with healthy person-alities while others display varying levels of mistrustfulness and/or shame and doubt and/or guilt. During their school careers, the school helps some to develop a sense of industry, of achievement and, at the same time, interacts with others in such a way as to lead them to devalue themselves, to develop feelings of inferiority, of self-doubt. In the high school, some are in the process of finding their identity; some are lost in a morass of identity confusion. The school is a powerful force affecting the self-concepts of children.

Determinants of Variability in Personality Characteristics

Human characteristics are both complex and multiply determined. Researchers who have pursued the environmental origins of these characteristics may be categorised into two broad groups: those who have concerned themselves with broad personality characteristics, and those who have worked within a more restricted framework and sought to relate specific child-rearing practices to specific personality outcomes.

Much of the attention of the former group has focused on social class, and there exists some agreement among findings on the relationship between social class and child-rearing values and practices, educational and vocational aspirations, achievement motivation, levels of academic achievement and general style of life.

The difficulty of predicting child outcomes from such broad and crude environmental variables, and the reality of within-class as well as between-class differences, have been stressed by a number of recent writers.[33] Jessor and Richardson, for example, urge the need for progress toward an analytic understanding of the effects of the psychological environment, and suggest that such progress would be facilitated if researchers distinguished between *distal* (remote) and *proximal* (immediate) environments.

On this basis, they classify gross environmental variables such as social class as distal variables, their effect on behaviour being mediated by proximal variables. Predictions about an individual's characteristics and behaviour based only on distal variables such as social class, are likely to be inaccurate. Although there is a positive correlation between such distal variables as social class and some child characteristics, it is not a perfect correlation; knowledge of the more proximal environmental variables surrounding the child yields a better prediction of his likely characteristics.

Work on the analysis of environmental process variables which affect cognitive development has been carried out by Bloom and his associates. Analyses of the psychosocial environment of significance in the development of personality characteristics have not yet reached a similar stage of precision.

The following scheme, proposed by Jessor and Richardson, should aid in the search for precision.

Jessor and Richardson's approach will be followed here. A search for determinants of the child's characteristics will begin in his more distal settings and the causes of differences between groups will be sought. There will follow a scrutiny of the proximal environmental variables he encounters; this will provide an understanding of within-group differences and of the uniqueness of the child. These matters are taken up in the following sections.

Distal Environmental Variables As Sources of Variance

1. Ethnic Group Membership

Ethnic groups are here defined as those groups who for physical, linguistic, historical or cultural reasons, see themselves and are seen by others as having an identity separate from that of the mainstream culture. In Australia, ethnic groups would include the diverse migrant groups and people of Aboriginal and/or Torres Strait Islander descent.

The newcomers to Australia have come from a variety of cultures: from Britain, Northern Europe, Southern Italy, Asia, the United States; indeed from almost every country.

The Aborigines, although a single ethnic group, also form a highly heterogeneous group—ranging from the tradition-oriented to people of partial Aboriginal descent; the latter could be divided broadly into two groups: those who seek to become an integral part of the mainstream of Australian life and those who seek rather to establish and maintain a particularised group identity.

Illustrative Schema for Psychosocial Deprivation and Development*
Jessor and Richardson

Environment Attributes†		Person Attributes	Behaviour Attributes†	
A *Distal*	B *Proximal*	C	D *Proximal*	E *Distal*
Race	Social evaluation reactions	Skills	Reading deficiency	School failure
Social Class	Parental teaching modes	Beliefs	Aggressiveness	Delinquency
Ethnic Status	Affectional climate	Motives	Withdrawal-Isolation	Psychopathology
Institutional Structures	Discipline-control	Attitudes	Discrimination	Inter-group hostility
Biological Defect	Exposure to peer models	Interests	Striving	Successful Role Performance
Urban Ecology	Teacher expectations	Identities		
Etc.	Etc.	Etc.	Etc.	Etc.

* 'The items within each column are arbitrarily arranged. Further, the items on any row across the column are also arbitrary, that is, there is no intention to suggest point-for-point relations across rows. Each column, in short, is a "box of variables", relations among and between which must be empirically established.

† 'The distinction between proximal and distal under Behaviour Attributes is not elaborated in the text. Its logic is the same as that attempted for the environment. Proximal behaviour is described in psychological terms, while distal behaviour implies social or institutional description, social processing, or social categorization.'

Each of these many cultures, whose members form ethnic minority groups in Australia, has its own distinctive style and we would expect to find certain personality characteristics stressed by some groups and underdeveloped in other groups.

Ethnic Variability in Motives. McClelland sought to understand differential economic achievements between societies;[34] he found the forces within man himself—'in his fundamental motives and in the way he organizes his relationships to his fellow man'. In a massive set of studies across time and space, he explored the hypothesis that a particular psychological factor—*the need for achievement*—was responsible for economic growth and decline. He believed that the rate of economic development of a society was a function of the number of members of that society who had developed strong achievement motives. He was able to present convincing support for his hypothesis; it would appear from his studies that certain societies, at certain points in time, are achieving societies, and that at these times high levels of n. Ach. are displayed by members of these societies.

Many ethnic minorities can be characterised as affiliative rather than achievement subcultures. These are subcultures which place less stress on individual achievement and greater stress on the personal qualities of their members and on relationships. Ausubel's studies of Maoris are worthy of note.[35]

One would expect a cultural emphasis on the need for affiliation in groups where kinship ties are very strong. This is certainly the case with Australian Aborigines. Calley, for example, writes,

But to the Aborigine, particularly if he is a long way removed from the old way of life . . . what marks being an Aborigine is willingness to help kin and be helped by them, to live in close day-to-day contact with them, to emphasize interpersonal relations . . . An Aboriginal community . . . can do more for the lonely, sick or aged than can the modern welfare state with all its vast economic resources.[36]

Watts's research showed n. Aff. to be far more characteristic of Aboriginal adolescent girls than of white adolescent girls.[37]

Krupinski,[38] in discussing immigrant families, notes that the extended family is still predominant among the peasant populations of Southern Italy, Greece and Malta. He reports on a study of households in the Latrobe Valley, where a vast majority comprised nuclear rather than extended families, but where kinship ties among the Southern Europeans were still very strong. Zubrzycki noted, too, the strong kinship ties among the Maltese settlers.[39] Italians, both at home in Italy,[40] and in Australia,[41] are still characterised by the extended family.

The preceding survey indicates that one might expect to find motivational differences among ethnic minorities, and between ethnic minorities and the members of the majority culture. There are, however, differences within groups as well as differences between groups. Our later examination of proximal environmental variables will attempt to uncover the determinants of within-group differences.

Ethnic Variability in Values and Attitudes. Australia is a culturally pluralistic society. There is variety in style of life, in values and goals, in beliefs, in what is judged to be good and desirable and what is judged to be bad and undesirable. The various minorities are perhaps best described as culturally different, that is, different in their cultural style and value systems from the majority group. Here follows a brief documentation of some of the major value differences, of educational concern, between these minorities and the mainstream culture.

First, our indigenous people, the Aborigines. Their very heterogeneity makes it difficult to make broad statements about their characteristics. However, one finds constant comment from researchers on their strong sense of kinship. (See, for example, Calley's earlier comments).

Many urbanising Aborigines prefer to remain in their own close-knit groups, even in substandard conditions, than to aspire to higher material standards of living that would necessitate their moving away from their own people. This preference is, no doubt, partly due to a sense of identification and consequential feelings of security; in many cases it is, no doubt, due also to expectations of hostility and perhaps discrimination from the outside white world.

Questions of value are concerned here. Gale suggested that many Aborigines in Adelaide have been accepted into the lower-class and working-class sections of the city and have acquired the relevant social values.[42] Barwick,[43] in Melbourne, found that most of the dark people she studied aspired to urban standards of housing and regular employment but did not yet desire the other characteristics of urbanisation: the breakdown of kinship bonds and the achievement of material success on an individual or nuclear family basis. Berndt[44] and Calley both refer to the lack of desire among many Aborigines for the highly competitive and stressful way of life that leads to the attainment of material success. Calley writes,

> Aborigines do not set store by accumulated material possessions and the forward march of technology that other Australians do. Given sufficient food and some protection from the weather, they are often content to ignore the rat race of modern society, to live for the present.[45]

The values held by some members of some Aboriginal groups thus constitute a difference from the mainstream culture values.

Migrant groups, too, differ from the dominant Australian group in certain values. Again, a few brief illustrations of differences between some migrant groups and the majority Australian group are offered. Musgrave, for example, commenting on migrants wrote,

> . . . they learn in their families different expectations of behaviour and a different language. Greek parents have strong views about the nature and amount of mixing there should be between boys and girls, both within the school and on the way to and from school. The sanctions that are used in the migrant family and in the schools of their homeland differ from those they find here. Parents at home used, and their children are accustomed to, both much stricter punishment than they find in Australia and to a different pattern of what is indulged and what is punished.[46]

F. Campbell emphasises the differing conceptions of human relations held by Asian students: 'The Asian accepts as part of his basic view of life ties with kin and friends which are warm, close, intimate, trusting, enduring, all-embracing . . .' In contrast, the Asian student sees 'Australian friendships [as] weak, they do not endure, they are not intimate and intense, the degree of commitment is far less, the area of privacy is much greater and therefore people do not communicate so fully.'[47]

Ethnic Variability in Aspirations and Expectations. As ethnic groups differ in their values, so, too, they differ in some respects in their aspirations and expectations.

Young has analysed the socialisation problems of minority groups in North America; his thinking can, to some extent at least, be generalised to the Australian situation. He identifies one source of problems as the ascription to minorities of inferior status and roles in the social structure—

> Minorities identified by racial or cultural divergencies are a variety of social class. That is, they are groups of people to whom a particular social status in the hierarchical social structure, with attendant role expectations and limitations, has been assigned.[48]

Every person has multiple status positions. In the case of the minority group member, however, each possible status position, in Young's view, is affected by the limitations of his overriding minority-class status. Jessor and Richardson, analysing stigma as a factor in social interaction, make this same point. They note that the stigmatised person is not accorded acceptance in most interactions—

the characteristic which makes him inferior to the normal in one dimension (. . . possessing a dark skin) is very often extended to all dimensions of his person such that he is considered generally inferior.[49]

Further exploring this source of problems, Young saw minority-group members, in common with everyone else, as having aspirations for respect and economic well-being.

Ethnic Variability in Self-Concept. There are cultural differences between groups in the emphasis placed on derived and primary status. Ausubel found, for example, in New Zealand, that whereas the Pakeha adolescents are expected by their culture to strive for primary status by their own efforts, competence and performance ability, the Maori culture permits its adolescents to continue to find a major source of their self-esteem in derived status, through a broad-based system of mutual psychological support.

There is, consequently, for the Maori adolescent little pressure from the family, the culture and the peer group for achievement. Evans has reported this same lack of parental pressure in Mexican-American groups.[50]

Children belonging to any group in society may be subject to influences which undermine their feelings of confidence and which cause them to feel insecure and to hold themselves in low esteem. However, when the children are members of a minority group, especially of a minority held in low regard by the majority group, they encounter special threats to the development of feelings of positive identity, of pride in ethnic identity and of personal valuation of themselves.

In making their evaluations of the worth of the group to which they belong, and of themselves as individuals, children are influenced to a considerable degree by the opinions which they believe others hold about them. When they believe their ethnic group and themselves as members of that group to be held in low regard, they are likely to incorporate these negative evaluations in their judgements of themselves.

Aboriginal and other minority individuals in Australia must be influenced in their self-evaluation by the beliefs about their group held by members of the dominant white culture, by teachers and by members of their own ethnic group.

Aborigines are obviously affected by these attitudes. Two comments by individuals show the clarity of the perceptions—

I must prove myself everywhere I go. If I move into strange communities, white communities, people look at me and think, 'Oh, an Aboriginal person, he's probably a no-hoper.'—and I must prove myself. People just do not accept me as a person.[51]

So many people come round us—they are religious, queer or university people. Nobody ever comes round just to be friends, to talk to us as if we were people, instead of Aborigines.[52]

When the Aboriginal lives in a community where the members of the dominant white group hold prejudices such as these he is not perceived as an individual with his own unique characteristics; he is perceived as likely to possess the negative characteristics attributed to his ethnic group. His minority-class status becomes the overriding consideration.

Aborigines vary in their reactions to these stereotypes. Some reject the white evaluation, but some, insecure in their position in the wider community, accept as valid these adverse judgements.

Members of a minority group who are subject to stigma are constantly reminded of the low expectations held of them by the majority group. Many accept the majority's judgement and set low aspirations and expectations for themselves. These lowered expectations lead to reduced striving for mobility and alienation from the goals of the wider society. As a consequence, many Aboriginal children see school achievements as irrelevant to their own lives, expect to achieve positions only at the lower end of the socio-economic ladder, and drop out from school as soon as they may legally do so. Thus the marginal position of the Aboriginal group is to a large extent maintained from generation to generation.

The very small child is protected from these influences by the love and acceptance of his family and immediate group. However, as he encounters the dominant group face-to-face he is inevitably influenced by their judgements. The values he prizes are often not those prized by the majority; the skills he develops lead to only partial acceptance; often he cannot compete successfully, particularly in academic achievements, with white children; his family typically lives in poorer circumstances than those of his white classmates; the 'successful' people in the community tend to be white rather than black. With increasing age, many Aboriginal children feel more and more strongly the gulf between themselves and the whites.

2. Social Class Membership

It is at times difficult to disentangle the effects of social class from those of ethnicity. For example, as Encel points out,[53] most people of Aboriginal descent live in depressed socio-economic conditions; a strong middle class of Aborigines has yet to emerge.

Some migrant groups in Australia tend, too, to be socio-economically depressed. Philp, for example, reports that the migrant who does not speak English is likely to become disadvantaged and economically depressed.[54]

Smolicz shows that only one-tenth of Italian fathers are in white-collar occupations,[55] as compared with almost half the Dutch and a quarter of the Polish families. His research showed that relatively few Italian parents had had more than a few years of primary education. Zubrzycki found that the four Southern European groups 'can be said to hold the lowest position in the system of ethnic stratification in Australia'.[56]

Social Class Variability in Motives. Research (in the main overseas) has established differences between social classes in respect to dominant motives. In terms of Maslow's hierarchy, one would expect to find that children living in poverty do not have their basic needs satisfied. There are many such children in Australia, who come to school with inadequate or no breakfast, whose level of nutrition is markedly low. (See, for example, Jose, Self and Stallman, who discuss malnutrition among Aborigines).[57] The more basic needs preoccupy the thoughts and energies of those groups of children who live out their lives in conditions of gross overcrowding, social disorganisation and disintegration and family instability. School tasks are unlikely to be challenging or appealing to those students.

The need for achievement has been found to be positively related to social class by many investigators (e.g.[58]). This motive is more frequently found in the middle than in the lower class. As we shall see later, middle-class families are more likely than lower-class ones to practise behaviours conductive to the development of a strong need for achievement.

Researchers interested in studying n. Aff. have not typically considered social-class differences. However, students of locus of control have been concerned with social-class differences and, in general, research suggests that internality is more characteristic of the middle class and externality more characteristic of the lower class. Gruen and Ottinger noted, in explanation of these differences,

> Middle class children have had life histories characterized by greater success in problem-solving situations than lower class children. They perceive outcomes on problem-solving tasks as contingent upon their own actions and tend to be internally controlled or skill-oriented.[59]

These overseas findings are confirmed in an Australian study by Katz, who studied the aspirations of a group of New South Wales adolescents. Among other issues, he was interested in the adolescents' views on the means to achieve success—

. . . the majority of the sample suggests that the procedure for achieving success is personal exertion and personal worthiness. Adolescents of USK* and SK* class origin, however, also view achievement of success as dependent on conditions over which the individual has no control: 'Luck' and/or 'influence' are as important as hard work.[60]

*USK = Unskilled manual labourer
SK = Skilled manual labourer

Social Class Variability in Values and Attitudes. Social classes differ in their values and attitudes, their orientations to life. They vary in both their instrumental and terminal values. The middle class, as a group, are far more likely than the lower social class to embrace the achievement-value syndrome.[61]

Social Class Variability in Aspirations and Expectations. Several researchers have noted consistent differences in levels of aspirations and achievement between social classes. Within recent years, various models have been proposed to account for this relationship and to describe the temporal sequence of variables which lead ultimately to educational and vocational achievement.

Social structural factors such as social class are included in these models, but so, also, are social psychological characteristics such as developed intelligence, achievement values and attitudes and educational expectations. Rehberg *et al.*,[62] from analyses of extensive data, suggest that social-class membership directly, and also, through its influence on educational expectations and intelligence, indirectly, exerts an influence on the development of mobility attitudes. Their model shows these interrelationships:

Relationships among Variables Affecting Mobility Attitudes

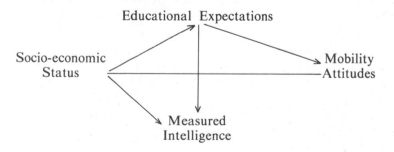

Social-class differences in the value attached to success have been claimed. Sociologists have been divided in their views as to the pervasiveness of the acceptance of success values within the American population. Some have maintained that all Americans espouse the same success values; others have argued that these values differ from one social class to another.

Wan Sang Han urged the need for a distinction between the acceptance of success goals,[63] and the definition of these goals. Variation in the latter between social classes has been well documented (for example, in the United States;[64] in Britain;[65] in Australia.[66] The essential difference between social classes has been well summarised by Kohn and Schooler—

Essentially, men of higher class position judge jobs more by intrinsic qualities; men of lower class position, more by extrinsic characteristics. That is, the higher the men's social class, the more importance they attach to pay, fringe benefits, the supervisor, co-workers, the hours of work, how tiring the work is, job security, and not being under too much pressure.[67]

Not only does the definition of vocational success itself differ from group to group, so, too, do the reasons for seeking vocational success. In his study of Maori youth, Ausubel found that Pakeha pupils not only had higher occupational prestige needs than Maori youth but also differed from the Maoris in their reasons for seeking job success.[68] The Pakehas gave higher ratings to prestige, wealth and advancement, while the Maoris were more highly motivated by considerations such as 'interest in studies', 'liking job', and 'to help others'. Such variations in motivations will again lead to the differential attractiveness of occupations.

Social Class Variability in Self-Concept. Social-class membership can affect the quality of parent-child relationships and hence the child's personality development, and particularly his concept of himself.

Ausubel and Sullivan offer a recent summary of some important social-class differences—

Middle-class mothers typically exercise much greater supervisory control and direction over their children's activities. . . They extend this supervisory role outside the home by placing restrictions on the child's freedom to come and go as he pleases, to attend movies alone, to keep late hours, to choose his own associates, and to explore the life of the streets. Nevertheless, within the home the middle-class parents value curiosity, happiness, consideration, and self-control more highly than do lower-class parents. Lower-class parental values tend to center on conformity to external prescriptions, whereas middle-class parents place greater emphasis on self-direction.[69]

Thus one might expect, in general, that members of different social classes will place differing values on personality characteristics. Bernard captures this difference—

> Hence, in the lower class he seeks to be tough, independent, physically strong, and not particularly interested in the academic; after all, his father and mother did not go to school very long and only on occasion do they cite the merits of education. The child from higher SES has a different concept of what behaviors to internalize says Kagan. He gets approval—is a good boy—when he does not fight, when he co-operates with the teacher instead of behaving autonomously. His parents constantly find occasion to praise his academic diligence and boast of his linguistic skills. Children from the contrasting classes seek identity in different ways and that identity is confirmed and conditioned by different responses.[70]

Social-class differences have been frequently noted, too, in respect to disciplinary practices. The lower-class parent is more likely than his counterpart to use unilateral techniques (commanding, bribing, physical enforcing and coercing). The child's view of himself is conditioned by these experiences.

The influence of these social-class variables become intensified with age and can be of major moment in determining the adolescent's judgement of himself.

3. Family Structure

Family structure is here classed as a distal rather than a proximal variable: size of family and position in family are likely to lead to certain parent-child interactions which will foster the development of certain personality characteristics. The link, however, is not direct. Not all larger families exhibit the same set of parent-child interactions; not all youngest children are treated in the same way. Clausen and Williams, in their reviews of the literature, conclude,

> . . . it is only by specification of the intervening processes of control, modeling and other modes of influence, along with the feelings which they engender, that one can begin to translate the social facts of family structure and functioning into psychological generalizations.[71]

Size of Family. Clausen has reviewed the research evidence on family size and parental behaviours and patterns of interaction,[72] and also the evidence which relates differences in child outcomes to their socialisation within large and small families. Parental behaviours found by him to characterise the large family, as contrasted with the small family, include:

1. More authoritarian parental behaviours, greater use of physical punishment and less frequent use of symbolic rewards as techniques of discipline
2. Delegation of responsibility for care of younger children to older siblings, the delegation resting upon explicit rules
3. Lower occupational and educational aspirations for their children
4. Less frequent setting of high goals and failure to impose standards of excellence

Differences between children from large and small families were noted. Children from large families

1. Made lower scores on intelligence tests, even with social class controlled.
2. Showed deficits in verbal ability.
3. Had lower achievement motivation and school performance— among Roman Catholics but not among Protestants.
4. Achieved a lower degree of occupational success.

Clausen concluded:

Family size, then, does appear to make a difference in the way children are reared and in the attitudes they develop, but the effects are small and depend on a number of circumstances . . .[73]

Rosen has exhibited particular concern with family size and its relation to the development of achievement motivation. In discussing family size and achievement motivation, he emphasised the greater likelihood in small than in large families that life would be organised around plans for the child's development and future, and that in such families parental reactions to a child's success/failure in competition with his peers would be likely to be immediate and strong. He also postulated that the pattern of independence training known to be related to the development of achievement motivation would be characteristic of the small rather than the large family. Other differences were in respect to patterns of discipline, with the large family more likely to make use of authoritarian techniques, which are not favourable to the development of high n. Ach. In his research, he found a clear inverse relationship between family size and achievement motivation.

In studies where the focus of interest is on child personality outcomes which are assumed to be affected by parent-child interactions during the early years, family size, as such, might not be the most useful independent variable. The crucial variable might be postulated as the number of younger siblings who are competing for the mother's time and attention. By the time a child is four years old, older siblings are away at school during a lengthy part of the day and the number of such older siblings has no direct effect on the mother's involvement with the four-year-old, and is, therefore, to some extent, irrelevant. The four-year-old with two or three younger siblings is in a significantly different situation from a child of similar age with only one younger sibling, even though both may belong to large families. The mother of the former is less likely than the mother of the latter, because of the greater demands on her time and energy, to use love-oriented techniques of discipline, to emphasise achievement behaviour over caretaking behaviour or to take pleasure in the child's own autonomous achievement efforts. These postulated differences in maternal behaviours should have consequences for the development of both identification and achievement motivation.

Ordinal Position of the Child. Clausen also reviewed the evidence relating to the child's birth order to his characteristics.[74] He found that the parent-child relationship is more intense for the only child and for the first-born in his initial years; that first-born children show higher achievement motivation in the academic, intellectual sphere; that affiliative tendencies may be stronger among first-born females than among first-born males.

Clausen has drawn attention to the fact that the influence exerted by ordinal position is determined to some extent by the operation of other variables—

Each child has to work out his own identity within the network of relationships and social roles that characterizes his place in family, kinship and neighbourhood. Each member of a group of siblings has a somewhat different set of capacities at birth and each finds a somewhat different environment.[75]

4. Parental Values

The issue of child-rearing values has been investigated within a framework of social-class differences. In general, studies over several decades suggest that working-class parents want their children to be neat and clean, to obey and respect adults and to please adults, while middle-class parents emphasise such characteristics as curiosity, happiness, consideration, self-control.

Kohn, in a series of studies,[76] has explored differences in values between parents of different social classes, the origins of these differences, and their effects on parent-child relationships.

He explained differences in values between social classes as a function of their conditions of life, and, in particular, of their occupational circumstances. He described three significant differences between middle-class and working-class occupations. The former are concerned with the manipulation of interpersonal relations, ideas and symbols, while the latter deal with the manipulation of things; the middle class, in their work situation, are more subject than the working class to self-direction, and progress is more dependent for the middle class upon the individual's own action, and, for the working class, on collective action.

Kohn believed there was a congruence between occupational requirements and parental values. He suggested that their occupational experiences affected parents' conceptions of desirable behaviours for adults and for children.

The third issue explored by Kohn in an early study was the effect of values on parent-child relationships. Analysis of the circumstances under which parents used physical punishment showed that middle-class parents, concerned with developing self-direction in their children, reacted to the intent of their children's actions; working-class parents reacted to the consequences of their children's actions. He drew on other research evidence to propose a further effect: middle-class parents, because of their sensitivity to the children's internal dynamics, were more supportive of children; working-class parents, with their emphasis on conformity to external rules, imposed constraints upon their children. Support for this conclusion is to be found in a study of Kamii and Radin.[77] They found that while middle-class mothers expected obedience to be combined with considerateness, disadvantaged mothers wanted complete obedience to those in authority.

Parental values will obviously help shape their educational and vocational aspirations for their children. In turn, these aspirations will shape the child-training practices they employ, the degree of support they give to their children's educational endeavours, the behaviour in their children that they reward or fail to reward.

Parental aspirations will, as we shall see shortly, be internalised by their children, according to the quality of parent-child interactions.

The preceding review has shown that distal environmental variables such as ethnicity, social class, family structure and parental values seem to be associated, in some degree, with certain child personality characteristics. However, as we pointed out earlier, these distal variables have no inevitable outcome—their effects are mediated by more proximal variables.

We turn now to a study of parent-child interactions and peer group-child interactions to understand more precisely the factors which shape a child's characteristics. This approach will allow us to understand the determinants of individual rather than of group differences.

Proximal Environmental Variables As Sources of Variance

1. Parent-Child Interactions

The primacy of the home as the major agent of socialisation is unquestioned. This is not, however, to suggest that researchers have yet achieved a full understanding of the precise influence of the home upon the child.

Even research efforts which focus solely on the home and family are beset with problems arising from the complexity of the setting and of the subtle interrelationships between the various components. The limitations of methodology force researchers to examine only a small proportion of the total elements, and, as a result, as Swift has pointed out, the complex relationship between the environment and the developing personality is often simplified to a caricature.[78]

Specific parental practices derive their significance, insofar as they constitute an influence upon the developing child's personality, from the total context of interactions within the home. Maccoby,[79] for example, emphasises that the effect of particular disciplinary practices depends on the history of the relationship that has developed between the child and the socialising agent. Given this point of view, it becomes difficult for the researcher to draw conclusions about the effects of such practices unless he can make detailed longitudinal studies of children in the home.

Furthermore, the effect of a particular parental practice is often contingent upon the presence or absence of other conditions. Argyle and Delin analysed a number of studies which showed that socialisation variables have different effects, depending on the values of 'critical variables' such as sex, personality traits, warmth of relationship with parents, strictness and social class. They concluded that the laws of socialisation are not universal; they apply only to members of certain subpopulations.[80]

The complexity of the problem of finding meaningful relationships between parental practices and child outcomes is further intensified by the fact that the meaning of specific practices derives not only from the total home context, but also from the wider social context.[81]

Another problem facing researchers lies in the determination of direction of effect. To what extent are child characteristics the outcome

of parental behaviours, and to what extent do the child's own characteristics help determine parental reactions and practices? This problem
has been widely discussed in the literature (e.g[82], [83]). Research which
would allow exploration of the problem is, however, difficult to design.

The idiosyncratic response of the child to parental practices is a
further complicating factor. He is not the passive recipient of parent-
initiated interactions. Church has emphasised that the child's selectivity
and autonomy operate early—

> Through empathic participation, they (babies) take on cultural styles
> and values, they form cultural identifications so that they come to
> be like the people around them . . . [They pick up] the styles of their
> families, but in idiosyncratic ways that suit and express their own
> individual temperaments.[84]

This review of the problems associated with determining the influence
of the home has been presented to help put into cautious perspective
the research findings on the antecedents of values and motives which
follow.

Parent-Child Interactions As Sources of Variability in Motives. The
achievement motive is assumed by the theorists to be a learned
motive, acquired by association with primary biological pleasure and
pain. It is, moreover, believed to develop during the very early period
of socialisation and to become, by pre-adolescence, a relatively stable
characteristic of the personality.

The theorists concur on the specific conditions of early childhood
which foster the development of the achievement motive. These are
demands by the parents for achievement, with emphasis on competition
with standards of excellence, accompanied by strong affective parental
reactions. The child, as a consequence, comes to perceive performance
in terms of these standards of excellence.

Veroff,[85] in examining early parent-child interactions associated with
strong affiliative motives in children, emphasised variables such as
association of bodily contact with pleasurable emotions, and approval
in spite of failure or misbehaviour; he saw intense expression of
acceptance or rejection coupled with early consistent body contact as
a supporting condition for the development of strong n. Aff.

With respect to the antecedents of locus of control, Katkovsky,
Crandall and Good theorised that

> It seems likely that the more a parent initiates and encourages his
> child's achievement behaviour and the development of his skills, the
> more the child will learn that it is his own behaviour, and not external

factors, which will determine the reinforcements he receives. The extent to which parents are positively or negatively reinforcing also may have a significant bearing on the child's belief in internal versus external control . . . Another possible antecedent of beliefs in internal versus external control is the degree to which the parent is nurturant, supportive and accepting.[86]

The data supported the importance of nurturance, supportiveness and acceptance in generating internality.

A.P. MacDonald confirmed these antecedents when he studied children's perceptions of their parents and the controls exercised on them by their parents. He found that externally oriented children described their parents as using techniques likely to give an impression that one's reinforcements are externally controlled, that is techniques such as overprotection, deprivation of privileges and affective punishment.[87]

Parent-child Interactions As Sources of Variability in Values and Attitudes. The home is the first agent of socialisation, but in the course of development, the child meets with other socialising agents. Goodman has described the child's social world as comprising three groups: those in his personal community, those in his immediate community and those in his vicarious community. With development, and increasing cognitive sophistication, interactions with the immediate community, and, to an extent, with the vicarious community, increase.[88] These increasing interactions open the possibility of new influences on the child's value system. Some of these influences will be compatible with home influences, while others will be at variance with the values espoused by the parents.

Recognition of the importance of the home leads to an examination of the processes by which parents transmit their values to their children.

A study of the literature discloses two main schools of thought on this issue: the one emphasises a learning-theory approach and the other follows the psycho-dynamic theory with its stress on identification and consequent internalisation of parental values. The views of learning theorists are represented by Hill[89] and Bandura;[90] issues central to the theory of identification are explored by Bronfenbrenner[91] and Sears, Rau and Alpert.[92]

A review of these two broad approaches which seek to account for the transmission of values from parent to child would suggest that children learn their values in many ways: through observation, through imitation, through identification; moreover, reinforcements—both direct and vicarious—play a necessary role.

Both groups of theorists stress this role of reinforcement, and both groups emphasise the necessity for a nurturant environment. Both groups would regard parental use of love-oriented techniques of discipline as a necessary, if not sufficient, condition for the transmission of values. Becker has commented that parental warmth variables have repeatedly been found to be associated with the use of praise and reasoning, while hostility variables have been found to be associated with the use of physical punishment. He maintained that both kinds of variables—discipline and affectional relations—have similar consequences for child behaviour.[93]

Parent-child Interactions As Sources of Variability in Attitudes, Aspirations and Expectations. Positive parental attitudes towards education, accompanied by active encouragement of the child, are significantly related to school performance. Douglas, in his study of 5,362 children from every type of home in England and Wales, found a cumulative effect of parental encouragement on school achievement. He concluded that

> The attitude of children to their school work is deeply affected by the degree of encouragement their parents give them and by their own level of emotional stability. The children who show few symptoms of emotional instability and whose parents are ambitious for their academic success have an increasing advantage during the years they are at primary school, largely because they pursue their studies with greater vigour and concentration than the less favoured children are prepared or able to do.[94]

Analysis of the data of the 1964 National Survey of Parental Attitudes and Circumstances Related to School and Pupil Characteristics and of the Manchester Survey also provided evidence on the importance of the home in shaping the child's attitude to and success in school.[95]

The attitudes that parents exhibit towards education and the consequential degree of encouragement that they offer their children in school activities are, in part, a reflection of the value they place on education and an indication of their perception of the relevance of educational achievement to their own life purposes and to their aspirations for their children.

Earlier in this chapter, reference was made to studies of Negroes by Katz[96] and of Maoris by Ausubel. In these studies both researchers found that although parents had high educational aspirations for their sons, the boys had not developed the behavioural mechanisms requisite for achieving the goals. Both noted that the parents did not match their aspirations for their sons with a comparable degree of effort devoted to their educational needs—

> . . . they have not yet been able in the main to provide the active and wholehearted support that are necessary if their children are to succeed in school and reach the higher rungs of the educational ladder.[97]

Ausubel noted that the Pakeha pupils perceived their parents as demanding higher school marks than Maori pupils did, and also rated 'parental approval' as a more important reason for seeking school success. Maori parents were much more permissive about homework, school marks, regular school attainment and sitting for the terminal examination.

Similar characteristics have been noted in some groups of Australian Aborigines. Watts[98] found that the major differences between the mothers of high-achieving and low-achieving Aboriginal adolescent girls were that the former had higher educational aspirations for their daughters and attached a greater value to good school marks than the latter.

Level of aspiration is, to some extent, influenced by knowledge of the higher education structure, or of job requirements and potentialities. Limited knowledge must affect the level of aspiration; many parents in the Australian community have extremely limited knowledge in this area.

Parent-child Interactions As Sources of Variability in Children's Self-concept. The child initially builds his concept of himself and makes his associated self-evaluations and self-judgements on the basis of reflected appraisals from his parents who, in his early years, are the main significant others in his world. Parental reactions to his attempts at the developmental tasks of infancy and early childhood determine whether he sees himself as capable and successful or inept and clumsy. He brings these new judgements to the tasks set by the school, and accordingly faces up to school demands with confidence, or assumes a doubtful, hesitant role as school learner.

The disciplinary practices adopted in the home will affect not only the child's attitudes towards authority but also his attitudes to himself and his basic orientation to the world. Thus children from warm, permissive homes are likely to be socially outgoing, friendly and creative, while those from cold, restrictive homes are likely to be socially withdrawn.

2. Peer Group-Child Interactions

Researchers have tried to establish the extent to which other influences, notably the peer group, take precedence over the home in the individual's development of characteristics. This issue has been reasonably widely examined in relation to the educational plans of adolescents. The findings are not unanimous. Some have found support for the hypothesis that parents are more influential than peers, while others have gathered data which led them to conclude that peer influences outweigh parent influences.

Overall, there would appear to be some justification for regarding the home as the most potent single influence on the adolescent in respect to the values he holds. Usually, under conditions of social stability, there is a reasonable degree of concurrence on values among the various agents of socialisation; the peer group tends to complement rather than conflict with the home influence.

As the child grows towards adolescence, the peer group exerts an increasing influence upon his self-concept and core personality characteristics. Ausubel and Sullivan see several functions of the peer group as a force influencing the individual's development: it furnishes primary status; it is a source of derived status; it helps the child to weaken the bonds of emotional anchorage to his parents; it is a socialising agency; it provides a particularised social identity for the child.[99]

The response the child makes to his various peer groups is partly dependent on his earlier experiences within the home. The child brought up by warm, reasonably permissive parents is likely to develop those personality characteristics which will foster his enjoyable and growth-promoting interactions with peers.

Not all children, however, find satisfying acceptance within the peer group. Those rejected by their peers not only suffer the demoralising and self-deflating experience of rejection but, furthermore, they are deprived of the very experiences which would help them to interact successfully with the group.

Acceptance by the peer group is likely to be affected by such variables as the child's ethnicity and social class, his physical characteristics and skills, and his values and behaviours.

It must be remembered that not all children seek to spend significant proportions of their time with peers. This is too often interpreted as revealing maladjustment. In some cases this may be true; in other instances, however, the child seeks to be alone not because of ineptness with or rejection by his peers but rather because he prefers his individual and private pursuit of his own concerns.

3. School-Student Interactions

Whatever the child's background, the nature of his school experiences will help shape his aspirations and, perhaps even more importantly, his expectations.

Teacher expectations play an important role here. Rosenthal and Jacobson[100] and others have recently documented the Pygmalion effect in classrooms; children tend to behave academically in a way which corresponds to the expectations of their teachers. Teachers of Aboriginal children in the past worked in a climate of opinion which held low expectations of the Aboriginal people as a group, and taught in difficult educational circumstances. It would not be surprising if the comparatively limited success that attended their efforts (a limitation almost guaranteed by the circumstances) led to a lowering of their own expectations of the children, and to the consequent operation of the self-fulfilling prophecy in the classrooms of the Aboriginal communities.

Success, at any task, tends to develop in the individual a positive orientation to that task and to related tasks; he holds expectations of further success and takes appropriate action. Thus the individual who experiences early success is likely, other things being equal, to continue to be successful, partly through the development of appropriate aspirations and expectations. On the other hand, the pupil who experiences early failure (because of mismatch between his home and school experiences) is likely to continue along the path of failure. This continuing failure is explicable only partly in terms of cognitive factors; unrealistically high or low aspirations which are his defence against failure also heighten the likelihood of continuing failure.

The school often prizes and rewards activities which serve a narrow range of aspirations. If the child's and the school's aspirations are congruent, the child's abilities are likely to be tapped by the school. School speech-nights single out, for public recognition and approval, those who achieve in two areas: academic and sporting prowess. There is no (or little) recognition for those whose values direct their aspirations and their energies towards other goals: goals such as sensitivity, courage, concern for others, or social justice. In short, the school system often fails to place the seal of its approval on the wide variety of aspirations to be found among its students. In failing to take account of and to value individual differences in this sphere, it disadvantages many of its students.

The school (primarily through its staff, its expectations and its judgements) either reaffirms the child's view of himself as worthy and valued, or undermines his faith in himself.

The Child Himself As a Determinant of His Personality

We have studied the forces which emanate from the child's wider social surroundings and from his more intimate circles. Yet, as we pointed out earlier, he himself helps determine the influences these forces will have on his further development.

The child's sex helps determine certain outcomes of adult-child interactions. For example, in respect to the development of motives, it seems that girls do not respond to achievement cues in the same fashion as boys[101]. Some researchers have sought an explanation of such differences in terms of social sex roles. It is suggested that achievement motivation of women is engaged only when they perceive achievement as an appropriate sex-role activity. Cultural factors are involved here. In some cultures, it is seen as appropriate for women to be achievement-oriented; in other cultures such an orientation is seen as diminishing the femininity of women. One might expect a lessening of this social stereotype in recent years with the growing emphasis on women as individuals in their own right.

We must ask the question: are there genetic determinants of specific motives? McClelland would respond to this question with a vigorous 'No'.

However, while taking the view that specific motives are learned, that is, that they develop on the basis of certain experiences, it may well be that genetic forces exert an indirect influence upon the development of specific motives. Ausubel and Sullivan list six categories of distinct and stable individual differences which have been identified in infants during the early months of life: placidity and irritability, activity level and distribution of activity, tone, length and vigorousness of crying, tolerance of frustration or discomfort and reaction to stress situation, under-stimulation and over-stimulation, differential sensitivity to stimulation in various sense modalities, and smiling and other types of positive emotional responses. While the uterine environment may have exerted some influence, Ausubel and Sullivan believe that genotypic diversity is probably the most determining factor.[102]

The placid baby will attract responses from his social environment quite different from those attracted by the restless, irritable baby. Each is likely to meet quite different demands from the parents and to respond quite differently. The placid baby may, because of his placidity, enjoy more cuddling and body contact with his mother. On the other hand, of course, it may be the fretful, restless baby who demands more nursing and who therefore has increased body contact with his mother.

The highly active child may act as a stimulus to parents to increase their demands on him—particularly demands for independence. The child with high frustration-tolerance is likely to persevere longer with tasks, in this way achieving success and receiving warmth and approval from his parents.

Earlier we saw that Ausubel emphasised the influence on the child's growing personality of his view of his social world rather than the social world itself.

The child's view of his family and the way in which he interprets parental actions and intents will influence his personality development. Warmth has been identified by researchers as a critical variable in the mother's influence on the child, particularly in her transmission of her values. The critical variable, is, however, perhaps not the warmth of the mother *per se*, but rather the child's perception of her as warm and nurturant. In homes where the child loves the mother and desires her affection and where he perceives her as warm, concerned for him and interested in him, presumably the optimal conditions for identification, and hence value-transmission, are present.

In the field of achievement motivation, McClelland and Heckhausen both pointed out that demands for achievement foster the development of the achievement motive, provided these parental behaviours are not evidence of rejection. Again, the child's interpretation of the intent behind the parental demands is the critical issue.

Just as the family influences the child in the light of his perceptions, so, too, does the community. The values to which the community, a normative group, subscribes can only act as a compelling force on the individual if he accurately perceives these values; his actions are governed by what he believes are the views of significant others. Similarly, the community in which the child and adolescent grow up makes demands and offers rewards and opportunities. Whether these will have an influence on the individual in directing the course of his aspirations and development depends on the degree to which he finds them attractive and personally relevant.

In the case of a minority-group member, the relative attractiveness to him of his group and of the majority group determines which group has the greater influence upon his aspirations and behaviour.

Furthermore, the impact of adverse attitudes held by the majority group towards his own stigmatised group will be dependent upon his reaction to the restrictions thus imposed on him. Young has described the range of possible reactions and the determinants of these reactions—

for some it may be a spur to intellectual effort, material achievement or the adoption of a leadership role. For others, the result may be low achievement motivation, resignation, frustration, animosity toward the more advantaged, open revolt, self-hatred, or a variety of other socially disadvantageous reactions. Just what the reaction will be depends on an unmanageable multitude of factors such as the experience and culture of the group to which an individual belongs, on his personal qualities, his background, his self-image and reference models and the details of the situation in which he finds himself.[103]

In this review, we are thus brought to the conclusion that we must look at specific motives, values, attitudes, expectations and self-concepts as learned characteristics, and seek to understand individual differences in the light of each child's idiosyncratic experiences created in part by himself, in part by his socialising environment, and in part by his perceptions and interpretations of that socialising environment.

As was pointed out earlier, we cannot speak of the whole child at once. In this chapter we have looked at some of his personality characteristics. In Chapter 3 we shall examine other aspects of the individual child's functioning, particularly in relation to his cognitive and linguistic performance; as in this chapter, we will seek to uncover the determinants and the significance of individual differences among children in those aspects of their functioning that are so important in their school lives.

References

1. Rogers, C., 1961, *On Becoming a Person*. Houghton-Mifflin: Boston, Mass.
2. Havighurst, R.J., 1972. *Development Tasks and Education*, 3rd edn, David Mackay: New York.
3. Maslow, A.H., 1954. *Motivation and Personality*. Harper & Row: New York.
4. Murray, H.A., 1938. *Explorations in Personality*. Oxford: New York.
5. McClelland, D.C., Atkinson, J.W., Clark, R.A., and Lowell, E.L., 1953: *The Achievement Motive*. Appleton-Century-Crofts: New York.
6. Heckhausen, H., 1967. *The Anatomy of Achievement Motivation*. Academic Press: New York and London, pp. 4–5.
7. Atkinson, J.W., 1964. *An Introduction to Motivation*, University Series in Psychology. Van Nostrand: Princeton, N.J., p. 244.
8. Atkinson, J.W. and Feather, N.T. (eds), 1966. *A Theory of Achievement Motivation*. John Wiley & Sons: New York.
9. Zigler, E. and Child, I.L., 1969. 'Socialization', in Lindzey, G. and Aronson, E. (eds), *The Handbook of Social Psychology*, 2nd edn, vol. 3, Addison-Wesley Publishing Co.: Reading, Mass., pp. 450–589.
10. Rotter, J.B., Seeman, M., and Liverant, S., 1962. 'Internal versus External Control of Reinforcement: A Major Variable in Behavior Theory', in Washburne, N.F. (ed.), *Decisions, Values and Groups*, vol. 2, Pergamon: London.
11. Kelley, H.H. and Thibaut, J.W., 1969. 'Group Problem Solving', in Lindzey and Aronson (eds), *op. cit.*, p. 11.

12. Campbell, W.J., 1967. 'Excellence or Fear of Failure: The Teacher's Role in the Motivation of Learners'. *Australian Journal of Education* 11, 1: 1–12.
13. Ausubel, D.P. and Sullivan, E.V., 1970. *Theory and Problems of Child Development*, 2nd edn. Grune & Stratton: New York, p. 461.
14. Rokeach, M., 1968. 'A Theory of Organization and Change within Value-Attitude Systems'. *Journal of Social Issues* 24, 1: 13–23.
15. Havighurst, 1972. *op. cit.*
16. Allport, G.W., Vernon, P.E., and Lindzey, G., 1951. *Study of Values*. Houghton-Mifflin: Boston, Mass.
17. Kluckhohn, F. and Strodtbeck, F.L., 1961. *Variations in Value Orientations: A Theory Tested in Five Cultures*. Row, Peterson & Co.: Evanston, Illinois.
18. Krech, D., Crutchfield, R.S. and Ballachey, E.L., 1962. *Individual in Society*. McGraw-Hill: New York.
19. Coleman, J.A., 1961. *The Adolescent Society*. Free Press: New York.
20. Spindler, G.D., 1963. *Education and Culture*. Holt, Rinehart & Winston: New York.
21. Campbell, W.J., 1970. 'The Peer Group Context', in Campbell, W.J. (ed.), *Scholars in Context*. John Wiley & Sons: New York.
22. Thompson, O.E., 1961. 'Student Values—Traditional or Emergent', *California Journal of Educational Research* 12, 3: 132–43.
23. McSweeney, R.V., 1970. 'The Nature and Correlates of Adolescent Values', in Campbell (ed.), *op. cit.*
24. Bernard, H.W., 1973. *Child Development and Learning*, Allyn & Bacon: Boston, Mass., pp. 15–16.
25. Mussen, P.H., Conger, J.J. and Kagan, J., 1969. *Child Development and Personality*, 3rd edn, Harper & Row: p. 702.
26. Rosen, B.C., 1956. 'The Achievement Syndrome: A Psychocultural Dimension of Social Stratification', *American Sociological Review* 21: 203–11.
27. Allport, G.W., 1955. *Becoming: Basic Considerations for a Psychology of Personality*, Yale University Press: New Haven, pp. 39–40.
28. Ausubel, and Sullivan, 1970. *op. cit.*
29. Erikson, E., 1963. *Childhood and Society*, W.W. Norton & Co. New York.
30. Rosenblith, J.F., Allinsmith, W. and Williams, J.P., 1972. *The Causes of Behaviour: Readings in Child Development and Educational Psychology*, 3rd edn. Allyn & Bacon: Boston, Mass. p. 295.
31. Aronfreed, J. *et al.*, 1971. *Developmental Psychology Today*. C.R.M. Books: Delmar, Calif., p. 375.
32. Jessor, R. and Richardson, S., 1968. 'Psychosocial Deprivation and Personality Development', in National Institute of Child Health and Human Development, *Perspectives on Human Deprivation*.
33. Warden, S.A., 1968. *The Leftouts: Disadvantaged Children in Heterogeneous Schools*. Holt, Rinehart & Winston: New York.
34. McClelland, D.C., 1961. *The Achieving Society*. Van Nostrand: Princeton, N.J.
35. Ausubel, D.P., 1961. *Maori Youth: A Psychoethnological Study of Cultural Deprivation*. Holt, Rinehart & Winston: New York.
36. Calley, M.J.C., 1968. 'Family and Kinship in Aboriginal Australia', in Throssell, H. (ed.), *Ethnic Minorities in Australia*. Australian Council of Social Service: Sydney.
37. Watts, B.H., 1970. Some Determinants of the Academic Progress of Australian Adolescent Aboriginal Girls. Ph.D. thesis, University of Queensland.

38. Krupinski, J., 1968. 'Problems of the immigrant family', in Throssell (ed.), *op. cit.*
39. Zubrzycki, J., 1964. *Settlers of the Latrobe Valley.* Australian National University: Canberra.
40. Iacono, G., 1968. 'An Affiliative Society Facing Innovations', *Journal of Social Issues* 24, 2: 125–30.
41. Tully, J., 1960. 'Experiences in Integrating Italian Families into an Extension Programme and into the Farming Community of the M.I.A.', in Price, C.A. (ed.), *The Study of Immigrants in Australia*, Australian National University: Canberra.
42. Gale, F., 1964. 'Administration As Guided Assimilation (South Australia)', in Reay, M. (ed.), *Aborigines Now.* Angus & Robertson: Melbourne.
43. Barwick, D., 1964. 'Self-Conscious People of Melbourne', in *ibid.*
44. Berndt, C., 1969. 'A Time of Rediscovery', in Hutchison, D.E. (ed.), *Aboriginal Progress, A New Era?.* University of Western Australia Press: Nedlands.
45. Calley, 1968. Op. cit. p. 11.
46. Musgrave, P., 1971. 'The School and Migrants', *Migrant and the School, Consultation Report, Australian Frontier.*
47. Campbell, F., 1968. 'Asian Students in Australia', in *Throssell* (ed.), *op. cit.*
48. Young, D.R., 1969. 'The socialization of American Minority People', in Goslin, D.A. (ed.), *Handbook of Socialization Theory and Research*, Rand McNally & Co.: New York, p.1111.
49. Jessor and Richardson, 1968. *Op. cit.*, pp 50–51.
50. Evans, F.B., 1970. 'The Psychocultural Origins of Achievement and Achievement Motivation: The Mexican American Family'. Paper presented to AERA Conference.
51. Moriarty, J., 1969. 'Development in South Australia', in Hutchison (ed.), *op. cit.*, pp. 101–20.
52. Barwick, 1964. *Op. cit.*, p. 25.
53. Encel, S., 1970. *Equality and Authority: A Study of Class, Status and Power in Australia*, Cheshire: Melbourne.
54. Philp, H., 1968. 'Education and Ethnic Minorities', in Throssell (ed.), *op. cit.*
55. Smolicz, J.J., 1971. 'Is the Australian School an Assimilationist Agency?'. *Education News*, August.
56. Zubrzycki, J., 1968. 'Migrants and the Occupational Structure', in Throssell, (ed.), *op. cit.*
57. Jose, D.G., Self, M.H.R. and Stallman, N.D., 1969. 'A Survey of Children and Adolescents on Queensland Aboriginal Settlements, 1967'. *Australian Paediatrics Journal* 5: 71–88.
58. Rosen, B., 1964. 'Family Structure and Value Transmission'. *Merrill-Palmer Quarterly* 10: 59–76.
59. Gruen, S.E. and Ottinger, D.R., 1969. 'Skill and Chance Orientations As Determiners of Problem Solving Behaviour in Lower and Middle Class Children'. *Psychology Reports* 24: 207–14.
60. Katz, F.M., 1964. 'The meaning of Success: Some Differences in Value Systems of Social Classes'. *Journal of Social Psychology* 62: 141–48.
61. Rosen, 1956. *Op. cit.*, p. 211.
62. Rehberg, R.A., Schafer, W.E. and Sinclair, J., 1970. 'The Educational and Early Occupational Attainment Process'. *American Sociological Review* 35, 34–48.

63. Wan Sang Han, 1969: 'Two Conflicting Themes: Common Values Versus Class Differential Values', *American Sociological Review*, Vol. 34, No. 5.
64. Kohn, M.L. and Schooler, C., 1969. 'Class, Occupation and Orientation'. *American Sociological Review* 31: 659–78.
65. Swift, D.E., 1966, 'Social Class and Achievement Motivation', *Educational Research*, III, 2, 83–95.
66. Katz, 1964. *Op. cit.*
67. Kohn, and Schooler. 1969. *Op. cit.*
68. Ausubel, D.P., 1961. *Op. cit.*, p. 164.
69. Ausubel and Sullivan, 1970. *Op. cit.*, pp. 292–93.
70. Bernard, 1973. *Op. cit.*, p. 334.
71. Clausen, J.A. and Williams, U.R., 1963. 'Sociological Correlates of Behaviour', *N.S.S.E. Yearbook*, University of Chicago Press, Chicago, p. 99.
72. Clausen, J.A., 1966. 'Family Structure, Socialisation and Personality', in Hoffman, L.W. and Hoffman, M.L. (ed.), *Review of Child Development Research*, vol 2. Russell Sage Foundation: New York.
73. *Ibid.*, pp. 14–15.
74. *Ibid.*, pp. 15–26.
75. *Ibid.*, p. 26.
76. Kohn and Schooler, 1969. *Op. cit.*, p. 676.
77. Kamii, C.E. and Radin, N.L., 1967. 'Class Differences in the Socialisation Practices of Negro Mothers'. *Journal of Marriage and Family* 29, 2: 302–10.
78. Swift, 1966. *Op. cit.*
79. Maccoby, E., 1961. 'The Choice of Variables in the Study of Socialisation'. *Sociometry* 24: 357–71.
80. Argyle, M. and Delin, P., 1965. 'Non-Universal Laws of Socialisation'. *Human Relations* 18, 2: 77–86.
81. Maccoby, 1961. *Op. cit.*, p. 368.
82. Bell, R.Q., 1968. 'A Reinterpretation of the Direction of Effects in Studies of Socialisation', *Psych. Review*, 75, 2: 81–95.
83. Goodman, M.E., 1968. 'Influence of Childhood and Adolescence', in Norbeck, E., Price-Williams, D. and McCord, W.M. (eds), *The Study of Personality: An Interdisciplinary Appraisal*. Holt, Rinehart & Winston: New York, p. 176.
84. Church, J., 1966. *Three Babies: Biographies of Cognitive Development*. Random House: New York, p. 290.
85. Veroff, J., 1965. 'Theoretical Background for Studying the Origins of Human Motivational Dispositions'. *Merrill-Palmer Quarterly of Behaviour and Development* 11: 3–18.
86. Katkovsky, W., Crandall, V.C. and Good, S., 1967. 'Parental Antecedents of Children's Beliefs in Internal-External Control of Reinforcements in Intellectual Achievement Situations'. *Child Development* 28: 765–76.
87. MacDonald, A.P., 1971. 'Internal-External Locus of Control: Parental Antecedents'. *Journal of Consulting and Clinical Psychology* 37, 1: 141–47.
88. Goodman, 1968. *Op. cit.*, p. 178.
89. Hill, W.F., 1960. 'Learning Theory and Acquisition of Values'. *Psychological Review* 67, 5: 317–31.
90. Bandura, A., 1969. 'Social-Learning Theory of Identification Processes', in Goslin (ed.), *op. cit.*
91. Bronfenbrenner, U., 1960. 'Freudian Theories of Identification and Their Derivatives'. *Child Development* 31: 15–40.
92. Sears, R.R., Rau, L., Alpert, R., 1965: *Identification and Child Rearing*, Stanford University Press: Stanford.

93. Becker, W.C., 1964. 'Consequences of Different Kinds of Parental Discipline', in Hoffman, M.L. and Hoffman, L.W. (eds), *Review of Child Development Research* Vol. 1, Russell Sage Foundation: New York, pp. 169–208.
94. Douglas, J.W.B., 1964. *The Home and the School: A Study of Ability and Attainment in the Primary Schools*. MacGibbon & Kee: London, pp. 67–68.
95. H.M.S.O., 1967. *Children and Their Primary Schools*.
96. Katz, I., 1967. 'The Socialisation of Academic Achievement in Minority Group Children', in Levine, D. (ed.), *Nebraska Symposium on Motivation*. University of Nebraska Press, Nebr.
97. Ausubel, 1961. *Op. cit.*, p. 81.
98. Watts, 1970. *Op. cit.*
99. Ausubel and Sullivan, 1970. *Op. cit.*
100. Rosenthal, R. and Jacobson, L., 1968. *Pygmalion in the Classroom: Teacher Expectations and Pupils' Intellectual Development*. Holt, Rinehart & Winston: New York.
101. Klinger, E., 1966. 'Fantasy Need Achievement As a Motivational Construct'. *Psychological Bulletin* 66, 4: 291–308.
102. Ausubel and Sullivan, 1970. *Op. cit.*, p. 123.
103. Young, 1969. *Op. cit.*, p. 1120.

2. The Mental Health of School Children

Introduction

What is the relationship between emotional disorder and learning retardation? Which is primary? How do they interact? Is there a basic neurophysiological dysfunction? If so, is it genetically determined or acquired? These are only some of the vexing questions in a multivariate field. Unfortunately, the complexity of learning difficulties had led some to postulate oversimplified causative connections (15 per cent of children have been said, for example, to suffer from 'dyslexia', a 'neurological' disorder), or, on the other hand, to reject the traditional diagnostic approach and to concentrate on the removal of undesirable behaviour and the shaping of desirable behaviour, without reference to dubious physical variables.

The usefulness of a static classificatory approach which is not linked to a rational and proven programme of management has been questioned, with good reason. Unfortunately, we are as yet far from the ideal. It is wise to approach the problem with an open mind, from a (justified) stance of moderate ignorance.

A discussion of the interrelation between emotional disorder and learning disability requires the consideration of a number of developmental and related issues. These will be discussed under the following headings:

1. Potential, competence and performance
2. Emotional and cognitive development
3. The causes of psychological disorder
4. Factors required for scholastic achievement
5. Patterns of behaviour disorder
6. Primary emotional disorder and learning disability
7. Management
8. The future

Potential, Competence and Performance

Man is born with *potentials* which are related to his inherited genetic endowment. If he is exposed to a satisfactory environment, these potentials will evolve, by a process of *realisation*. Realisation is a result of two factors: 1. *maturation* of the central nervous system; 2. an *interaction* between internal structures (to do with the cognitive, affective and psychomotor domains) and external people, objects and events. Provided this interaction is consonant with maturational level, it will lead to the *differentiation, articulation, integration* and *super-ordination* of those mental structures which are the basis of social and scholastic competence in childhood.

At any particular time, the individual has a profile of *competencies* through which he adapts to social and ecological pressures. Through socialisation and education each culture fosters the development in its children of those competencies required to cope with the particular ecological pressures to which they are exposed.

Competencies may (or may not) be expressed in a particular situation in the form of performance. Competence can only be inferred from performance.

We do not fully understand the competencies required to succeed at primary school; the following are but reasonable speculations:

1. Affective Domain

    (a) Ability to tolerate separation from parents
    (b) Ability to relate, with pleasure, to peers
    (c) Ability to tolerate some tension and to attend and concentrate
    (d) Pleasure in achievement and responsiveness to verbal reward
    (e) Sense of individuality and of self-worth

2. Perceptual-Motor Domain

    (a) Ability to integrate percepts from a number of modalities
    (b) Ability to imitate the sequence of an acoustically or visually presented stimulus array
    (c) Age-appropriate lateralisation of motor and speech function
    (d) Body-image knowledge
    (e) Control of motility

3. Cognitive Domain

    (a) Ability to use standard syntax
    (b) Adequate vocabulary
    (c) Ability to exploit language in the service of representational thought

(d) Age-appropriate memory capacity

These competences, usually, act in co-ordinated fashion. The child with adequate cognitive competencies will not express them in school unless his affective competencies are developed. Inadequate performance (learning disability, for example) may be due to one, several, or all of the following:

1. Defective potential due to genetic disorder (e.g. mongolism)
2. Defective potential due to damage to the nervous system in antenatal or postnatal life (e.g. head trauma)
3. Inappropriate realisation experiences (e.g. growing up in a culturally disadvantaged home)
4. Inadequate application of established competence (e.g. lack of motivation to achieve in school)

Emotional disturbance applies to (3) or (4) or both. Emotional disturbance is relevant to (1) and (2) in a secondary fashion; that is emotional disturbance may be a consequence of genetic or organic defect which reduces scholastic competence.

Emotional and Cognitive Development

Erikson (1950) and Piaget (1970) have described the realisation of competence in terms of stages:

1. Early infancy (0 to 1½ years)
2. Late infancy (1½ to 3½ years)
3. Early childhood (3½ to 7 years)
4. Late childhood (7 to 12 years)
5. Adolescence (12 to 18 years)

In order that he should reach and successfully negotiate each stage it is necessary that he

1. be genetically normal and physically intact;
2. receive adequate supplies from his environment; and
3. satisfactorily resolve the problems of previous stages.

The environmental supplies required are *physical, psycho-social* and *socio-cultural. Physical supplies* involve adequate nutrition and protection from injury or disease. *Psycho-social supplies* involve the sense of being loved and of having someone to love in return. *Socio-cultural supplies* involve the sense of belonging, to family, group and culture. In brief: being healthy, loving and being loved, and belonging.

If these supplies are not available, or if the individual must face a traumatic accidental crisis (e.g. loss of a parent, shift of home, physical illness) he may not pass through a developmental stage (*fixation*), or he may fall back to an earlier stage of functioning (*regression*). Regression involves a relative *disintegration, disarticulation* and *de-differentiation*. This is the basis of psychological disorder and explains why emotional regression is frequently associated with a falling-off or immaturity in cognitive performance.

The Causes of Psychological Disorder

Behaviour disorder may be derived from damage to the central nervous system. The *continuum of reproductive casualty* (Kawi and Pasamanick, 1958) correlates with low socio-economic status, poor antenatal and postnatal nutrition, toxaemia, kidney disease, prematurity, malfunction of the placenta and respiratory disorders of the newborn. Postnatal damage may be produced by such factors as head trauma, infection or lead poisoning. Learning ability is likely to be affected because of general retardation or specific learning difficulties, or because the child is hyperactive, with brief attention span.

The developmental problems of earlier stages may not be resolved if psycho-social supplies are deficient or inappropriate. Common factors are: parental indulgence and inconsistency, without supportive limits and guidelines; deprivation of parental attention due to absence, preoccupation or psychological unavailability; and parental rejection, hostility or ambivalence.

Psychological problems may also occur if the child must face a severe accidental problem for which he is ill-prepared, for example, the death or severe illness of a parent.

These factors reduce affective competence and are likely to produce transient or enduring reduction of cognitive performance (and, ultimately, competence). They therefore affect the realisation and expression of basic competencies.

Factors Required for Scholastic Achievement

Seven broad requisites must be fulfilled if a school-age child is to learn:

1. He must have adequate general intelligence.
2. He must have adequate specific perceptual, language and motor abilities.

3. His peripheral senses must be intact.
4. His physical health must be adequate.
5. He must have a good teacher, with adequate facilities.
6. He must be motivated to learn. He must share with his teacher the values (future-orientation, impulse-control, need for achievement, responsiveness to praise, sense of independence, experience of success, sense of worth, and ability to exploit the possibilities of language) required to make a learning contract.
7. He must be emotionally free to learn (free from disrupting affects, able to relate to adults and learn from them, and sufficiently mature in cognitive and affective competence).

The remainder of this chapter deals with (6) and (7): those children who, for psychological reasons, are not able to express or have not realised the affective, cognitive and psychomotor competencies required to succeed in school, despite the fact that their potential, originally, was adequate.

Patterns of Behaviour Disorder

How is a perceptive teacher to recognise a child with emotional disorder? One of the most sensitive indices of adjustment is school performance. It is unlikely, however, that a deterioration in performance will occur without other discernible signs. There are five major syndromes: *restlessness, immaturity, anxiety* or *depression, unruliness* and *isolation.*

The *restless child* is overactive, fidgety, unable to concentrate and sometimes prone to attacks of rage if frustrated. He is difficult to handle in the classroom and prone to be provocative if he detects hostility in his teacher.

The *immature child* has not solved problems of earlier developmental stages. He has trouble separating from home, is likely to be fearful of new situations, and is often away from school for trivial reasons. He has difficulty coping with his peers. He may lack control of bladder or bowel and show other habit immaturities such as thumb-sucking or body stimulation.

The *anxious or depressed child* often has tears on arrival at school and may have frequent absences. He complains to the teacher that others persecute him. He may be fussy and over-meticulous about school work and over-react to the threat of failure.

The *unruly child* is disobedient, defiant, oppositional and aggressive. Either alone, or with a group of other children, he stands against authority and may bully weaker children. Sometimes he lies, steals and truants. He is likely to come from a disorganised home and to have experienced marked inconsistency or rejection in his early years.

The *isolated, shut-in child* may be the most seriously disturbed of all, and yet the easiest to miss. Friendless, self-contained, eccentric, and alone, he may be conspicuous only if, in addition, he is picked on by others. Conscientiousness may enable him to keep up with his schoolwork, but his staying power is weak and his increasingly invalid fantasy-life is likely to cause a marked deterioration in school performance during adolescence.

The above syndromes overlap. All may cause a deterioration or lag in school performance. All, on the other hand, may be the result of difficulties in school performance. Eventually school difficulties and psychological disorder interact in a vicious circle.

Learning disorders may be classified as follows:

1. Generalised intellectual malfunctioning due to psychological disorder
2. Scholastic learning problems
   (a) secondary to brain dysfunction
      (i) *acquired* (due to brain damage)
      (ii) *inherited* (due to genetic anomaly)
   (b) secondary to psychological disorder
   (c) mixtures of (a) and (b)

Primary Emotional Disorder and Learning Disability

Learning disability may be part of a generalised retardation due to very severe emotional privation or trauma in earlier years. More commonly, poor school performance is one of the symptoms of psychological disorder in a child who shows evidence, otherwise, that he is capable of achieving better. The scholastic difficulty may be general or affect particular subjects such as reading or number work. Learning problems may become predominant in a disturbed child's symptomatology if school and parents concentrate their concern upon it.

The influence of the child's social background in shaping his attitude to authority and to learning must be stressed. School difficulties are likely in: children who have never formed adequate primary attachments to others (for example, children institutionalised as infants); children whose early training has been premature and coercive and who have developed an oppositional attitude towards adults; children who have been overprotected and who cannot separate from the home sufficiently to relate to teachers; and children whose natural curiosity has been crushed, particularly if the home atmosphere is heavy with a family secret.

Learning requires the control and constructive deployment of aggression. The child who has not learnt to check aggressive feelings and to tolerate some tension is likely to be hyperactive and disorganised. The child whose natural aggression has been submerged is likely to be passive, listless and unresponsive in school, and excessively dependent at home.

A common family interaction involves a struggle for dominance between parent and child. The parents who for economic reasons were unable to fulfil their own educational aspirations (for example, the mother whose brothers were offered the opportunity she was denied, the father blocked by the unsympathetic attitudes of his own family) may hound and nag the child, who is expected to compensate the adults for what they have lacked. A particularly serious variant of this theme occurs when the father is a failure (alcoholic, for example) and a dominant mother projects on to her son both a demand for success and an expectation of failure. The problem is compounded if the father shows resentment towards the son for the mother's involvement with him.

In other families it appears that one or both parents have assigned to a child a low status in the family. Sometimes it seems that the child has become identified with a parent's hated sibling. The role of family 'dope' may be as difficult to cast off as it is to counteract the family's expectation that one will be a failure.

It appears that symbolic problem solving is compromised by uncontrolled effects. Anxiety, depression or hostility which are unbound disrupt decentred thought with emotionally charged imagery of egocentric nature. Anxiety or hostility may become associated with learning in general, or with a particular school subject, or with a particular teacher.

For some children learning means growing up, and growing up means separation from parents. They may resist school as a symbol of a feared outcome. Another group of children appear to have attempted to preserve infantile ideas of omnipotence and to be unwilling to accept criticism or to learn from mistakes. A third group associate scholastic achievement with the danger of retaliation from a rival parent. Some children fear to be conspicuous and to run the risk of rejection by peers if they do well in school; they thus condemn themselves to mediocrity rather than break step with the prevailing cultural anti-educational ethos. Others, still more disturbed, and often depressed, are self-defeating, and seem to court failure with a bitter satisfaction.

Management

The teacher is in the key position to recognise children with emotional disturbance, or learning disability, or both. By the time a vicious circle has been established it may be a theoretical question as to which was primary—the learning disorder or the psychological problem? In any case, the comprehensive diagnosis of such condition is not the teacher's responsibility. The teacher's province is the recognition of children with established problems, the discernment of those at risk, the referral of those who need help, and collaboration with referral agencies in continuing management.

Recognition

The common patterns of behaviour disorder have already been de-scribed: hyperactivity, anxiety, immaturity, unruliness and isolation. Serious psychological problems are not transient; they affect many areas of psychological functioning. Learning disability alone, without a variety of other psychological symptoms, is unlikely to be primarily of emotional origin. Learning disability due, basically, to an inherited or acquired perceptual-motor or language dysfunction may also produce and become integral to an emotional disorder. If a child deteriorates markedly in performance, or if his performance is much below his apparent ability, or if he shows persistent psychological symptoms, then referral should be considered.

Discernment of Those at Risk

The teacher should be aware of the possibility of learning difficulty in children who, when they enter school, are delayed in language develop-ment, or who appear to have marked difficulty in co-ordination or concentration. The possibility of unresolved emotional disorder should be kept in mind in those children who come from disorganised homes —especially if there is interparental conflict or separation—, who are from foster homes or institutional homes, or who have recently experienced a serious emotional crisis. Other children at risk are those with a physical handicap (e.g. harelip, stammer, absence of a limb) or with problems in sex-role differentiation (e.g. the effeminate boy). Children of ethnic minority groups (e.g. Aborigines and recent mi-grants) are at risk, also, if, at the time of entry into school, their competence in standard English has been poorly realised.

Referral

If a school counselling service is available, initial referral presents no difficulty. If not, the teacher or principal must discuss the problem with the child and parents, to arrange for assessment at an educational or child psychiatric assessment unit. Parents are most likely to become resistant if they detect a spirit of accusation in those who would refer them. Everybody seems to have heard the damaging and invalid adage 'There are no delinquent children, only delinquent parents'. Actually, direct parental malevolence towards a child is not a common cause of emotional disturbance.

Whether the child is referred to an educational or child guidance clinic depends upon whether the referring agent considers that educational or psychological problems are predominant. It should not matter; both types of service are capable of a diagnostic assessment that leads to a rational plan of management and determines whether the main strategy should be educational or psychotherapeutic (or both). Cases can be transferred from one service to the other, if more appropriate.

If the family are to be referred to a child guidance or child psychiatry clinic, it is important for them to know what to expect. The idea is associated, in many peoples' minds, with insanity, imputations of parental responsibility, syringes of truth serum, couches and other cinematic devices. Parents can be reassured that they will be interviewed by a clinic worker to elucidate the nature and urgency of the problem. The child will be seen, also, and (if relevant) psychologically tested in regard to general intelligence, perceptual-motor abilities, language development, school achievement and personality. At a conference the clinic workers design the plan of management and convey this, later, to the parents and child. The family, then, have the option of making or rejecting a therapeutic contract.

If a child has both an emotional disorder and a learning disability, regardless of which is primary, it is unlikely that attention to the emotional disorder alone will be adequate. Almost always the child's lag in school achievement will need special attention (for example, by coaching outside of school, individual attention in the classroom, or a more specialised remedial programme); otherwise the frustration of poor school achievement will hinder the child's emotional improvement. Similarly, even when the child's central and primary problem is scholastic, attention to his general adjustment will be required, at some level. Parental involvement and enlightened management in school are the basis of this.

Collaboration

The teacher should be able to communicate directly with the referral agent, about the nature of the problem. The school principal will foster this and regard it as a legitimate part of the teacher's function. The teacher and principal will expect clear, jargon-free communication from the referral agency.

Where possible, the child should be helped in the classroom. If necessary, special remedial teaching may be required, but this should be in the same school, if possible. Transfer to a special school should be envisaged only in extreme circumstances (for example, for those psychotic children who need highly specialised management).

In most cases, the burden of management will return to the teacher, assisted and advised by the educational or child guidance service.

The Future

The current educational system will be examined closely. An attempt will be made to determine, with more clarity, the competencies required by children at the time they leave school. Greater parental involvement in the educational process will be expected and actively sought. Education will not be a time-limited compartment but a process continuous throughout life and throughout the community. Educational strategies will be individualised to develop the child's competencies and to compensate where he needs help. Ethnic minorities will be taught in such a way as to support their sense of cultural identity, yet to offer them the opportunity to share in the surrounding technological culture, if they so wish.

The training of doctors, psychologists, teachers and allied workers will be such that they share a common pool of knowledge, have purposes that are seen as overlapping, and expect to collaborate. Medical services will have a major preventive function and will communicate to the universal pre-school and school systems about the children who are at risk of learning or emotional disorders. School counselling services will be greatly developed. Each school will have its own counsellors. A proportion of referred children will be treated or managed in the extensive child psychiatry and educational services that operate in close liaison with schools. Great concern will be exercised about the confidentiality of records. The operation of these community services will be supervised by committees of citizens from the community.

Research will be directed, particularly, towards answering the following questions: How is language acquired? What is the interrelation of language and thought? What is the neurology of body-image, perceptual and language development? How do affective-relational and cognitive structures interact? What are the competencies required to cope with school? Which early childhood experiences foster the realisation of these competencies? How can the powerhouse of language be exploited best in the service of thought, and how can the school promote this?

The future is in the direction of openness, continuity, clarity of questions, and collaboration, on the basis of a genuinely universal education. The polemics and the reductionism of the current scene will be understood, then, as premature attempts to grasp simple straws in a sea of complexity.

Bibliography

Erikson, E., 1950. *Childhood and Society*. Norton: New York.

Kawi, A.A. and Pasamanick, B., 1958, 'The Continuum of Reproductive Casualty'. *Journal of the American Medical Association* 166: 1420–26.

Kessler, J., 1966. *Psychopathology of Childhood*. Prentice Hall: Englewood Cliffs, N.J.

Menkes, J.H. and Schain, R.J. (eds), 1971. *Learning Disorders in Children*. Report of the Sixty-First Ross Conference on Pediatric Research. Ross Laboratories: Columbus.

Nurcombe, B., 1976. *Children of the Dispossessed*. Culture Learning Institute Monograph, East-West Center. University of Hawaii Press: Hawaii.

Piaget, J., 1970. *Genetic Epistemology*, trans. Eleanor Buckworth, Columbia University Press: New York.

3. Individual Differences in Cognitive and Linguistic Functioning: Psychological and Sociological Perspectives

Introduction

The Complexity of Cognitive Functioning

As pointed out in the introduction to Chapter 1, the child functions as a whole. While there is a need to distinguish his various characteristics for the purposes of examination and discussion, this process of partition must not lead us to ignore the complexity of his functioning.

The term 'cognition' refers to a complex of mental activities or processes through the operation of which the child comes to know his world. These processes include sensing, recognising, remembering, abstracting, analysing and reasoning. Even though we may consider each of these as a discrete process, there is an intimate interrelatedness among them, and the child, in his commerce with his environment, utilises all of them.

Furthermore, even though language acquisition and the development of linguistic competence are specific aspects of child development, from the age of two onwards, it becomes extremely difficult to separate language and thinking. While language and thought are not coextensive, and while language can be exhibited without thought, and vice versa, growth in logical thinking does seem tied to growth in language capability. Language, for many individuals, acts as a patterning or limiting factor in their cognitive development.[1] Luria is among the theorists who discusses the ways in which internal speech helps the child to mobilise and utilise his past experiences in his present encounters with his environment.[2]

Not only is there an interrelationship between language and thought and among the various mental processes, but, additionally, cognitive development and functioning are closely affected by personality factors.

Furthermore, the level of cognitive functioning displayed by a child at any point in time is dependent partly on the level of his developed

86

abilities, but also, importantly, upon his motivation to utilise those abilities—upon the degree to which he is fully engaged by that particular situation. Crandall has pointed out that motivational factors (for example, confidence in one's ability to perform well in an achievement task) facilitate the cognitive processes of discrimination, abstraction, integration and recognition and thus affect problem solving. She believes that ability itself does not constitute a dynamic, activating variable—it lies dormant unless or until it is aroused by motivational factors.[3]

Most major theorists, in fact, emphasise that cognitive activity does not take place in a vacuum; non-intellectual factors are always implicated in the quality of cognitive output.

Structure of This Chapter

The complex interrelatedness of aspects of cognitive functioning, the comparative brevity of this chapter and an assumption about the interests of readers have led to the selection of the following topics for detailed discussion: cognitive abilities, cognitive style and language. The nature of each characteristic will be examined, its significance in the classroom and the range of variability among pupils will be discussed, and finally, there will be a search for the determinants of these characteristics.

Cognitive Abilities

The Nature of Abilities

Intellectual abilities are of central significance to psychologists and educators; they have been a focus of continuous research interest during the whole of this century. We may adopt one or more of several perspectives in our quest to understand this characteristic of man.

First, we may question the nature of intelligence itself—what is it that constitutes intelligence? This question can be answered by considering the nature of intelligence-in-action, that is by examining the characteristics of intelligent behaviour. Binet and Simon, early pioneers in the field, believed that

> . . . in the intelligence there is a fundamental faculty, the alteration or lack of which is of utmost importance in practical life. This faculty is judgement, otherwise called good sense, practical sense, initiative, the faculty of adapting oneself to circumstances.[4]

Binet saw the essential activities of intelligence as judging well, reasoning well, comprehending well.

Echoes of this early definition can be discerned in more recent attempts to define this quality: Munn's flexibility and versatility in the use of symbolic processes; [5] Wechsler's aggregate or global capacity of the individual to act purposefully, to think rationally and to deal effectively with his environment; [6] the Ausubels' general capacity for processing information and for utilising abstract symbols in the solution of abstract problems.[7]

Implicit in the views above is a notion of intelligence as a unitary or general ability. A second perspective offered by the theorists takes up this issue and addresses itself to the structure or composition of intelligence. This group of theorists presents a diversity of conclusions about the structure, but common to all is an acceptance of the multidimensionality of intelligence. Some, as we shall see, argue for a general or unitary ability together with a number of separate and distinct more specific abilities; others concentrate on a range of specific abilities and aptitudes and see no need for an assumption of a general ability.

Initial statements on the structure of intelligence, based on statistical analyses of test scores, were made by Spearman,[8] who presented in the 1920s a two-factor theory of intelligence. He identified a general factor of intelligence (g) which was implicated in all intellectual activities, and a number of specific factors (s), which affected an individual's functioning in various specific areas.

During the later fifties, Vernon further modified the prevailing British view, in a hierarchical view of intelligence, and postulated a general factor, but, in addition, two major types of abilities: verbal-educational and spatial-perceptual-practical; he suggested that these major ability types could be broken down into more specialised ones.[9] He emphasised that these group factors were statistical abstractions, not psychological entities. He also emphasised the need to take account, in examining an individual's cognitive performance, of personality factors, including interests and industriousness.

Meantime, on the North American scene, Thurstone had rejected the notion of a general mental ability, replacing it with a view of intelligence as consisting of a number of primary mental abilities: verbal comprehension, word fluency, number, spatial relations, associative memory, perceptual speed and induction.[10] Thurstone's thinking was highly influential in the United States, not only in the construction of intelligence tests, but also in educational practices.

A third perspective, while arguing, as above, the multidimensionality of intelligence, placed a primary emphasis on mental processes as well as the products of intellectual activity, varying according to the types of material being dealt with. Eysenck, in Britain, in 1953, described intelligence through an analysis of what is measured by intelligence tests. He proposed a model comprising three elements: speed and power of mental functioning (relating to quality), special facility for dealing with different types of material, and special excellence of different types of mental processes (perception, memory, reasoning).[11] Eysenck, like Vernon, urged the need to recognise the involvement of non-intellectual factors such as persistence, which he saw as of great importance in determining a person's effective intelligence—his power to solve problems of higher and higher difficulty and complexity.

Guilford, in 1955, also held the viewpoint that there was no one single, comprehensive ability. In conceptualising his view of the structure of the intellect, he proposed three bases of classification:

1. the process or operation—cognition, memory, convergent thinking, divergent thinking and evaluation;
2. the material or content involved—figural (concrete), symbolic, semantic and behavioural;
3. type of product—units, classes, relations, systems, transformations, implications.

'The kind of organism suggested by this way of looking at intellect is that of an agency for dealing with information of various kinds in various ways'.[12]

Guilford made a major contribution to theorising about the nature of intelligence by distinguishing between processes, products and contents, and also by introducing divergent thinking, i.e. creative abilities, into the ambit of a theory of intellect; earlier theorists had tended to emphasise the convergent-thinking operations. These divergent-thinking abilities include word fluency, spontaneous flexibility, associational fluency, expressional fluency, adaptive flexibility and originality.

The sixties and seventies were characterised by a major upsurge of research activity into the phenomenon of creativity (for example, 1967 saw the launching of a new journal, *Creativity*), and, on the educational scene, by considerable effort aimed at identifying and fostering the development of creative, divergent thinkers.

By 1967, Guilford was able to present in greater detail his conclusions on creative thinking.[13] He stated that there were two categories of abilities most relevant to creative thinking. One category is *divergent-production abilities*, pertaining to the generation of ideas, with creative talents being strongly dependent on the media in which the individual works. The second category is *transformation abilities*, through which the person revises what he experiences and knows in order to produce new forms and patterns.

The most recent attempt to capture the multidimensional nature of intelligence is represented by the work of Warburton in the development of the British Intelligence Scale.[14] Warburton points out that, in arriving at a rationale, the test constructors considered three principal sources of evidence: psychometric work on the structure of ability, knowledge of the nature and sequence of cognitive structures obtained from developmental psychology, and experience gained by clinical testers. They arrived at a model incorporating both contents and mental processes:

Contents	Processes
Shapes	Perception
Symbols	Memorisation
Numbers	Recognition
Objects (and pictures of objects)	Conceptualisation
Words	Convergent reasoning (classification)
Sentences	Convergent reasoning (operational)
	Divergent reasoning (creativity)

As will be seen, the Warburton model also recognises divergent reasoning as being one of the mental processes that underlie intellectual functioning.

A fourth perspective on the nature of intelligence, or cognitive abilities, is provided by Piaget, who has focused on the structures of the developing intellect. His basic concern is the understanding of knowledge—its nature and the way in which it is acquired;[15] that is, how the child understands his world. Thus his orientation is to the qualitative growth of the child's abilities, as he proceeds towards the end-state of adult Western logical thought.

He believes that intelligence is the ability to adapt to the environment and that this adaptation is achieved through the two complementary processes of assimilation and accommodation. As the child interacts with his environment (there is an active seeking out and exploring of the environment by the child), he internalises his world, in the form of mental schemata or structures.

In assimilation, the child relates what he perceives to his existing understandings; new information may be distorted to fit in with these existing understandings. In accommodation, the child alters existing structures to accommodate new facts or new information. Thus adaptation is achieved through a balance of assimilation and accommodation.

Piaget notes the human tendency to adaptation and a second tendency to organisation, which is the tendency for all species to systematise or organise their processes into coherent systems, either physical or psychological. This organisation occurs as the individual interacts with his world, and progressively integrates his existing structures into higher-order systems or structures.

McVicker Hunt also sees intelligence as involving adaptation, with a hierarchy of learning sets, strategies of information processing, concepts, motivational systems and skills acquired through the child's ongoing interaction with his environment.[16]

Sharing this fourth perspective is the work of Bruner, based on research conducted at the Center for Cognitive Studies at Harvard. Piaget frames his theory in terms of adaptation and organisation, Hunt stresses adaptation and Bruner focuses on integration—

> the means whereby acts are organized into higher order ensembles, making possible the use of larger and larger units of information for the solution of problems.[17]

In summary, we have outlined above a number of theoretical perspectives on the nature of intelligence. But have we arrived at a clearer understanding of the concept of intelligence itself?

We shall, in a later section, explore the relative fruitfulness of the various models for the classroom teacher concerned with individual differences.

Growth in Cognitive Abilities

It is possible to view a child's cognitive development in quantitative terms—as he grows older, he can solve more difficult problems at greater speed; in terms of intelligence tests, he can, with increasing age, pass more items.

A generalised growth curve shows that the growth of intelligence is most rapid in the early years—in infancy and early childhood; during the later years of childhood and adolescence the rate of growth slackens markedly.

However, generalised growth curves conceal individual variation. Work by Bayley shows plots of growth curves for individual children;[18] these reveal idiosyncratic spurts and plateaux, reminding us of the essential uniqueness of each child. Furthermore, as Ausubel and Sullivan comment,[19] there is evidence that bright, dull and average children grow intellectually at different rates and differ with respect to the organisation and qualitative pattern of cognitive abilities.

Of perhaps greater interest than quantitative changes in intelligence are the qualitative changes that occur as the child, in constant interaction with his environment, grows and develops.

Bruner, as we noted earlier, sees intellectual growth as dependent on the emergence of competence in representation and integration. Thus he described the developing child as passing sequentially through three modes of representation.

enactive	(representing past events through appropriate motor response);
iconic	(summarising events by the selective organisation of percepts and of images); and
symbolic	(representing things by design features that include remoteness and arbitrariness).

These modes appear in the order as listed, each depending on the previous one, but each mode remaining intact.

A major factor in this successive emergence is language, because it releases the child from immediacy, from the domination of perceptual representation, and permits the development of higher-order techniques for processing information.

Piaget, as he traces the child's evolving cognitive growth towards maturity, focuses on qualitative changes as the child passes through a series of maturational stages—the period of sensori-motor intelligence, the pre-operational stage, the period of concrete operations and finally the period of formal operations. In the first period, motor activity is the basis for mental operations. At the onset of the pre-operational stage, the child begins to construct symbols and to use language, and the range of his cognitive functioning is extended. However, during the period of concrete operations, although he is mastering logical acquisitions such as classification, seriation, reversibility and conservation, he is still tied to the concrete level. In the final stage he can deal with abstract relationships: with problems of proportionality, probability, permutations and combinations.

These stages are universal—the order, but not the rate, of achievement of the stages is invariant, since the emergence of new capacities depends on mastery of the prior stage as new capabilities are incorporated into and integrated with previously existing ones.

There follows a brief summary of the essential characteristics of each of the Piagetian stages; the summary is based on an analysis by Smart and Smart:*

---

*Excellent detailed discussions of Piaget's view of development. Smart and Smart's presentation is recommended for detailed consideration by the reader.[20]

Sensori-motor period   (Approximately 0–2 years)
Intelligence works through action schemes; object permanence is achieved; the child learns control of his body in space; he begins to use language to imitate and to make internal representations of reality.

Pre-operational period   (Pre-conceptual stage—approximately 2–4 years; intuitive stage—approximately 4–7 years)
The beginning of symbolising; increase in flexibility of thinking; child becomes more able to draw on past experience and to consider more than one aspect of an event at a time.

Concrete operations period   (Approximately 7–11 years)
The child can think about real, concrete things in a systematic way, but has difficulty in thinking about abstractions; achieves conservation, seriation, class inclusion and reversibility; his thinking becomes socialised.

Formal operations period   (Approximately 11–15 years)
The individual has the mental operations for adult thinking; can think and reason in purely abstract terms; can think systematically; can form and test hypotheses.

Of particular interest to teachers are differences between the way children function at the pre-operational and concrete operational stages and differences between children and adolescents. Differences between the pre-school child and the seven-year-old are summarised by Mussen, Conger and Kagan as follows:

> . . . the former does not have a mental representation of a series of actions; he cannot conserve—that is, he does not realize, as he will a little later, that liquids and solids can be transformed in shape without changing their volume or mass, nor does he realize one-to-one correspondence; he does not understand relational terms (darker, bigger) but, rather, tends to think in absolutes; he cannot yet reason simultaneously about parts and wholes.[21]

Elkind, Barocas and Johnsen suggest that child/adolescent differences are of three kinds: quantitative—the child's logic is restricted to simple combinations, whereas the adolescent can synthesise several factors; qualitative—the child works at the concrete level of symbolic representation, while the adolescent can reason in a sophisticated way and manipulate symbols in novel ways; affective—the child is less certain than the adolescent of the adequacy and efficiency of his own thought processes and is therefore more suggestible.[22]

Clearly, optimal cognitive development requires integrity in sensory functioning. The child who suffers visual, auditory or other perceptual impairment is handicapped in the encounters with the environment through which he actively develops his intelligence. These disadvantages are most marked in the case of the severely or profoundly deaf child.

This is not to say, of course, that all children with sensory defects are below average in cognitive or linguistic competence. However, they do require from their environment special help to actualise their genetic potential. Much depends, in their case, on early parental practices and attitudes and later school endeavours.

Individual Differences in Cognitive Abilities and Performance

Table 1 shows the distribution of intelligence, the proportion at various levels one would expect to find in an unselected population, and the descriptive labels commonly applied to the different levels:

Table 1
Distribution of Intelligence

Range of I.Q.	Percentage of Population	Descriptive Label
140+	1.3	Very superior
120–139	11.3	Superior
110–119	18.1	High average
90–109	46.5	Average or normal
80–89	14.5	Low average, dull normal, slow learning
70–79	5.6	Borderline
50–69	2.4	Mildly intellectually handicapped
20–49	0.2	Moderately intellectually handicapped
Below 20		Severely and profoundly intellectually handicapped

One must not impute a false accuracy to the I.Q.s cited above; they must, because of errors such as errors of measurement, be regarded as approximate only.

Children in the one classroom will be heterogeneous in respect to each of the dimensions discussed in the preceding section.

All levels of intellectual ability, as assessed by intelligence tests, will be represented, from borderline to low average through to the highly gifted. Some classes, in school systems which follow a policy of integration, will contain children categorised as mildly intellectually handicapped; this will, of course, be the situation also in schools with no access to special schools or classes. In most Australian schools, children classified as moderately, severely or profoundly intellectually handicapped will normally not be present.

As we consider individual differences in intelligence among the pupils in the classroom we will immediately think in terms of levels of intelligence—so we will distinguish the bright from the average, and the average from the dull. However, individual variability is much more complex than this, as we might expect from our earlier analyses of theories regarding the multidimensionality of intelligence. These theories draw our attention not only to further more subtle differences between pupils but also alert us to intra-individual variability—that is that each child presents a unique profile of cognitive strengths and weaknesses. Following Guilford, we can expect marked differences among the pupils in respect to the results of the application of the various processes or operations to different content areas. Some, for example, will exhibit their major strengths in convergent thinking applied to semantic material as they seek to achieve systems, transformations and implications; these are the children one would expect to find as high achievers in the traditionally structured learning experiences emphasising verbal competence. Others, still skilled in convergent thinking, will perform best when they deal with concrete or figural rather than with verbal materials. There will be other children whose skills lie more markedly in the area of divergent thinking, some of whom will do their best thinking with symbolic materials but others of whom will excel in the semantic area. Among these divergent thinkers will be found the creative children—those who exhibit fluency, flexibility and creativity in their interactions with their environment. Recognition of the existence and value of this group of children has been relatively recent on the educational scene.

Following Vernon, we would expect children with equal general ability to differ from each other in respect to the relative strengths of their verbal-educational and practical-spatial-mechanical abilities. Again, our present educational system is likely to advantage the former rather than the latter in many areas of the curriculum. Children with adequate general ability and high practical-spatial-mechanical abilities are those likely to succeed in some areas of mathematics, handwork, technical and scientific subjects.

A greater range in special abilities and talents can be expected in the secondary than in the primary classroom—

> By the time an individual reaches adolescence, differential factors of interest, relative ability, specialization of training, motivation, success and failure experience, and cultural expectation operate selectively to develop certain original abilities and to leave others relatively undeveloped.[23]

Following Bruner, we would expect to find in classrooms some children still operating mainly in the iconic mode, while others will have achieved the symbolic mode of representation. As we shall see later, in our discussion of cognitive style, children from certain subcultures may, throughout the years of their schooling, seem to maintain a preference for the enactive over the symbolic mode. Differences in efficiency of utilising the symbolic mode would, expectedly, be associated with differences in language skill and orientation to language use as well as with differences in level of intelligence.

Piaget, in his theorising, was not concerned with individual differences. Nevertheless, researchers who have worked within the Piagetian framework have emphasised the fact of individual differences. For example, some six-year-olds will be functioning entirely at the pre-operational level while other six-year-olds will be reaching forward, in some of their interactions with the environment, towards the concrete operational stage; the modes of the two groups in adapting to their school worlds will differ markedly.

In primary classrooms some children will have achieved security in conservation, others will be in a transitional stage, and yet others will still not have mastered the notion of reversibility.

Piaget's theory, too, allows for intra-individual variability. It is presumed that children acquire different conservations at different ages; a child may well have achieved conservation of length and weight but not yet of volume. Furthermore, children do not make a sudden leap from one stage to the next. It seems likely that a child, for example, in the early years of managing concrete operational thinking, will revert to pre-operational thought in situations of stress or of marked unfamiliarity; he is likely to achieve the new stage first in those areas in which he feels most competent.

One would expect an even greater diversity among children in actual levels of performance than of abilities. This arises from the lack of a one-to-one relationship between ability and performance. The operation of intervening variables—such as background, experience, motivation, preferred cognitive style, language competence, teacher expectation, teacher-child match—will mean that some children will utilise their talents to the full in the classroom and operate at their optimal level. The remainder will vary in the degree to which their achievements in the varied areas of classroom concern reflect only some of their ability.

Group differences (e.g. sex, ethnic and social class groups) will be considered in the final section of this chapter.

Significance of Individual Differences in Cognitive Functioning for the Classroom

To some degree the classroom significance of individual differences in this aspect of a child's functioning seem obvious: the brighter the child, the more easily will he master the tasks of the classroom—especially those involving higher cognitive processes such as reasoning. The brighter the child, the more profit he will have gained from his interactions with previous learning environments and the greater and richer will be the store of concepts and understandings he brings to the present learning situation. To the degree that the child is passing through the developmental stages expected of his age group (e.g. acquiring conservation in the later years of the infant school), to that extent he is likely to find demands made by the teacher compatible with his existing cognitive structures; the degree of his likely success in thus predictable.

But the significance of individuality in intelligence is greater and more far-reaching than this.

Some intellectual abilities are prized more than others by many teachers, and children who excel in these preferred abilities are likely to be rewarded, through their own success, and through the positive response of their teachers. The emotional climate of many classrooms, governed as it is by teacher characteristics, will favour the convergent over the divergent thinker. Thus the teacher's own value system helps determine what significance individual differences will hold.

As we shall see later, appropriate stimulation and encouragement tempt the child further along the route to full realisation of his intellectual capacities. But the stimulation must be appropriate to his present level of functioning. Unless the teacher is aware of each child's level, he is unlikely to offer optimal stimulation to all. Sometimes it is the bright who suffer—they are understimulated and thus deprived of the opportunity to stretch themselves to the full—to enjoy the fruits of meeting challenge. At least as often, it is the duller class members who suffer—often the gap between what they can do and what they are asked to do is so great that they cannot profit from the classroom experiences. As a result, their feelings of competence and confidence are assaulted and it is highly probable that, as they pass through the school classes, the gap between their potential and their actual performance widens. By the time they reach the upper primary and secondary school years, they have become underachievers.

On the basis of his interactions with his pupils (and sometimes on the basis of the results of intelligence tests), the teacher comes to form judgements about his pupils' intellectual competence. These judgements exert a major influence on the teacher's expectations of the pupils. His expectations, in turn, determine the ways in which he continues to interact with them, the level of functioning he demands, what he rewards from among his pupils' behaviours. The pupil responds to these encounters with the teacher, subtly (and sometimes not so subtly) receiving the non-verbal (sometimes verbal) judgements of the teacher about his ability. He absorbs this judgement by the teacher into his self-judgement. If the original teacher judgement was favourable, he is doubly advantaged in the learning situation—by the quality and nature of the learning experiences provided by the teacher, and by his feelings of confidence in his abilities. When the original judgement about a child is negative, he is doubly disadvantaged.*

These outcomes would merit our close attention even if teacher judgements were always accurate. But there is a growing research literature which attests to teacher error in this regard. Many bright children escape identification. Many children from disadvantaged minority groups and many children from the ranks of the poor are underestimated by their teachers, and set on a path of failure.†

Differences in cognitive functioning lead to a further set of repercussions in the classroom. Each teacher will have in his class children of varying abilities. Labels will be assigned in terms of level of I.Q.

Many teachers find it difficult to withstand the effects of labelling. Additionally, many generalise beyond the label assigned to a child— assigned in the light of his intellectual functioning alone. Thus, the bright child, because he is bright, is likely to be seen by the teacher as having a range of virtues in fact quite uncorrelated with brightness. The link between his higher I.Q. and the favourable attributions made by the teacher are a function of the value system of teachers—a value system which accords high status to brightness. Such teachers equate brightness with worth, and perceive the bright as better and more

*See refs nos 24, 25 for a discussion of the self-fulfilling prophecy.
†See discussion in the later section *The School as a Source of Individual Differences*.

valuable than their duller peers and as more likely to be sensitive, mature, sociable and popular. The poor achiever is likely to be judged by the teacher as dull or mildly intellectually handicapped, and, given the traditional school system, is likely, at the same time, to be perceived as an unsatisfactory student with negative personality traits.

The demonstration by researchers of the existence of individual differences in each classroom and their documentation of the uniqueness of each child needs to be matched by teacher understanding and valuing of diversity.

Cognitive Style

Nature of Cognitive Style

Children certainly differ in levels of intellectual ability and cognitive functioning. Importantly, they also differ in their preferred modes of cognitive interaction with the world.

Following Sigel,[26] cognitive style subsumes a variety of cognitive behaviours—'it refers to modes an individual employs in perceiving, organizing and labelling various dimensions of the environment'. Theorists concerned with cognitive style emphasise the existence and importance of individual differences in this aspect. Thus Sigel argues that individuals have preferences for particular modes of categorisation, these modes possessing certain distinctive properties. Ausubel and Sullivan emphasise not only the fact of individual differences but also the self-consistency and enduring nature of these individual styles.[27]

At the moment, and in particular in any learning situation, the individual is surrounded by a host of potential stimuli. He cannot attend to all of these and it is suggested that his particular cognitive style determines those environmental stimuli to which he will attend. Additionally, a child's style determines specifically his utilisation of his intellectual abilities.

Ausubel believes that differences in cognitive style reflect differences in personality organisation as well as differences in cognitive capacity and functioning.[28] He sees cognitive style as mediating between motivation and emotion on the one hand and cognition on the other. Witkin,[29] a major worker in the field, shares Ausubel's view.

Individual Differences in Cognitive Style

Different theorists have been attracted to the exploration and understanding of various aspects of cognitive style.

Nations has postulated that learning styles differ in terms of the combinations of three components: sensory orientation, responsive mode and thinking pattern.[30] Pupils differ in their preferred sensory orientation —some, for example, pay more attention to aural than to visual cues from their environment; some experience the world primarily through their eyes, others through touch. As an extension of this issue of sensory orientation, Bruner, as we saw earlier, suggests that there are three ways in which the child represents experience in his thought: *enactive* (resulting from motor activity), *iconic* (internal images of what is perceived through the senses) and *symbolic* (through the use of language).

Although Bruner postulates these as sequential stages, research shows that some children retain a preference for the enactive or motoric mode of orienting themselves to their world; these children are basically action-oriented.[31, 32, 33, 34, 35, 36]

Nations's second component is 'responsive mode'. Here he is concerned with the fact that some individuals work best in a group, whereas others work best independently; some are active participants, while others are observers; some accept conclusions and suggestions which are proferred to them, while others, because of their responsive mode, are likely to challenge presentations.

The third component—thinking pattern—has been widely explored. Nations contrasts individuals whose preferred pattern is a deliberate, methodical gathering of information with those who prefer, in their problem solving, to make giant intuitive leaps. Kagan has explored this same attribute, naming it the reflection-impulsivity dimension.[37]

Witkin has documented another attribute of cognitive style, which he calls field independence-dependence.[38] The perceptions of field-dependent children are dominated by the total or overall organisation of the field, and they display an inability to perceive the parts of a field as discrete. The field-independent child, on the other hand, is not dominated by the embedding context, but can experience the parts of the field as distinct from, rather than fused with, the organised background. The field-independent children seem to engage in a more active analysis of stimuli and are more adept at breaking a problem down into its constituent parts.

Confirming Ausubel's notion of style as reflecting personality orientation, children with these contrasting styles exhibit different motivational orientations, with the field-dependent child being socially oriented, the field-independent child task oriented.*

A final example* of individual differences in cognitive style which

---

*See ref. no. 1 for discussion of other areas of difference in cognitive style.

is relevant to teachers is to be found in respect to styles of categorisation, employed by individuals. Kagan, Moss and Sigel have distinguished three such styles or ways of analysing the environment.[39] Some make a more minute analysis than others—the theorists refer, for example, to children as 'splitters' or 'lumpers'. They have documented preferences among individuals for one of these three styles:

Categorical groupings	made on the basis of common features;
Relational-contextual groupings	made on the basis of relationships between items;
Analytic or descriptive groupings	made on the basis of similarity in objective elements.

Preference for the third mode appears to be associated with longer attention span, greater reflectivity, greater emotional control and more marked social independence.

Significance for the Classroom of Individual Differences in Cognitive Style

The picture that emerges from the above discussion is one of classrooms composed of pupils with highly individual personality and cognitive styles.

We might expect that strategies which facilitate the pupil's use of his own distinctive cognitive style would have a motivating as well as an enhancing effect upon his learning. If teachers are to create effective learning situations, they must obviously know each pupil's preferred mode of categorisation. Gage, for example, concludes that . . . 'properly organized subject matter presented to learners whose cognitive development *and processes** are correctly understood will produce learning'.[40]

Many schools favour the abstract, conceptual style; according to Olsen,[41] the typical classroom suffers from 'the verbal hangover of the Middle Ages'. This favouring of the abstract conceptual style will promote a ready response in some, but not all, pupils. Others will exact more benefit from multisensory approaches, from teaching strategies which appeal to their action style, to their physical way of learning, for example, simulation, role playing, socio-drama.[42, 43]

Most teachers are middle-class† mainstream-culture members. Most have demonstrated, through their own educational history, the

*Author's italics.
†By birth, or through upward mobility.

particular cognitive styles, values and motives our schools have always been able to use effectively. The challenge to these teachers is to help children with abilities and orientations different from their own to learn. Guiding the learning process involves highly personal and intimate transactions between teacher and pupil. There must be appreciation by the teacher of the child's perception of a situation, of the cues in a given situation that are significant to him. He must be able to sense the value the child is exacting from a particular experience if he is to guide him; he must know each child's distinctive preferred cognitive style.

Not only is it important that teachers recognise diversity in their pupils; it is critical that they value these alternative styles—that they see them as educationally viable and valid. Otherwise, even if appropriate strategies are developed and made available to teachers, there may be little demonstrable gain to pupils: the strategies, if used, will be used unwisely, without insight and without expectation of success. In contrast, the teacher who prizes this diversity will in his day-to-day interactions with his pupils, be alert to recognise a variety of styles and to use these to tempt his pupils forward toward optimal development.

There is a further implication of individual differences in cognitive style for the classroom teacher. Riessman believes that we have a responsibility to aid each student to gain power from his style, because this is going to be the source of his power.[44] If, for example, an individual has a physical style, Riessman affirms that he needs to learn the special attributes of this style and how to use them.

Asking the learner to master school tasks through the use of his own cognitive style, where this is possible, not only makes good educational sense, but also confirms for the student his teacher's respect for and valuing of him. Perhaps this is a major factor in the motivating force of such strategies.

Language

The Nature of Language and Linguistic Development

It is perhaps necessary to draw the distinction which exists between language and speech. One of the distinctions drawn by Miller and McNeill is between language as the cognitive component that a language user must know and speaking as a behavioural component of a vocal communication event.[45] This distinction between language and speech is associated with the difference emphasised by Chomsky between *competence* (the knowledge the person must have to understand or generate any of the infinitely large number of sentences permitted in the language) and *performance* (the actual use of language in specific situations).[46] As we shall see later, a child's performance does not always reflect his actual developed level of competence.

The language that a child acquires is, in Lewis's words, made up of systems of, structures and systems of meanings which are systematically related to each other; the child acquires his language with little or no awareness of the systematic relations between structures and meanings.[47]

There are three components of the language system. *Phonology* refers to the sound system, *grammar* or *syntax* refers to the way in which elements are organised and combined into well-formed sentences, while *lexicon* or the *semantic system* is concerned with words—particularly their definitions or meanings.

As educationists, usually interacting with the child from the age of four or five onwards, we shall look a little more closely at syntax and semantics.

There are two major aspects of a language—its structure and its meaning. Understanding language means that one must understand structure and meaning, and these two broad aspects are, in fact, associated. This association can be understood through the two aspects of structure: the surface structure of a sentence refers to the sound of the sentence, while the deep structure of the sentence refers to its meaning.[48] Chomsky has proposed a transformational grammar,[49] formulating rules that link surface and deep structure and specifying how meaning (deep structure) is transformed into sounds (surface structure).

Grammatical competence is illustrated in rules for generating sentences and for the construction of individual words. The young child very early acquires the grammar of his language. Miller and Erwin,[50] summarising research evidence, conclude that by the age of four most children have learned the fundamental structural features of their language and many of the details; this early mastery is followed by a period of consolidation. Ausubel suggests that at four years, the only major syntactic forms that are not completed are the transformations for negatives, questions and passives; these are completed during the primary school years.[51] Miller and McNeill suggest that these remarkable achievements are routinely performed by every pre-school child.

During the primary school years, the child completes his mastery of transformations and learns to become adept in the formulation of longer and more complicated sentences—both compound and complex.

Semantic aspects of language—the area of meaning and vocabulary

—are of critical importance to educators, and, as we shall discuss later, a wider range of individual differences, within a given speech community, is likely to obtain in semantic than in syntactic performance.

Several distinctions must be remembered as the semantic aspects of a child's development are considered. First, the child, by school entry and thereafter, possesses two vocabularies—a passive vocabulary (listening) and an active vocabulary (speaking); for most individuals the passive is more extensive than the active vocabulary. The schooling processes introduce the child to the secondary language uses of reading and writing.

Second, the individual develops different vocabularies for different purposes—the vocabulary the child uses with his peers may differ in important respects from that he uses in communication with his parents and, again, from that he uses with teachers and other non-family adults. As he grows he develops situation-specific and activity-specific vocabularies.

A child's semantic competence/performance cannot, of course, be divorced from the linguistic community in which he grows up. He acquires not only the structures or syntax of the language which surrounds him, but also the particular meanings and nuances, both cognitive and affective, assigned by his culture or subculture to specific words and phrases.

Whereas the school entrant has almost mastered the syntax of his language, he will continue throughout childhood and adolescence to develop and expand his semantic mastery of his language. He extends his vocabulary; he assigns greater precision to particular words; he achieves greater command of this tool of thought and of communication. There is an interrelationship between this greater command and his growing cognitive sophistication.

Ausubel, using a meaningful verbal learning theory, believes that the most basic type of meaningful learning is representational learning—that is, learning the meanings of single symbols (typically words) or learning what they represent (vocabulary learning). He distinguishes between learning the meaning of single symbols and learning the meanings of ideas expressed by groups of words. He sees concept learning, or learning the meaning of concepts, as a third type of learning.

During the early stages of vocabulary learning, words tend to represent actual objects and events and are hence equated in meaning with the relatively concrete and specific images such referents signify; 'naming' involves the establishment of representational equivalence between first-order symbols and concrete images. Later, words become concept names and are equated in meaning with more abstract, generalised, and categorical cognitive content. Denotative and connotative meanings are acquired. After the pre-school years, the meanings of most new words are learnt by definition or by being encountered in appropriate contexts.[52]

Bruner sees the learning of references (the semantic function of language) as a slow process, since it involves learning the semantic markers of a word, the senses that it has or the contexts into which it fits.[53]

The burden of learning is increased by the fact that varying social contexts impose constraints on the child's use of language—he must learn the ways appropriate to his culture of speaking (how, to whom, under what circumstances). As he does this he acquires socio-linguistic competence; that is he acquires a variety of styles to suit the social contexts of verbal exchanges in which he participates.[54]

Our understanding of children and of the differences among them is enhanced if we consider the functions which language serves. Language is seen as fulfilling a number of functions: communication, facilitation of abstract thought, self-control and social self-identification.

The role of language in communication seems obvious, but there are some aspects that require stressing. Language is part only of a whole matrix of events in which communication occurs. Miller and McNeill describe three aspects of the social matrix of verbal communications —linguistic, paralinguistic (voice qualities and other socially significant vocalisations), and kinesic (e.g. body actions and attitudes). On the linguistic dimension, they point to the fact that lexical choice is a function of perceived relationships; thus our use of language reflects the social situation in which we find ourselves.

Fishman, in an introduction to socio-linguistics, emphasises, too, the social situation—two interlocutors must recognise the role relationship that exists between them at any particular time; this recognition is part of the communality of norms, without which communication would be severely impaired.[55]

The second function of language listed earlier is the facilitation of abstract thought. It is true that there is some disagreement between theorists about the exact relationship between language and thought, but language plays a key role in the thinking of most people most of the time. As Lewis summarises, we use language for recalling what has happened, for recording for the future, for solving problems, for anticipating and planning.[56]

As the child acquires language, his cognitive abilities undergo modification and his learning becomes increasingly controlled and regulated by words.

Bruner sees the internalisation of language as a cognitive instrument enabling the child to represent and transform experience with greater power and flexibility.[57] Ausubel emphasises the dependence on linguistic competence of transfer from concrete operational to formal operational thinking.

The third role of language was postulated as self-control. The relationship between language and self-control is obviously linked with that between language and thought. It was Luria who traced the parallelism between the development of language and emerging self-control.[58] This control is exercised through 'inner speech' and Luria notes the concurrent emergence of inner speech and self-control at about four and a half years of age.

Finally, language serves a function of social self-identification. Individuals identify themselves, both consciously and unconsciously, with their own speech community; similarly, outsiders frequently identify an individual's social class and/or ethnic and/or educational background through his linguistic style. In fact, in this latter instance, a particular language variety or dialect can serve to reinforce stereotypes held by others about members of that linguistic community.

Young writes,

> Language is a uniquely revealing type of behaviour. It identifies a person with amazing effectiveness. Language habits reflect one's past life, the geographic area where childhood years were spent, grammatical errors copied from uneducated associates, and the critical or kindly attitude of the speaker.[59]

Individual Differences in Linguistic Development

Children are genetically programmed to acquire language; through interactions with speakers in their linguistic community they achieve language.

There is, as would be expected, variability among the pupils in a classroom in their linguistic performance, even if we were to envisage a classroom composed entirely of middle-class members of a single cultural group.

As the children develop, individual differences in semantic development become more marked than differences in structural development. That is, meaning rather than structure becomes the important issue. The pupils vary in the vocabulary they command, the sophistication and precision of the concepts they have developed, their abilities to facilitate problem solving through the use of language, their verbal fluency and creativeness.

Lewis associates these differences with differences in natural giftedness in the area of potential language ability, with differences in hearing, with differences in intelligence and with differences in temperament. Obviously environment, too, is implicated. This underlines the continual emphasis in this analysis of individual differences on the interrelatedness of all aspects of a child's development. This interrelatedness, this interdependence of characteristics itself guarantees the uniqueness of each individual.

We will, in the final section of this chapter, explore the sources of these individual differences. At present, we merely note their existence.

Reality, in the Australian setting, would, however, oblige us to people our illustrative classroom with not only middle-class mainstream-culture children but also with pupils from the various other sectors of the Australian society: children from the working class and lower class, children of English-speaking parents who were born overseas, children whose parents' first language was a language other than English, Aboriginal children. In each of these subgroups there will be marked heterogeneity in respect to their linguistic competence in their own first language, in their linguistic competence and performance in the language of the classroom—Standard English—, and, furthermore, in their socio-linguistic competence.

The pupils in the multicultural classroom will differ, also, in a further respect—in their orientation to language use. Bernstein[60] has drawn our attention to the ways in which modes of social relationship within the family and language code are intimately related. Some families socialise their children in ways that promote an emphasis on contexts and particularistic meanings in language use, while in other families (typically the middle class) social-personal relationships orient the members more to universalistic orders of meaning, to the use of language to explore, to question, to hypothesise. Pupils from the former type of home will be less skilled than the latter in school uses of language, particularly as the school is necessarily concerned with the transmission and development of universal orders of meaning.

Significance of Individual Differences in Linguistic Functioning in the Classroom

Because of differences in their linguistic development children are differentially ready to profit from what is offered in the classroom. We might consider two examples of this.

First, it seems to remain true that children spend a major proportion of their within-class time listening; or, more accurately, we might say that a considerable proportion of the school day is spent in teacher talk. In addressing himself to his pupils the teacher makes assumptions that he is communicating, that he is understood. In this, he is assuming also that the words he uses have the same meanings and implications for his pupils as for himself; he is assuming also that all pupils share his orientation towards universalistic orders. Enough has been said above to indicate that for some pupils in the classroom these teacher assumptions are, in fact, untenable; communication is impaired; the learning stimulus that is offered is not appropriate; the pupils thus affected do not learn. Furthermore, they are likely to develop feelings of incompetence and self-doubt and tune out from the teacher talk.

A second example: as we have indicated above, the expansion and refinement of vocabulary takes place, after the infant school years, increasingly through verbal rather than concrete contexts. The child with less than average linguistic and/or intellectual competence finds too large a gap between his existing knowledge and the new knowledge to be acquired through verbal mediation, and failure is again the result.

Situations such as those described above have two negative outcomes for the less competent child: he fails to master the ideas and concepts presented in a range of subject matter; he fails, also, to develop further, to the extent to which he is capable, his language competence.

The socio-linguists offer a further perspective on the significance for classroom teachers of differences among children.[61] Individual pupils will differ from one another in their social background and hence in the social norms and role expectations that rule in their families; they will be socialised differentially into language behaviour with correspondingly different outcomes in cognitive style, world view, the uses of language and the language or dialect they speak. Each of these variables affects educability. (It is important to comment that educability is not an absolute; the degree to which a child is educable is highly dependent on the match between what he offers and what the school demands.)

There is, however, an intervening variable: the teacher's judgement of educability. How are these judgements influenced by the child's language performance, socio-linguistic competence and dialect?

First, teachers are prone to see Standard English as the only correct form of English and to judge non-standard forms as inferior. In these views teachers have until recently been supported by researchers and writers who have described non-standard dialects as deficit dialects. For example, Bereiter and Englemann claim that the language of the culturally deprived is basically a non-logical mode of expressive behaviour.[62]

They describe further deficits in the language of these children: giant word units, rather than distinct words, inability to deal with sentences as sequences of meaningful parts, marked lack of ability to use language as a device for acquiring and processing information.

Recent work by linguists, psycholinguists and socio-linguists has, however, demonstrated this view of language as 'sheer nonsense'.[63] In 1970 the Linguistic Society of America set up a Committee on Language and Cognitive Development to publicise linguists' knowledge about the nature of language, the adequacy of different languages or forms of language for formulating thought, and the nature of language development in the individual.[64] Labov sums up the view of the linguists—

Linguists are in an excellent position to demonstrate the fallacies of the verbal deprivation theory. All linguists agree that non-standard dialects are highly structured systems. They do not see these dialects as accumulations of errors caused by the failure of their speakers to master standard English . . . Nor do they believe that the speech of working-class people is merely a form of emotional expression, incapable of expressive logical thought.[65]

Many teachers, however, continue to judge non-standard forms of English as inferior, and, in making this judgement, make further judgements about the intellectual inferiority of the speakers of such language forms. In these circumstances they are likely to make a negative judgement about the child's educability. This judgement is often confirmed by the child's failure to learn. But his failure is not, in fact, caused by incompetence but, rather, by lack of teacher understanding and hence the failure of the teachers to provide effective teaching-learning situations. They frequently do not understand the non-standard speaker's linguistic system (its content or its potency) and are unaware of the demands they make when they expect him to operate in standard English; they do not appreciate the socio-linguistic interference from the contrasting communicative demands in and outside the school.[66] Consequently the child's motivation is impaired; he sees himself presented with almost insuperable obstacles to his academic progress; school learning seems unconnected with his real life, seems of no personal importance, and often failure is the logical end-point.

Second, people (including teachers) tend, as we saw earlier, to use a child's speech to infer a range of characteristics about him—characteristics relevant to their notions of educability. Entwisle quotes Rist's work,[67] which showed that teachers used children's speech as a criterion for grouping them on their initial enrolment at school; this initial grouping determined teacher-pupil interactions and teacher expectations. A number of researchers (e.g. [68]) have convincingly demonstrated that pupils' speech and voice cues affect teacher judgement about their intelligence.

Determinants of Variability in Cognitive and Linguistic Functioning

In Chapter 1 we began our search for the sources of variability in personality characteristics in distal environmental variables, and then progressed to examine proximal environmental variables, and finally looked to see the role the individual plays in shaping his own development. This path was pursued in respect to each of the characteristics under review.

In this chapter, we vary our approach in two ways. First, we begin with an examination of the contribution of heredity to individual differences in cognitive and linguistic functioning; we begin here because of the clearly established genetic influence. Second, because of the interdependence of cognitive and linguistic abilities and the high degree of communality in their antecedents, as we examine each of the variables we will analyse their effects on both aspects of the child's development and hence their contribution to individual variability.

Heredity As a Source of Variance

Theorists in earlier decades of this century emphasised heredity as the main determinant of an individual's level of intelligence; that is intelligence was conceived as an innate ability, affected only to a minor degree by environmental circumstances—(e.g.[69]). Researchers began to demonstrate that variations in environment could be associated with variations in intelligence, and gradually psychologists seemed to align themselves with one of two groups: those who claimed the major source of variance as genetic, or their opponents who urged the influence of environment.

There is no doubt that, at the moment of conception, the individual-to-be receives genes from both parents which predetermine his level of intellectual potential; some are advantaged in their gene-pool, others (to a greater or lesser extent) disadvantaged. However, few contemporary theorists discount the importance of environment in the actualisation of that potential. Cognitive functions cannot develop without an environment with which the individual can interact. Furthermore, research has identified wide variation in those aspects of the growing child's environment that are significant for his cognitive development. Thus the commonly held view today is (a) that an individual's intellectual potential is set at conception, individuals varying in the level of genetic potential; and (b) that environment determines the realisation of that potential, individuals again varying in the environments provided by their societies and families for their nurture. Thus an individual's level of functioning—his effective intelligence—is determined by complex interactions between heredity and environment.

A child who receives a favourable genetic endowment will, if raised in stimulating circumstances, realise this potential, theoretically, at least, to the full. However, the same child may well encounter environments adverse to his development; if so, he will be functionally duller than he might have been. The same holds for the child with low potential. Environmental stimulation, appropriate to his level, will enable him to realise that potential; inappropriate environments will ensure that he realises or actualises only some degree of that already limited potential. Environment, however favourable, cannot raise his achievement beyond the genetic potential. Many children are advantaged by both heredity and environment while many others are doubly disadvantaged.

As we seek to understand heredity/environment interaction, we find that Ausubel has offered a very useful concept in the 'growth matrix'.[70] Development results from continuous interaction between various stimulating factors and the individual's prevailing growth matrix. This growth matrix, encompassing the results of all prior interactions between heredity and environment, consists of selective predispositions both to undergo change and to respond to the environment in particular ways. A child favoured by genes and early experiences will respond quite differently to the challenge and the opportunity of a new learning experience from a child who, because of factors associated with heredity and/or environment, brings less competence to the new situation. Each child helps determine the effect that the new situation will have on his further development. For the first child, cognitive functioning, further stimulated, advances; for the second child, there is no or little stimulus to further advancement.

With respect to language development, it is accepted that man possesses an inborn capacity for language; the potential is carried in the genes. Obviously, however, the particular language a child learns, and how well he learns its various aspects, are subject to environmental influence.

Sex differences in intellectual and cognitive functioning provide a useful illustration of the interaction of heredity and environment in shaping the child's development.

If we examine the overall level of cognitive functioning of boys and girls we find no group differences between the sexes. However, there are differences in some aspects of intellectual functioning—in general, as groups, girls surpass boys on verbal aspects, particularly verbal fluency, and also in rote memory, while boys exhibit superior performance in mathematical reasoning and spatial understanding. These differences become more marked with age, particularly by adolescence.[71]

Differences, in favour of the girls, in the verbal domain emerge early in the developmental cycle—girls talk a little earlier and exhibit superior performance during the pre-school years in articulation and intelligibility and learn grammar and spelling more readily.[72] However, there are no sex differences in vocabulary.

Sigel documents sex differences in cognitive styles.[73] These are particularly noticeable in the trait field-dependence/field-independence. Women are more field-dependent; men more field-independent; women are more influenced in their problem solving than men by the structure of the total situation.

The complex interactions between genetic potentialities and environmental variables probably account for sex differences in patterns of abilities. A major environmental variable which is implicated is social sex role. Most cultures assign different sets of socially desirable and culturally sanctioned roles to boys and girls. As the children are socialised into their culture they are strongly influenced by these social sex roles and learn to develop behaviours and skills appropriate to their social sex role. Parents are an important influence in this learning, as they reward and encourage, or discourage, behaviours in terms of perceived appropriateness.

Distal Environmental Variables As Sources of Variance

1. Race, Ethnicity, Social Class

Ethnicity and social class are conceptually distinct. However, in Western societies at least, those theorists who have pursued the contribution of race or ethnicity to variability in cognitive and linguistic functioning have concerned themselves with ethnic groups the majority of whose members are disadvantaged lower-class members of the total society.* It thus becomes difficult, if not impossible, to disentangle the effects of ethnicity and social class. This is particularly so in Australia.

The major figures of note in this area are Jensen and Eysenck. Jensen,[74] from his studies in North America, concluded that genetic factors are strongly implicated in the average Negro/white intelligence difference. Jensen also concluded, from his studies, that two broad categories of mental abilities, abstract reasoning ability and associative learning ability, appear to be distributed differentially in various social

*See ch. 1.

classes and racial groups. Essentially, Jensen has argued that race differences are more consistent with a hypothesis of genetic rather than environmental causation. Eysenck[75] concurs with Jensen.

Jensen's 1969 paper raised a storm of protest, and arguments against his position, both rational and emotive, were advanced.

Gage in a careful analysis of the data,[76] is one of a number who suggests that Jensen has underestimated the impact of environment; he shows that 'given environments different or "apart" enough, we can produce major differences in I.Q. or, even more important, school attainment, even among persons with the same genetic composition'.

As we pursue our investigation of environmental variables associated with differences in cognition, readers will be in a better position to study and evaluate the conflicting theories on race and intelligence currently in force. This writer believes that environmental factors are strongly implicated not only in differences between individuals but also in differences between groups.[77]

Social class, as we saw in Chapter 1, is a pervasive variable and social class differences in intelligence, cognitive style and language, favouring the middle over the lower class, have been consistently documented and are reported in almost all books written on child development.

Other environmental variables to be pursued in the following pages include a number closely associated with social class and through the mechanism of which social class probably operates: family structure, parental values, parent-child interactions and school-student interactions.

One further aspect, particularly related to social class, merits specific mention. This is the matter of health and nutritional status. As North points out,[78] ill health can keep a child from fully exploiting his environment and, thus, we would add, from developing his intelligence through active exploration of his environment. Low socio-economic status is associated with a higher incidence and prevalence of many health problems, including malnutrition and anaemia; it is associated, too, with a higher incidence of premature births—prematurity and impaired I.Q. have, in turn, some degree of association.

Ethnicity and social class are also related to preferred cognitive style. For example, various ethnic groups within the United States (in studies replicated in New York and Boston) foster the development of different patterns of mental ability; these studies show Jewish children superior in verbal ability and black children relatively inferior on spatial and numerical tasks, but average in verbal ability, Chinese children high on spatial conceptualisation, and Puerto Ricans lowest of all the groups on verbal ability.[79]

If we examine the life styles and values of the various social classes we would expect to find group differences among the adults (and hence the children, through child-rearing practices) in preference for the various cognitive styles described earlier. As one example, Pavenstedt found low lower-class families to be impulse-determined, giving little evidence of planfulness. Such families are likely to produce children displaying impulsive rather than reflective cognitive styles.[80]

Ethnicity and social class are associated with children's language development. The link is obvious with respect to the particular language or dialect the child learns. In societies such as ours, composed of multiple social-class and ethnic groups, value judgements about the inadequacy of non-standard forms of the language are made. In an earlier section we discussed the lack of validity of such judgements in the light of linguistic criteria.

2. Family Structure

Size of Family and Position in Family. A number of investigations have reported a negative relationship between I.Q. and size of family. Nisbet had early hypothesised that, because of the close link between language development and abstract thinking, the environment of the large family had its depressing effect on I.Q. because of the limited amount of contact between parent and child.[81] This limited contact will, as we shall later see, reduce the opportunity for stimulation of the child,* resulting in impaired cognitive and linguistic development. As a result, one would expect group differences in the characteristics with which we are presently concerned, in favour of the children from low-density families.

First-born or only children tend to be more verbal and exhibit higher I.Q.s than other children. The explanation for this lies in the quality and quantity of parent-child interaction.

3. Parental Values

A review of the discussion of parental values presented in Chapter 1 suggests that parental values will determine child-training practices which have a marked effect on children's cognitive and language development. Parents who value curiosity and a seeking method of problem solving will foster the development of these traits in their children, whereas those who value obedience and conformity will place a lower premium on these traits. Similarly, parental values, and hence child-rearing practices, will foster or inhibit divergent and convergent thinking skills.

*See detailed discussion of family size in Ch. 1.

Proximal Environmental Variables As Sources of Variance

1. Parent-Child Interactions

Hunt has made a major contribution to our understanding of the role of the child's early environment in the stimulation of his intellectual growth—

> It was commonly believed before World War II that early experience was important for emotional development and the development of personality characteristics, but unimportant for the development of intellect or intelligence . . . It looks now as though early experience may be even more important for the perceptual, cognitive and intellective functions than it is for the emotional and temperamental functions.[82]

The importance of an environment rich in sensory stimulation is evident when one considers Piaget's theory of the first basic developments during the period of sensori-motor intelligence.

Language is very important, too. The degree of contact a child has with his parents, the nature of the contact, the quality of the language model they provide for him and the language demands they make upon him are important determinants of his language and cognitive abilities.

Hess,[83] after a careful analysis of the research literature on parental variables associated with cognitive growth, scholastic achievement and educability, suggests three groups of variables:

1. *Intellectual relationship*
   demand for high achievement
   maximisation of verbal interaction
   engagement with and attentiveness to the child
   maternal teaching behaviour
   diffuse intellectual stimulation

2. *Affective relationship*
   warm, affective relationship with the child
   feelings of high regard for child and self

3. *Interaction patterns*
   pressure for independence and self reliance
   clarity and severity of disciplinary rules
   use of conceptual rather than arbitrary regulatory strategies

Mothers differ in the degree to which they help their children to become more effective problem-solvers, and these differences are linked to social class: some provide more specific feedback and allow the child to work at his own pace, offering general suggestions about how to search for a solution, while others make more controlling and disapproving comments and provide highly specific suggestions that do not emphasise basic problem-solving strategies. Again, some mothers (more typically middle-class ones) are more responsive to their children's questions and give more accurate and informative answers.[84]

It is important to note that there are sex differences in parent-child interactions related to intellectual development. Honzik, for example, found that optimal intellectual growth in boys requires a warm close relationship with a mother as well as a masculine model who achieves and is also concerned about his son's achievement. However, the same does not hold true for girls; in their case intellectual growth appears relatively independent of close maternal emotional relationships, but bears more relationship to parental ability.[85]

Finally, in this section, it is worth emphasising that the parent-child interactions which foster cognitive and linguistic development are more typical of middle-class than of lower-class families. However, there is heterogeneity within each class and a child's developmental pattern is determined, not by his social-class membership, but by the practices his particular parents use as they act as the agents of socialisation.

2. School-Student Interaction

It is reasonable to assert that the school itself is a source of variability among its pupils. Children enter the doors of the schoolroom already presenting differing intellectual and linguistic profiles to the teacher. To the extent that a teacher fails to lead each child on from where he is, so that teacher causes the gap to widen between the more and the less competent children.

The research literature of the forties, fifties and sixties documents the lower I.Q., the below-average school performance, the high illiteracy rates, the high drop-out rates among many of the culturally different groups—especially those where a majority of the members live in depressed socio-economic conditions.

Explanations of these limited achievements have been sought in the home circumstances of the children. Correlational studies have linked diminished achievement with membership of large families, overcrowded homes, poor nutritional status, lack of stimulating environment, lack of pressure for language development and for achievement motivation.

Factors such as these are undoubtedly obstacles to the academic progress of many children. But it may be that these 'explanations' are too simplistic in their approach. They focus on discontinuities between home and school, but in a one-sided fashion: the home does not promote the development of abilities the school believes important. But does not the home promote the development of other abilities? What are these other abilities and why does the school not make use of them?

Many contemporary writers see a major cause of this condition as residing in the school itself, primarily because of a mismatch between the school and the child. They argue that it is the school's responsibility to plan learning situations which capitalise on the child's developed concepts, styles, understandings and skills and which lead him forward to new learnings from a secure base.

Unless this happens, the child of the poor, of the disadvantaged minority, suffers what has been graphically called the 'cumulative deficit' phenomenon—the longer he stays at school, the more he falls behind his socially advantaged peers. When this occurs, the school must face the charge of failing to be a positive environmental influence.

Whether the school succeeds in providing a match between itself and the child is a function, ultimately, of teachers' knowledge, understandings and values. They need to be concerned with ways of offering effective education for all. Each new proposed variation in school architecture, curriculum, methodology and evaluation needs to be assessed in terms of its effect on each pupil, not in terms of its probable effect on the majority, or, as sometimes happens, its probable appropriateness to the middle-class mainstream pupils.

Conclusion

We have emphasised throughout the dangers that may arise when we consider, in isolation, one characteristic or group of characteristics of a child. Cognitive and linguistic styles and abilities are but a few of his characteristics. They are influenced in both their *development* and *utilisation* by his view of himself and his perceived place in the world and his confidence in the future. Thus knowing a child's intellectual abilities may be but the teacher's first step in devising and implementing an appropriate educational programme for him. This programme needs to be refined in the light of the teacher's understanding of his preferred cognitive style, and of his psycholinguistic and socio-linguistic competence. But, beyond this, the teacher must be always cognisant that a child's response to the programme is determined by the particular constellation of characteristics—affective, cognitive and psychomotor—that define his uniqueness.

References

1. Ausubel, D.P. and Sullivan, E.V., 1970. *Theory and Problems of Child Development*, 2nd edn. Grune & Stratton: New York, chs. 14 and 16.
2. Luria, A.R., 1957. 'The Role of Language in the Formation of Temporary Connections', in Simon B. (ed.), *Psychology in the Soviet Union*. Stanford University Press: Calif.
3. Crandall, V.C., 1969. 'Sex Differences in Expectancy of Intellectual and Academic Reinforcement', in Smith, C.P. (ed.), *Achievement-Related Motives in Children*. Russell Sage Foundation: New York, p. 15.
4. Binet, A. and Simon, T., 1916. *The Development of Intelligence in Children*, trans. E.S. Kite. Williams & Wilkins: Baltimore, p. 42.
5. Munn, N.L., 1946. *Psychology: The Fundamentals of Human Adjustment*. Houghton Mifflin: Boston Mass.
6. Wechsler, D., 1952. *The Measurement and Appraisal of Adult Intelligence*, 3rd edn. Williams & Wilkins: Baltimore.
7. Ausubel, D.P. and Ausubel, P., 1966. 'Cognitive Development in Adolescence'. *Review of Educational Research* 36: 403–13.
8. Spearman, C., 1923. *The Nature of Intelligence and the Principles of Cognition*. Macmillan & Co.: London.
9. Vernon, P.E., 1961. *The Structure of Human Abilities*. Methuen & Co.: London.
10. Thurstone, L.L., 1938. *Primary Mental Abilities*. University of Chicago Press: Chicago.
11. Eysenck, H.J., 1953. *Uses and Abuses of Psychology*, Penguin Publications: London.
12. Guilford, J.P., 1959. 'Three Faces of Intellect'. *American Psychologist* 14: 469–79.
13. Guilford, J.P., 1967. 'Creativity: Yesterday, Today and Tomorrow'. *Creativity* 1: 3–14.
14. Warburton, F.W., 1970. 'The British Intelligence Scale', in Dockrell, W.B. (ed.), *On Intelligence: The Toronto Symposium of Intelligence, 1969*. Methuen & Co: London.
15. See, for example; Ginsburg, H. and Opper, S., 1969. *Piaget's Theory of Intellectual Development: An Introduction*. Prentice Hall: Englewood Cliffs, N.J.
16. Hunt, J. McV., 1975. 'Psychological Assessment in Education and Social Class', in Maehr, M.L. and Stallings, W.M. (eds), *Culture, Child and School: Sociocultural Influences on Learning*. Brooks-Cole Publishing Co.: Monterey, Calif.
17. Bruner, J.S., 1964. 'The Course of Cognitive Growth'. *American Psychologist* 19: 1–15.
18. Bayley, N., 1956. 'Individual Patterns of Development'. *Child Development* 27: 45–74.
19. Ausubel and Sullivan, 1970. *Op. cit.*, p. 655.
20. Smart, M.S. and Smart, R., 1972. *Children: Development and Relationships*, 2nd edn. Macmillan Co.: New York.
21. Mussen, P.H., Conger, J.J. and Kagan, J., 1969. *Child Development and Personality*, 3rd edn. Harper International: New York.
22. Elkind, D., Barocas, R. and Johnsen, P., 1969. 'Concept Production in Children and Adolescents'. *Human Development* 12: 10–21.
23. Ausubel and Sullivan, 1970. *Op. cit.*, p. 662.

24. Rosenthal, R. and Jacobson, L., 1968. *Pygmalion in the Classroom: Teacher Expectation and Pupils' Intellectual Development.* Holt, Rinehart & Winston: New York.
25. Rubovitz, P.C. and Maehr, M.L., 1975. 'Teacher Expectations: A Special Problem for Black Children with White Teachers', in Maehr & Stallings, *op. cit.*, pp. 249–59.
26. Sigel, I.E., 1963. 'How Intelligence Tests Limit Understanding of Intelligence'. *Merrill-Palmer Quarterly of Behaviour and Development* 9: 39–56.
27. Ausubel and Sullivan, 1970. *Op. cit.*, p. 638.
28. *Ibid.*, p. 112.
29. Witkin, H.A., 1969. 'Social Influences in the Development of Cognitive Style', in Goslin, D. (ed.), *Handbook of Socialization Theory and Research.* Rand McNally & Co.: New York, p. 688.
30. Nations, J.E., 1967. 'Caring for Individual Differences in Reading through Non-Grading'. Referenced in Bernard, 1973. *Op. cit.*, p. 199.
31. Eisenberg, L., 1967. 'Strengths of the Inner City Child', in Passow, A.H. Goldberg, M.L. and Tannenbaum, A.J. (eds), *Education of the Disadvantaged.* Holt, Rinehart & Winston: New York.
32. Riessman, F., 1962. *The Culturally Deprived Child.* Harper & Row: New York.
33. ———, 1967*a*. 'Blueprint for an Educational Revolution', in Kvaraceus, W.C., Gibson, J.S. and Curtin, T.J. (eds), *Poverty, Education and Race Relations.* Allyn & Bacon: Boston, Mass.
34. ———, 1967*b*. 'The Strategy of Style', in Passow, Goldberg and Tannenbaum (eds), *op. cit.*
35. Goldberg, M.L., 1967. 'Adapting Teacher Style to Pupil Differences: Teachers for Disadvantaged Children', in Passow, Goldberg and Tannenbaum (eds), *op. cit.*
36. Beilin, H. and Gotkin, L., 1967. 'Psychological Issues in the Development of Mathematics Curricula for Socially Disadvantaged Children', in Passow, Goldberg and Tannenbaum (eds), *op. cit.*
37. Kagan, J., 1966. 'Body-build and Conceptual Impulsivity in Children'. *Journal of Personality* 34: 118–28.
38. Witkin, H.A., Dvk, R.B., Paterson, H.F., Goodenough, D.R. and Karp, S.A. 1962. *A Psychological Differentiation.* Wiley & Sons: New York.
39. Kagan, J., Moss, H.A. and Sigel, I.E., 1963. 'Psychological Significance of Styles of Conceptualization'. *Monograph of the Society for Research in Child Development.* 28, 2: 73–112.
40. Gage, N.L., 1963. 'Paradigms for Research on Teaching', in Gage, N.L. (ed.), *Handbook of Research on Teaching.* A.E.R.A.
41. Olsen, J., 1971. 'The Verbal Ability of the Culturally Different', in Joyce, W.W. and Banks, J.A. (eds), *Teaching the Language Arts to Culturally Different Children.* Addison-Wesley Publishing Co.: Reading, Mass.
42. Banks, J.A. and Joyce, W.W., 1971. *Teaching Social Studies to Culturally Different Children.* Addison-Wesley Publishing Co.: Reading, Mass.
43. Joyce, W.W. and Banks, J.A. (eds) 1971. *Teaching the Language Arts to Culturally Different Children.* Addison-Wesley Publishing Co.: Reading, Mass.
44. Riessman, 1967*b*. *Op. cit.*
45. Miller, G.A. and McNeill, D., 1969. 'Psycholinguistics', in Lindzey, G. and Aronson, E. (eds), *The Handbook of Social Psychology*, 2nd edn, vol. 3, Addison-Wesley Publishing Co.: Reading, Mass., ch. 26.

46. Chomsky, N., 1965. *Aspects of the Theory of Syntax.* M.I.T. Press: Cambridge.
47. Lewis, M.M., 1969. *Language and the Child.* N.F.E.R.: Slough.
48. McNeill, D., 1960. 'The Development of Language', in Mussen, P.H. (ed.), *Manual of Child Psychology.* Wiley: New York.
49. Chomsky, N., 1957. *Syntactic Structures.* Mouton: The Hague.
50. Miller, W. and Erwin, S., 1964. 'The Development of Grammar in Child Language', in Bellugi, U. and Brown, R. (eds), *The Acquisition of Language. Monograph of Social Research and Child Development* 29: 9–34.
51. Ausubel, D.P. and Sullivan, E.V., 1970. *Op. cit.,* p. 524.
52. *Ibid.,* pp. 526–27.
53. Bruner, J.S., Oliver, R.R. and Greenfield, P.M., 1966. *Studies in Cognitive Growth.* Wiley & Sons: New York.
54. Entwisle, D.R., 1975. 'Socialization of Language Behaviour and Educability', in Maehr, M.L. and Stallings, W.M. (eds.), *Culture, Child and School: Sociocultural Influences on Learning.* Brooks/Cole Publishing Co., Monterey: Calif.
55. Fishman, J., 1970. *Sociolinguistics: A Brief Introduction.* Newbury House Publishers: Rowley, Mass.
56. Lewis, 1970. *Op. cit.*
57. Bruner, 1964. *Op. cit.*
58. Luria, A.R., 1961. *The Role of Speech in the Regulation of Normal and Abnormal Behaviour.* Pergamon: London.
59. Young, F.M., 1959. 'Language Growth and Development', in Garrison, K.C. (ed.), *Growth and Development,* 2nd edn. Longmans Green: New York.
60. Bernstein, B., 1970: 'A Sociolinguistic approach to socialization: with some reference to educability' in F. Williams (ed.) *Language* and *Poverty,* Markham Press, Chicago.
61. Entwisle, 1975. *Op. cit.*
62. Bereiter, C., Englemann, S., Osborn, J. and Reidford, P.A., 1966. 'An Academically-Oriented Pre-School for Culturally Deprived Children', in Hechinger, F. (ed.), *Pre-School Education Today.* Doubleday: New York.
63. Labov, W., 1970. 'The Logic of Non-Standard English', in Williams, F. (ed.), *Language and Poverty,* Markham Press: Chicago.
64. Carroll, J.B., 1972. 'Language and Cognition: Current Perspectives from Linguistics and Psychology', in Rosenblith, J.F., Allinsmith, W. and Williams, J.P., (eds) *The Causes of Behaviour: Readings in Child Development and Educational Psychology,* 3rd edn. Allyn and Bacon: Boston.
65. Labov, W., 1970. *Op. cit.* p. 184.
66. Cazden, C.B., 1970. 'The Neglected Situation in Child Language Research and Education', in Williams, F. (ed.), *Language and Poverty.* Markham Press: Chicago.
67. Rist, R.C., 1970. 'Student Social Class and Teacher Expectations: The Self-Fulfilling Prophecy in Ghetto Education'. *Harvard Educational Review* 40: 411–51.
68. Williams, F., 1970. 'Psychological Correlates of Speech Characteristics: On Sounding Disadvantaged'. *Journal of Speech and Hearing Research* 13: 472–88.
69. Goddard, H.H., 1912. *The Kallikak Family: A Study in the Heredity of Feeblemindedness.* Macmillan Co.: New York.
70. Ausubel and Sullivan, 1970. *Op. cit.,* pp. 50–53.
71. Elkind, D., 1968. 'Cognitive Development in Adolescence', in Adams, J.F. (ed.), *Understanding Adolescence.* Allyn & Bacon: Boston, Mass, 128–58.

72. Tyler, L.E., 1965. *The Psychology of Human Differences*, 3rd edn. Appleton-Century-Crofts: New York.
73. Sigel, I.E., 1953. 'How Intelligence Tests Limit Understanding of Intelligence'. *Merrill-Palmer Quarterly of Behaviour and Development* 9: 39–56.
74. Jensen, A.R., 1969. 'How Much Can We Boost I.Q. and Scholastic Achievement?' *Harvard Educational Review*. Winter: 1–123.
75. Eysenck, H.J., 1971. *Race, Intelligence and Education*. Sun Books: Melbourne.
76. Gage, N.L., 1972. 'I.Q. Heritability, Race Difference and Educational Research'. *Phi. Delta Kappan*, January.
77. Kearney, G.E. and Davidson, G.R., 1976. *The Psychology of Aboriginal Australians*. Australian Institute of Aboriginal Studies: Canberra.
78. North, A.F., 1969. 'Research Issues in Child Health: An Overview', in Grotberg, E. (ed.), *Critical Issues in Research Related to Disadvantaged Children*. E.T.S.: Princeton, New Jersey.
79. Lesser, G.S., Fifer, G. and Clark, D., 1965. 'Mental Abilities of Children from Different Social Class and Cultural Groups'. *Monograph of the Society for Research in Child Development*.
80. Pavenstedt, E., 1965. 'A Comparison of the Child-Rearing Environment of Upper-Lower and Very Low-Born Class Families'. *American Journal of Orthopsychiatry* 35: 89–98.
81. Nisbet, J.D., and Entwisle, N.J., 1967. 'Intelligence and Family Size, 1949–65'. *British Journal of Educational Psychology* 37, 2: 188–93.
82. Hunt, J. McV., 1964. 'The Psychological Basis of Using Pre-School Enrichment As an Antidote for Cultural Deprivation'. *Merrill Palmer Quarterly of Behaviour and Development* 10: 209–48.
83. Hess, R.D., 1969. 'Parental Behaviour and Children's School Achievement Implications for Head Start', in Grotberg, E. (ed.), *Critical Issues in Research Relating to Disadvantaged Children*. E.T.S.: Princeton, New Jersey.
84. Entwisle, 1975. *Op. cit.*, p. 90.
85. Honzik, M.P., 1967. 'Environmental Correlates of Mental Growth: Prediction from the Family Setting at Twenty-One Months'. *Child Development* 38: 337–64.

Part Two

GUIDELINES FOR EDUCATIONAL PRACTICE

Introductory Comment

In this second part of the book the attempt is made to formulate guidelines for educational practice which take account of the general aim of trying to cater for individual differences and of the factual evidence about the nature of these differences presented in Part One. These guidelines necessarily touch educational practice at virtually every point—school organisation, teaching methods, guidance programmes, curricula, evaluation, and the school's relationship with its community.

The term *guideline*, although commonplace, has been chosen with care. Alternatives such as *principle* or *rule*, which convey the idea of regularity and predictability, have been deliberately avoided. The term *guideline*, being less prescriptive, takes account of the baffling range and type of difference—physical, psychological and sociological—that any teacher has to deal with, and the need for him to interpret each situation appropriately, rather than try to apply standard formulas. It thus conveys better the professional character of teaching, which involves the capacity of teachers to interpret and apply evidence in harmony with a commitment to the educational ideal of equalising opportunity for each student.

This commitment cannot be taken for granted, in spite of the glib use of the phrase 'teaching for individual differences' in educational literature. The warning given by Broudy should be taken seriously—

> The blithe idiocy with which we repeat the refrain 'Treat every pupil as an individual' is revealed when we ask how many people does anyone treat as an individual human person. A half dozen is about par for most of us; the modern novel moreover, often has as its subject our failure to reach even this small number. Indeed parents are indicted a thousand times a day for not treating their own children as individuals deserving the dignity of persons.[1]

It is obvious that unless teachers want to understand their students as individuals and treat them as such, they will be unlikely to value information about individual differences, and to try to use it sensitively and imaginatively. Accordingly priority should be given in pre-service and in-service programmes to activities that sensitise teachers to the desirability of getting to know each student as well as possible, and that assist them to put this knowledge to use in a creative way that expresses their own personal style.

The guidelines presented and discussed in the following chapters are relevant to all levels of the school from kindergarten to secondary although of course space does not permit a comprehensive presentation of all possible applications of them. Nor is this necessary. Their greatest value is in the interpretation made by particular teachers and schools trying to solve specific problems in their continuing search for more effective practices. While the guidelines may have some relevance to special schools catering for handicapped students, and others widely divergent from the normal, they are not intended to apply in any substantial way to them. Both the scientific description of differences of this extreme kind and the pedagogical treatment of them lie outside the scope of this presentation.

As foreshadowed in the Introduction the guidelines discussed in succeeding chapters are grouped in the following areas:
1. Home and Community Influences
2. School Organisation
3. Curriculum
4. Teaching
5. Evaluation

Reference

1. Broudy, H.S., 1972. *The Real World of the Classroom.* Harcourt Brace Jovanovich: New York, p. 44.

4. Home and Community Influences

Guidelines Relating to Home and Community Influences on Children's Success in School

1.1   A school should establish liaison with its students' homes if it is to provide effectively for their progress and gain parental support for its work.

1.2   A school should establish liaison with the local community in which it is situated if it is to relate its work closely to its students' experience.

1.3   The school's knowledge of the home and community background of students should enable it to compensate, in some degree, for the cultural deprivation which some students suffer. There should be awareness of this need at all levels of the school, pre-school, primary and secondary, and emphasis should be placed on individual teaching using a variety of means such as lower staff-student ratio, specialised curriculum material, and the assistance of teachers with special knowledge (for example in language, and counselling) to supplement the work of the regular staff. Cultural deprivation should not be confused with cultural difference. A multicultural society needs to provide different opportunities for compensation according to the needs of different cultural groups.

1.1 Liaison between School and Home

We have seen from Chapter 1 that the home is the major agent of socialisation. Accordingly, agencies such as the school, which are also concerned with the child's social development, cannot afford to ignore it. If the influences of home and school are antagonistic, the child is caught between these contrary influences, and must be adversely affected. At best, he attempts to live a divided existence, coming to terms with each as best he can; more likely, he experiences conflict and strain, affecting his life both at home and at school. Since both home and school are powerful influences in his development, particularly during school years, it is wasteful for them not to be in close harmony, and it is tragic for them to be in opposition.

In spite of the undoubted truth of these propositions, practical solutions to them are by no means obvious, and in some cases they may be difficult or even impossible. Home and school have different origins and circumstances; they often have different values, expectations and goals. In a country such as Australia, for most children the school is a creation of a state governmental authority. It is a standardised kind of institution, both organisationally and architecturally, with a state-wide curriculum policy, and teachers with broadly similar training, recruited from much the same socio-economic background. The homes from which the children are drawn, by contrast, vary enormously in such significant characteristics as class affiliation, financial status, vocational interests, parental educational level and values, domestic harmony, patterns of discipline and cultural stimulation. Relating the culture of the school to the variety of specific home influences that the children display in school is probably the most difficult task that the school faces, and it must be accepted at the outset that schools alone cannot offset the disadvantages which some children suffer at home. These disadvantaged homes require assistance from other sources as well to compensate or assist them. It is a pathetic and dangerous fallacy to believe that social inequality can be redressed by educational programmes without the help of other forms of social amelioration; pathetic in that it is well intentioned, but futile; dangerous in that it diverts attention from other courses of action that are needed, inducing unwarranted complacency.

In spite of these rather disheartening propositions, it can be claimed that the spread of popular education has had a beneficial effect on the level of culture, and more specifically, that there is much that the school can do to improve its own effectiveness by more direct contact with the home.

As was explained in Chapter 1 the child's personality is an important element in his achievement in school. Personality is a complex product, varying in infinitely subtle ways from person to person. It is influenced broadly by factors such as social class, peer group, race, religion, home and school, but each of these is complex and interrelated. So far as their effects can be isolated, it is the home, as has been stated, that is the major influence for most children. This influence is particularly evident in the child's motivational pattern (his striving for achievement, his need for approval and his capacity for independent action), his attitudes, aspirations, and expectations, and his self-concept, all of which have a direct carry-over into schoolwork. His acceptance of school, his industry, his social relationships with teachers and other students, his capacity for concentrated and independent effort, his sense of discipline, his confidence, and his striving for achievement are largely determined in the home, as, by contrast, are his rejection of school, his social maladjustment, his insecurity and over-reliance on social approval and his lack of ambition.

These propositions are, of course, broad generalisations, and are not true in every case. There are many examples of children whose home influences have been altered, or even reversed, by external experiences. Nor should the statements be interpreted fatalistically by teachers, accepting that all the dynamic factors in the child's school life are quite outside their sphere of influence. This is certainly not the case. School and home interact in a significant way, and patterns of behaviour can be strengthened or weakened, impoverished or enriched, by this interaction. Of all the socialising agencies shaping the child's development, home and school are those that need each other's co-operation most. Whether this will continue to be true in an emerging social situation in which home influence appears to be changing remains to be seen. If present trends continue, particularly in the mother's role and the authority of parents generally, the social psychology of child development may have to be revised.

While our concern here is with the steps that schools may take to secure the home as an ally, it should be said that the home would serve its own interests well by actively seeking the school as an ally. From many points of view it is easier for individual parents to take co-operative action with the school than it is for the school to approach the home. It is a single task for the home, a multiple one for the school.

We turn then to a more practical consideration of the problem— the steps that schools might take to co-operate with the home. In doing so it is stressed that there could be many alternative steps to the ones suggested. If principals and teachers really believe that it is important to co-operate with their students' homes, it is likely that they will invent ways of doing it that fit the local scene. One principal, known to the author, arranged for the parents of a mid-secondary class to change places for a day with their sons and daughters. The parents came to school and followed the students' routine fully; the students stayed at home and, presumably, did the house work. In spite of some problems (working mothers, children below school age, etc.), the attendance was good, and the experiment was taken seriously. Some mothers even wore their daughter's school uniform. The impact on these parents was dramatic, and probably salutary. To catch a glimpse, even for a day, of what school was actually like for their children, would convey the lesson of home-school co-operation more realistically than many more conventional measures that might be taken. This novel kind of action could surely be multiplied many times if schools were seized with the need for them.

The practical measures suggested are listed and commented on as follows:

1. Explicit recognition of the importance of home-school co-operation and communication of it to students and parents
2. Making the school programme familiar to parents
3. Communicating with parents regarding their children's progress
4. Improving understanding of individual children through knowledge of their home background

An Explicit Policy of Home-School Co-operation

This first suggestion seems so obvious that it may be considered unworthy of comment; yet it is very important. If a school has a policy of co-operation with the home it should state it explicitly, express it operationally (that is, in terms of the kinds of objectives and programmes that it entails), and explain it to both students and parents.

It is a rather remarkable fact that all too frequently principals and teachers make policies directly affecting the student body without attempting to explain them to the students. Some teachers even teach their subjects (for which they have reasonably clear objectives) without considering it necessary to explain to the students what these objectives are, and how achieving them will benefit them. More generally, few teachers seem to discuss with their students educational principles (such as methods of learning), or educational philosophy (such as aims, concepts of discipline and authority, etc.), yet presumably they are making use of them all the time. Both principal (addressing himself to the school as a whole) and teachers (with their own students) could, with great advantage, discuss the general proposition of home-school co-operation, its advantages and problems, and ways of achieving it. This would alert students to its importance, help them to see the continuity (or discontinuity) of school and home in their own development, and dispel the idea that is so common, that the two are separate and incompatible. It might also lead to some good proposals from the students as to how the relationship could be improved.

Whereas the students are a captive audience, and can easily be contacted, the parents are not, and can be approached only with more difficulty. Moreover many parents have been conditioned to believe that school and home are separate worlds, and have to be convinced that liaison is possible and worthwhile. Many migrant parents, particularly, lack confidence about approaching the school, either because of their different traditions in relation to the school, or through a sense of cultural inferiority.

The most obvious medium for communicating with parents is print, in the form of memoranda, letters to parents, school publications, and so on. Print is a medium that requires effort on the part of those to whom it is addressed to read it and interpret it. Some parents are unable to do this, and some seem to be unwilling. The style of presentation is important. The use of jargon does nothing to make ideas clear to parents, and it tends to repel by its patronising tone.

Face-to-face discussion is much more effective, and this should be possible for at least some of the parents if the school is flexible enough to make it convenient. In such discussions doubts and queries can be voiced and answered.

It is assumed in all this discussion that home-school co-operation is understood in practical terms, at least by the school authorities. In the perspective of the school it might be spelled out as follows:

1. The interest of parents in their child's general adjustment to school and in his progress, and their general support for the importance of education.

2. The provision of conditions at home for the child to study, e.g. a regular routine, quietness, control of T.V. watching, a room (or a place) of his own.

3. Assistance in various ways, e.g. reading to young children, hearing children read, encouraging them to discuss work done recently at school. The capacity of parents to do these things varies greatly. We shall return to this point later in connection with innovative programmes.

Co-operation, however, is a two-way process, and no doubt there is a valid perspective on it from the side of parents which would differ from the preceding account. The parents' perspective is likely to be more specific in terms relating to their own children. In one case known to the author it was the parents who became concerned about their child's slow progress in learning to read. The school appeared to be unconcerned. Action taken privately by them to have the child's specific difficulties in reading diagnosed and remedied by private teaching saved the child from becoming seriously retarded. Parents also have views about unreasonable homework demands or unbalanced patterns of homework among secondary school subjects. The effect of their concern, if made known, should benefit schools. Parents often have observations to make on problems that would not occur to teachers.

Informing Parents about the School Programme

The problem of communication between school and home was raised in the preceding section. It is even more difficult to explain the school's programme to parents than it is to explain the need for their co-operation. It involves explicit analysis of objectives, methods and outcomes for a wide range of subjects and procedures, expressing them in an authentic but non-technical form, and relating them to wider social goals that concern the parents, such as vocation, citizenship and the use of leisure. Many teachers themselves often take for granted a great deal of what they do day-by-day, and are not very articulate when asked to explain or justify it. The task is better attempted in a series of talks and discussions. A single manifesto would be somewhat overpowering.

The parents' problems are intensified when methods and substance are different from those familiar from their own schooldays. In a mobile society with an ever-increasing provision of popular education, it is common enough for children to become better educated than their parents. Many parents who do interest themselves in their children's education, and endeavour to help, are reconciled to the fact that their capacity to do so falters somewhere in the secondary years. But it is disturbing to parents to be overtaken while their children are still in the primary school. New methods and new terminology cause disquiet to parents, particularly if at the same time the school is exhorting the parents to take an active interest in their children's progress. It is important that innovations be explained to parents. Indeed, it would be reasonable to expect that parents be consulted before an innovation is introduced. The rationale of the new scheme needs to be fully understood by the school, and an educational programme mounted to explain it to parents. Failure to do this obviously limits the parents' capacity to co-operate for the benefit of their own children. Also, it is likely to lead to criticism of the 'new-fangled' scheme, and, possibly, active opposition. It is a common human reaction to resent change, and especially so if it is quite outside one's own experience.

Undoubtedly, the most effective medium of communication is participation, and if parents can be involved in the school's affairs they are likely to learn about them in the most realistic way possible. What form the involvement may take will depend on the belief of each school in its value, and the originality of the people concerned. Some obvious, but important ways are as follows:

(a) to bring in parents with special knowledge to work with students;
(b) to include parents on a steering committee for an innovative project;

(c) to have open days when parents may see the children at work;
(d) to arrange discussion sessions in the evening at school or in parents' homes at which a teacher or group of teachers leads the discussion on some aspect of the school's work; and
(e) to encourage parents to spend time regularly at school helping in the classroom.

Of these the most heartening (as it seems to the author) is the participation of parents (usually mothers) in the regular work of the classroom. In many English primary schools visited by the author this was a common sight. The number of parents able and willing to do this may be relatively small, but the insight gained by them is undoubtedly considerable, and their general influence on the whole approach of the school to home-school co-operation is almost certainly encouraging. Unhappily this direct expression of interest by parents seems to diminish as their children progress up the school.

In secondary schools where the special accomplishments of some parents could be most profitably exploited to broaden the experience of the students, it is relatively rare. While this apparent slackening of interest by parents of older children appears to be a fact of life, there is no reason why it should be accepted as inevitable. It may well be altered by some imaginative action on the part of schools. To accommodate parents in a classroom it is desirable that the work be carried on in an informal way, and if the emphasis is on teaching children individually, this is likely to be the case. In the formal classroom visitors produce an uneasy feeling, as though privacy has been invaded. In this kind of classroom climate the parent may be regarded as an intruder.

Communicating with Parents regarding Their Children's Progress

A significant part of the communication process is reporting the progress of students to their parents. Probably to most parents this is the most important. The topic of assessment (and reporting) is dealt with separately in Chapter 8, and consideration of it can be deferred.

Seeking Greater Understanding of Individual Children

Of all the benefits that can be gained from a closer association between home and school, clearly the most beneficial is the more complete knowledge that the teacher can gain of each student as a person. This knowledge gives vital clues to his approach to schoolwork, enabling the teacher to deal with him much more sensitively. It may not turn failure into success, but it could turn frustration and dislike into understanding and toleration.

It should be said also that this kind of knowledge needs to be handled with care, and a high degree of professionalism. In no circumstances should it be used patronisingly, or in ways that would embarrass a student in the presence of other students or teachers. Knowing private details about a student's home life should enable a teacher to work with him with insight; it should not lead to his use of this knowledge as a threat to the child. It is information that one keeps to oneself, but it gives an added quality to one's transactions with the child.

To increase the teacher's chances of gaining greater knowledge of the child's background a system of class patrons or personal tutors may be used, additional staff may be appointed with special training for this work, or a small team of teachers may teach the same group of students over a number of years. Probably some combination of these would be best. The services of psychologically trained counsellors and social workers could strengthen greatly the school's capacity to deal with its students more sensitively and tactfully. Again, however, the need for discretion is stressed. These specialists will probably know more about some children than teachers and principals need to know, and judgement is needed as to what to pass on. They need to sift from their knowledge of the child's home situation those influences that bear upon his motivation for school work, the constraints that make it difficult for him to meet the school's requirements, and those talents and interests that seem to have been neglected at school, and to alert the teachers to these. Sensitively interpreted, the service of these specialists is invaluable. Probably most teachers cannot be expected to know their students intimately without this kind of help.

But, however gained, from parents in visits to the school, from counsellors and social workers, or from the teacher's own observation of the child in day-to-day contacts, it is quite clear that this knowledge is necessary if students are to be taught as individuals. If a school attempts to run its affairs in a self-contained world, remote from the most influential source of its students' life-style, to that extent it limits the possibility of its own effectiveness.

1.2 The School and Its Relationship with the Community

Much of the previous discussion of school-home relationships is relevant also to the school's relationship with the wider community, but there are additional features extending beyond the home. These may be conveniently discussed under the following headings:

1. School governance
2. Using community resources

School Governance

The way in which the school is governed may seem at first glance to be somewhat remote from the pedagogical question how to cater for the individual differences of its students, but the link is important. The capacity of a school to pursue an independent programme, relating its activities to its local setting and hence appealing to the children's special interests and experience, can be influenced very much by the nature of its governing body.

Most schools in Australia exist under the authority of governmental authorities (State Governments in the States and the Commonwealth Government in Commonwealth territories), and hence belong to a system of schools. Roman Catholic independent schools are also systematised to some extent, under teaching orders or other church jurisdiction. Usually the teaching orders are nationwide in their scope (indeed some have international affiliation), and hence are not exclusively identified with a particular State. Because of their link with an international (or universal) church and its associated culture their problem of localisation would be different from that of the state schools, and possibly more difficult. Most other non-government schools function as independent units, although many have common interests and similar policies (usually through a common allegiance to a religious denomination). Many of these schools are non-local in the sense that they cater for children who come from outside the immediate community, and who either board in the school or privately. These schools also have a special problem in relating their work to the local community.

Membership of a system generally increases the pressures on individual schools towards uniformity. These pressures may come from the authority or from the schools themselves. The schools are sensitive to equality of treatment, and naturally try to secure for themselves any advantages gained by others in the system. This kind of influence also occurs to some extent outside the system (as, for example, when schools in one State claim advantages secured by those in another) but the pressures towards uniformity are greater within a system. An authority usually applies its policies to all schools within its jurisdiction. The resultant degree of uniformity depends a great deal on what these policies are. A tight control over what is considered to be good teaching and an appropriate curriculum produces a high level of uniformity; a more open approach to them makes diversity possible, and hence makes it easier for schools to relate their work to their community.

The size of a system, with regard to the area and homogeneity of its jurisdiction and the numbers involved, also affects the style of its operation. A small system, within a relatively homogeneous area, adapts more readily to local needs than does a large system extending over a heterogeneous area. Australian state systems of education historically have had difficulties resulting from size (whatever advantages they may have had from greater financial competence and equality of treatment throughout all parts of the State). In attempting to treat all communities equally they have found it difficult to treat them differentially, as may be needed. This alien character of the school in the community is brought out well in the following quotation:

> The schools are built, staffed, equipped, paid for, and supervised outside the community. The curriculum that they follow comes by post from the capital city; teachers and headmasters come and go by means invisible to the local people, and for reasons that can, as a rule, only be guessed at. Some *deus ex machina* seems to be at work silently and inexorably arranging all these things.[1]

This problem facing centralised systems has been recognised for some time, and various steps have been taken to meet it, particularly in recent years. None of the measures adopted has been aimed at increasing the number of statutory authorities (other than the creation of an authority for the Australian Capital Territory in 1973). Decentralisation, in this sense, does not seem to be an acceptable option in the Australian political scene. The method rather has been administrative decentralisation, that is the delegation of authority from existing statutory authorities. This has taken two main forms: the creation of new administrative bodies (variously called areas and regions), and the strengthening of the independence of each school in the system.

The regional directorates have been staffed to carry out most of the administrative responsibilities of the authority within the specified area, subject to the general educational and financial policies of the authority. In varying degrees they have established links within their area, and have been able to respond to local needs. Because of their generally large size geographically (in rural areas) they are faced, in a smaller way, with the problem of a variety of communities, that the state authority is faced with. In metropolitan areas (where directorates have also been set up), the problems rather are those of large numbers of students, and poorly defined community consciousness. Speaking generally it could be said that the area scheme has increased the possibility that schools are able to function in a way that recognises individual differences. By itself, however, it could scarcely be claimed that it would guarantee it.

Concurrently with the development of regional authorities, has been the move to encourage principals and staffs in their own school to accept more authority for the character of their school. This has led in turn to schemes to encourage and assist school-based curriculum projects so that the freedom for schools to interpret statewide curricula in their own way (which has been constantly urged) can become more of a reality. The creation of the Curriculum Development Centre at the national level, the appointment of advisory teachers and the introduction of various in-service courses designed to assist schools in developing curricula of their own, are all part of this general plan to encourage and assist schools towards greater autonomy.

The most novel step to date has been the creation of school councils, representing both school and community interests, to assume a significant measure of responsibility in running the school. It would be expected that this new form of school governance would give schools their best chance to develop an individual character, and to become more closely associated with local community and family interests, although of course much would still depend on the way in which the councils and the school staff went about their task.

This belief in the virtue of a more open administrative system is expressed strongly in the Karmel Report which brought together in one document many of the reformist ideas that had been gathering strength during the sixties—

> The Committee favours less rather than more centralised control over the operation of schools. Responsibility should be devolved as far as possible upon the people involved in the actual task of teaching, in consultation with the parents of the pupils whom they teach and, at senior levels, with the students themselves.[2]

The federal influence in education, running more strongly now than at any time in Australia's history, is encouraging this trend towards greater autonomy in schools. The Schools Commission (a federal body) is encouraging it with schemes of financial assistance to schools, teacher development and the encouragement of innovative practices. How the 'new federalism' of the Liberal-National Country party coalition government will affect these trends remains to be seen. Greater emphasis on state control of education (if this is the outcome of the 'new federalism') should not significantly affect the trend towards greater autonomy for individual schools. State authorities have expressed it as policy, and it is now firmly entrenched in professional opinion.

Changes in the administrative pattern for schools and the various moves to increase the freedom of action of the schools, and strengthen the competence of principals and teachers to take advantage of this freedom are not always supported by explicit statements of the advantages to be gained. Terms such as 'democracy in education', 'openness in administration', and 'community involvement' are used freely, but they suggest reform rather than explain how it is to occur. A.W. Jones has warned against too naive an acceptance of automatic benefits from changes in administration—'There can be more bureaucratic or authoritarian action or disregard for the rights of individuals within schools than over occurs in the central administrative office'.[3]

A similar cautionary statement could be made with respect to the liaison with the community that the existence of a school council might be expected to foster. There are plenty of examples of council-controlled independent schools and tertiary institutions which have failed to create worthwhile contacts of their institution with the community. A decentralised form of control gives an institution the opportunity to relate its activities more closely to its community, and increase the relevance of the work done in it to the experience of its students, but it does not automatically bring these results about. To quote A.W. Jones again —'Central control and local control can both be bureaucratic if the decision makers are not readily available and accessible to their community'.[4] Given this accessibility and sensitivity there is a good chance that schools will become an integral part of their community (without sacrificing any allegiance to that more universal culture to which they also belong), and school programmes will cater better for children in terms that they understand, giving them a surer basis for the exploration of ideas outside their direct experience. There is a better chance, too, of the community's accepting the school as a local institution rather than as one manipulated from outside, of understanding and supporting its programmes, and making its resources available to it.

Using Community Resources

The community is a potentially rich laboratory for the teacher, but he needs to be sensitive to its value and also to have the confidence of those in the community whose help he needs. In Chapters 5 and 6, dealing respectively with school organisation and the curriculum, the value of local environmental study is dealt with in some detail. Here the emphasis is on establishing the link between school and community.

We take up first the problem that many teachers face through their own inexperience. In a state centralised system of education in which staffing is done centrally, it is inevitable that many teachers find themselves in communities that they only poorly understand, and with which they feel little affinity. Teachers brought up in the city are posted to country schools; those from mining towns find themselves in agricultural areas; those from inland towns are sent to communities that live primarily from the sea, and so on. Students thoroughly familiar with coastal vegetation find themselves teaching in a mountain or inland area where the vegetation is quite different; others well versed in the local history of their home area know nothing of the background of the communities in which they are sent to teach. Examples could be easily multiplied. A striking example is the young teacher, usually fresh from training, who is sent to an isolated rural community in charge of a one-teacher school. He is thrust into a conservative rural environment knowing little or nothing about it, insensitive to values, attitudes and practices that his students have been born into. Many young teachers, faced with this situation, act defensively, steering the curriculum towards their own experience rather than attempting to work through the experience of the children. This reaction to insecurity is understandable, but it is poor pedagogy, and gives point to the criticism made by many students that school is divorced from real life. It also reinforces the idea that the teacher is an outsider. A more constructive approach is for the teacher to acknowledge his ignorance, and set about remedying it by reading and by visiting his children's farms or other places of livelihood. A young teacher, known to the author, was appointed to a school in a cane-farming area. He was not well versed in the growing and manufacture of sugar, but he soon realised that it was a major influence in the lives of his children, and that his own ignorance was a handicap to his work. He made it a high priority to learn the details of the growing, harvesting and processing of the sugar cane and the marketing of the sugar. In a sense he learnt along with the class. The children's knowledge was highly personal, but conceptually unsophisticated. He was able to bring to the task a more disciplined intelligence and a broader perspective, particularly in dealing with questions of distribution and marketing where the study of sugar changed from science to social studies.

These comments about the rootlessness of teachers in a statewide system with a high degree of staff mobility apply also to principals, and because of their critical position in the school, their quick identification with the life of a community after appointment is important for all concerned. Any suggestion that the appointment is being used by the principal mainly as a stepping-stone to some more congenial one is most damaging to his prospects of harmony with the community.

An effective way of increasing the school's links with the community (and one within the principal's jurisdiction) is to allow the community to use the school's facilities, such as playing field, swimming pool, and the school building. This could be regarded as a defensible step in its own right, but whether this is so or not, it is certainly true that it is a major step in breaking down the separation between the two, increasing the prospect that the school will make greater use of community resources in its teaching.

The Karmel Report suggests an even more complete association of school and community in which the school becomes a community school—

> Educationally and from the point of view of efficient use of resources, it would make good sense to have the school as the nucleus of a community centre. Joint planning and even conduct of schools by educational, health, welfare, cultural and sporting agencies could provide additional facilities for the school, allow the community access to its resources, and thus generally increase its fruitfulness. In this way a link could be forged between school, family, peer group, and the society at large.[5]

The term 'community school' now has a wide currency, but it has a variety of meanings.[6, 7] Hedley Beare describes a highly novel plan which was proposed for Darwin in which the school as a self-contained institution virtually ceases to exist, its work becoming merged in community activities*. At the other end of the scale is the more orthodox development of the traditional school in which community and school share facilities and closely interact. Whatever form it takes (and there is no reason why only one form should be used), it is essential from the educator's viewpoint that the community's physical and human resources be accessible to the teacher if he is to capitalise on the student's out-of-school experience.

This is true even if the student's background is disadvantaged, and far below the level of civilised living that education should aim at. There are, of course, special problems in the community-school relationship when the student's home and their community life generally are impoverished. These are taken up in the following section dealing with compensatory education.

1.3 Compensatory Education

> In assigning a label to the seventh decade of the twentieth century, historians will have a wide range of descriptive terms from which to choose. Within the field of education, however, the choice could hardly be a difficult one, for it has assuredly been the decade of the disadvantaged child, especially the young disadvantaged child.[8]

---

*It was one of the casualties of cyclone Tracy in 1975.

Caldwell's judgement in the preceding statement was made with respect to the U.S.A., but to a substantial degree it is true also of Britain and Australia.

It may be useful as an introduction to the topic of compensatory education to give a brief résumé of the landmarks of this movement in these countries. Without doubt America has led the way, both in the amount of research and publication, and in the projects attempted, and it is appropriate to being with this country. It is important, in considering the problems and issues, to remember that each country is distinctive, and to recognise that the major preoccupation of American literature on compensatory education is with Negro education.

The research generated by the concern of the period with social inequalities, particularly in the Kennedy and Johnson eras, is enormous, and has attracted the attention of scholars in psychology, sociology, philosophy and education. Obviously full justice cannot be done to it in this brief account, but much of what appears in Chapters 1 and 2 of this book is also relevant. One rather cynical comment on much of the literature is worth quoting, if only for its refreshingly unacademic language—

> There is too much written about the disadvantaged child and his school-related corollary, compensatory education. It is fired by the gluttonous appetite of mediocre journals, and feeds on the insatiable demands of school and university promotion committees. The bulk of this literature is replete with unwitting lies, prejudices, misconceptions, stupidities, double talk, and worse.[9]

After such an assessment one hesitates to go on, since there is apparently something worse than unwitting lies, prejudices, misconceptions, stupidities, and double talk, but I shall at least try to heed this trenchant warning.

It is difficult to find a sure starting point, since the concept of compensatory education is inherent in all education, particularly in the U.S.A., where so much confidence has been placed in the public school system to improve the quality of social life. The Research Conference on Education and Cultural Deprivation held in June 1964, at the University of Chicago, has been chosen because of the authoritative nature of its deliberations, and because many of its recommendations were carried into effect, particularly in the 1965 Education Act and in major projects such as 'Head Start'. The participants were principally American, but some prominent overseas scholars such as Bernstein, from the University of London, also attended. The recommendations are too lengthy to reproduce here, but an abbreviated selection and summary is presented as follows:[10]

1. Compensatory education is recognised as a distinct type of education for socially disadvantaged students. It is not the reduction of all education to a least common denominator.

2. The school or associated agency, should make up for basic needs not satisfied in the home. These include an adequate breakfast, a midday meal, appropriate physical examinations by nurses, doctors, and dentists, and necessary clothing.

3.(a) Nursery schools and kindergartens should be organised to provide culturally deprived children with the intellectual and learning-to-learn stimulation which other children get at home.

  (b) A national commission of experts should be created to develop curricula guidelines, materials and methods for this special type of school.

  (c) Appropriate teacher-training courses should be given to help staff these schools.

  (d) The parents of the children should be directly involved.

4.(a) In the elementary school a screening process should be used to determine the level of the child on entry in perceptual development, language development, ability to attend, and motivation to learn. Each child should be treated in a way which is most appropriate for him. The emphasis in the first three years should be on continual success at small tasks, sequentially arranged.

  (b) A national commission on curriculum for these first three years, for culturally deprived children, should be set up.

  (c) Teaching staff should be carefully selected and have many opportunities for in-service education. Their major task should be to help the child master fundamental skills in language, reading, arithmetic and the general skills of learning.

  (d) Every effort should be made to strengthen the relation between the home and the school, particularly by parental participation in the programme.

5.(a) On entry to secondary education a major effort should be made to identify a sizeable group of deprived students who can, with appropriate help, be enabled to complete secondary education and proceed to higher education. Special programmes, tutorial help, increased counselling and help with basic skills should be given. Favourable comment is made, in this regard, on the Higher Horizons Project in New York City.[11] (Balson,[12] an Australian, also comments very favourably on this project).

  (b) Culturally disadvantaged adolescents who are having great difficulty with the regular school curricula should have a programme that emphasises the basic skills of language and reading, and should be allowed to specialise in an area in which they are interested.

(c) There should be work-study plans. This requires effective co-operation with industry and public agencies.

(d) Peer societies should be organised by appropriate community agencies with the co-operation of the school. These would, of course, be relevant to all youth.

In short it is claimed that there is an identifiable group of culturally disadvantaged students. These students require special programmes at pre-school, elementary and secondary levels. Research and development are needed to clarify the nature of these programmes, and special schemes of pre-service and in-service teacher training should be instituted to provide the skilled staff necessary.

In various forms all these objectives were realised in practical form during the late sixties and seventies. The most striking achievement was the 1965 Education Act, fostered, but unfulfilled in the Kennedy era, and brought to fruition in the presidency of L.B. Johnson. It was virtually a charter for education for the rest of the twentieth century, providing massive financial assistance for elementary and secondary education, with associated research and development, innovation, teacher education, and compensatory education.

Space does not permit a detailed reference to the multiplicity of projects, research and evaluation studies, teacher-education schemes and the like attempted during the decade 1965–75, but the overall effort and dedication to the task must be rated as outstanding by any impartial observer. Only a few of the more prominent federal schemes will be mentioned.

'Head Start', established in 1965 by the Office of Economic Opportunity, and carried on by the Office of Education (both federal bodies), is probably the best known of many pre-school projects which placed their hopes on early intervention, particularly in the area of language and personality development. 'Follow Through', initiated by the Office of Education in 1967, was aimed at continuing the work begun in 'Head Start', through elementary and secondary school. 'Upward Bound', initiated by the Office of Economic Opportunity, was aimed at identifying and assisting potential college students; other programmes with the objective of assisting potentially able students were designed for students who left school prematurely (drop-outs).

The early optimistic mood in which these programmes began has undergone some changes. Caldwell[13] describes the sequence as *enthusiasm* and *optimism* (1965, 'we all surfed on the excitement and hoped we would not drown in our own foamy rhetoric'), then *scepticism* (when in 1966 the first trickles of evaluation data began to appear), then *disillusionment* (in 1969 with the release of the Westinghouse/ Ohio Report,[14] dealing with the disappointing evaluation of 'Head Start', and Jensen's *Harvard Educational Review*[15] paper, with its emphasis on genetic determinism), finally to *consolidation* in the present (with the onus of unrealistic expectations removed, and enough left to work with; namely a theoretical base for interest in the effects of early experience, an awareness of the need for new concepts in terms of which to construct programmes, and a recognition of the need to search for ways to organise the learning environment so as to sustain as well as stimulate growth).

In Britain the concern with inequality of educational opportunity was more muted, with fewer mood swings than occurred in America, but there have been some substantial studies, some worthwhile projects, and some careful research. The most publicised studies were made by committees of inquiry, some of which commissioned important research. Briefly, these are the *Crowther Report*,[16] 1959 (revealing that the majority of able children who were early drop-outs came from the homes of manual workers), the *Robbins Report*,[17] 1963 (revealing that a much higher proportion of children with fathers in non-manual employment reached full-time higher education than those whose fathers were manual workers), the *Newsom Report*,[18] 1963 (which drew attention to disadvantaged schools and the associated high drop-out rate among 13–16-year-olds of average and less than average ability), and the *Plowden Report*,[19] 1967 (which focused attention on seriously deprived children at primary level, and which provided the major focus of effort in compensatory education).

Experimental projects and research on the scale attempted in America have not been possible in Britain, but there have been some significant developments.

One of the major recommendations of the *Plowden Report* was that there should be positive discrimination (not equality of treatment) in areas of greatest disadvantage. This was put into practice and financed by the Social Science Research Council and the Department of Education and Science. The overall director of the project is Dr Halsey, a noted English sociologist, and each project in the different areas is carried on with a large measure of autonomy. Some good action research has been done in their educational priority areas, notably in Birmingham (with pre-school and primary children), Liverpool (with trainee teachers of underprivileged children), London (with community schools) and the West Riding of Yorkshire (with experimental play groups devoted to intensive language study, and assisted by mothers).

The National Foundation for Educational Research (N.F.E.R.) has also initiated or assisted with a number of research and evaluation studies. Most notable among its own researches has been the N.F.E.R. Preschool Project, initiated in 1968 in five local nursery schools (Slough). This has given rise to a number of associated researches and has closely involved the headmasters and teachers in the schools. Matters stressed in the scheme were language development (using a revised form of the American Peabody Language Development Kit), basic mathematical concepts and visual and auditory perception. There was also very close contact with the parents and a study of the home environment of nursery-school children to try to give some clear meaning to the rather vague term 'cultural deprivation'. An interesting conclusion after four years' experience with the project was that children of all social classes and levels of general intellectual ability derive almost equal benefit from the programme.

The Schools Council, established in 1964, has also played a significant role in research and development in compensatory education. An important project was the Swansea study (associated with the Department of Education, University College of Swansea). Major aims were (1) to provide identification techniques for local children in need of compensatory education, (2) to study over a period the emotional development and response to schooling of infant children in deprived areas, (3) to develop teaching materials of special use for culturally deprived infant children (with a separate Welsh language project). Other projects have been concerned with the education of immigrant children, particularly at Birmingham and Leeds, and many curriculum development projects at both primary and secondary level which, while not exclusively undertaken as compensatory education, could well be considered as contributing to it. *Breakthrough to Literacy* (for infants) and the *Humanities Curriculum* for non-academic secondary students might be cited as examples.

Educational research in England in the universities is commonly interlocked with national committees of inquiry, the N.F.E.R. and the Schools Council, but it would be fair to mention specially the work of Chazan,[20] Floud,[21] Wiseman,[22] Blackstone,[23] Eysenck,[24] Bernstein,[25] Musgrove[26] Halsey[27] and Lawton.[28] There are, of course, many others.

As in the U.S.A., and no doubt partly because of it, optimism (for example, that of the *Plowden Report*) about the possibility of compensating in the schools for defects in the homes and the community, had turned to scepticism by the early seventies. The strength of genetic factors (as argued by Eysenck, particularly), the danger of identifying and labelling children as 'disadvantaged', the over-emphasis on the influence of the early years to change the course of a person's life, and the deflection of attention away from the main target of reform, the ordinary processes of schooling—all formed part of the substance of this disillusionment. In England, too, the present mood could be described as one of sober consolidation, and a realistic acceptance of the limits of hastily prepared programmes to deal with school failure, and a general scepticism about school programmes offsetting social abuses such as slums, poverty, and racial alienation.

In Australia the goal of equal opportunity has always been acknowledged in its educational programmes, and some notable past achievements should be recognised, particularly in rural education, in schemes of financial assistance at all levels to help offset economic inequalities, and in its statewide school staffing policies. The modern ferment, however, corresponding to the movements just described in America and England, is very recent, and could be fairly located in 1973 with the publication of the *Karmel Report*. Reference has already been made to this Report in the Introduction and its main objectives stated. At the risk of some repetition it may be helpful to stress some of its philosophy, and the subsequent reaction to it. With the record of events in America and Britain in mind, it is clear that this Australian study is grappling with quite similar problems, and is proposing similar solutions. There are signs, too, that a similar mood of disillusionment has already followed (irrationally enough, before most of the proposed programmes have had a chance to succeed).

The major guiding idea in the Report is the importance of social justice throughout Australian society and the failure of the doctrine of equal opportunity in education to play its part towards achieving it. The major solutions proposed are to discriminate in favour of the disadvantaged, to try to produce teachers better able to cope with disadvantaged children, to stimulate all teachers to accept a more creative interpretation of their role, and to try to relate schools more closely to home and community. The conception of the problem and the solutions proposed are thus very familiar. The setting, of course, is different. The same questions—Who are the culturally disadvantaged? What kind of deficiencies do they have that can be remedied through the schools? What kind of programmes are likely to be successful in compensating them for their deficiencies? How can we establish whether our efforts have been successful?—have to be asked, but clearly in a different society the answers will be different, at least in some respects. Not that we have final answers to any of the questions, or even good answers to some of them. Roughly we have identified the culturally disadvantaged as the poor, the children from inner city slums, Aborigines, migrants, and children in isolated areas. Yet clearly these groups are not uniform, and numerous exceptions can be found in each.[29]

Clearly, also, they are interrelated. Poverty, place of residence, and race commonly overlap, as is the case with many Aboriginal and non-English-speaking migrant communities. The Karmel Committee concentrated (no doubt wisely, from a practical point of view) on identifying schools as 'disadvantaged', and grading these in terms of need. There are many schools where the proportion of children needing intensive educational care is greater than average, for example, inner city schools that draw a great many pupils from non-English-speaking migrant families, or families dependent on social service payments, and schools in remote country areas. In determining need in quantitative terms (i.e. for financial support) the committee faced the same problem as was faced abroad in identifying warrantable criteria that have a known relationship with educational outcomes. The formula eventually arrived at is, no doubt, an ingenious attempt to create a socio-economic scale to assess the communities in which schools are set. The group variables used in the formula were *parental occupation, housing, schooling, employment, migration, residential mobility, family, ethnicity, religion;* and within each there were individual variables, for example, within *ethnicity* the number of Aborigines was determined, within *occupation* there were fourteen subdivisions, within *employment*, the number of unemployed as a proportion of the work force, and within *schooling* there were subdivisions for the number of children at school, and those undertaking various levels of study.[30]

The educational programme proposed in the Report to try to ensure that the additional funding to these disadvantaged schools was designed to improve physical facilities, establish or improve libraries, assist teacher development through in-service programmes and innovative projects, and assist appropriate research.

The Schools Commission, in its first triennial report (for the years 1976–78), basically followed the plan of reform proposed by the Karmel Report, although there are differences of emphasis and detail. This stillborn report was revised because of governmental financial difficulties and the present plans are a scaled-down version of the original. The new deal, by means of large-scale federal intervention in the nation's education system, has undoubtedly given an initial impetus to change, but the period involved is short, and there have been few innovative projects or researches on the scale witnessed overseas. More money has been spent, there is a good deal of talk and writing about reform, and some heartening moves in in-service education, innovation and teacher-education programmes, and perhaps, most significant of all, an enlivening of teacher interest, but there are signs that we have reached our 'disillusionment and consolidation' period without having gone very far with the original practical expression of the period of 'optimism'.

In the light of these exciting events abroad and at home, how then shall we view compensatory education? There is a danger in giving names to complex processes, as there is a strong pressure towards a 'hardening of the categories'—a disease to which educationists seem to be particularly prone. Thus 'compensatory education' tends to be thought of as a 'package'—a set of prescriptions for dealing with clearly identifiable groups. It cannot be overemphasised that it is not a 'package' (although some components such as language, specialised curriculum material, and social experiences calculated to increase the students' self-image are likely to be common ingredients), and that the children are not groups, no matter how convenient it is to use collective terms like *Aborigines, migrants, isolated children, culturally disadvantaged,* and *poor.* There are, no doubt, significant common elements within these groups, such as the role of the native language for non-English-speaking children, but basically we are dealing with individuals, not categories of disadvantaged children.

An American, Ginsburg,[31] writes of the 'myth of the deprived child'. He does not, of course, doubt that some children are deprived in various ways; but he attacks the categorisation of such children. The approach that he wishes to see is similar to that expressed above. Discussing the early training programmes, he writes as follows:[32]

> . . . poor children are typically confronted with an inadequate educational system, a system that assumes poor children cannot do well and that is not designed to foster their unique potentialities. It should come as no surprise that poor children do badly in a situation like this, that a few years of early compensatory education cannot prevent later academic failure and that the only way to improve the situation is to reform the schools at all levels.

He is sceptical about the possibility of satisfactory innovation within the traditional system, and advocates open education as more promising. He describes it as a 'delicate maneuver in designing educational experiences relevant to the lives of individual children.'[33]

What is to be counted a deficit for which compensation has to be made? When social life is homogeneous the criteria of success and failure are relatively clear to all. Deficiencies (for example, in income, housing, entertainment, vocational qualifications and job opportunities) are easily recognisable, and programmes of compensation are also clear, at least in intention. But when wide cultural differences exist, neither deficiency nor remedy is so clear cut; and the priorities of one group may differ markedly from those of another.

Multiculturalism is a relatively recent condition for Australian society. Aborigines, of course, have existed as a minority racial group, but the dominant white population has been so relatively alike, racially and culturally, that we have not questioned the idea that Australia is culturally homogeneous. What educational provisions there were for Aboriginal children seemed designed to assimilate them into the main stream of Australian life and work. The influx of migrants since World War II has dramatically changed the population pattern, and created substantial cultural diversity.

Many educational problems have been created by these changed circumstances. Probably the most common interpretation of the concept of assimilation is for the migrants to become like Australians, and correspondingly the most common interpretation of compensatory education for them is that of remedying deficiencies in their knowledge of English and of Australian vocational, cultural, and institutional life. Apart from this ideological view of assimilation, the education system has not been well equipped to deal constructively with individual differences, even among Australian children, and the greater spread of differences created by migrant children has intensified this difficulty.

There are some signs that the monolithic concept of assimilation is giving way to a more cosmopolitan view, and it may well be that Australia will come to accept, or even appreciate, being a multicultural society. The bilingual approach with Aboriginal children is an indication of the change of outlook in some of the schools.

The idea of compensatory education itself may well be changed by this attitude of greater toleration of cultural differences. It may come to be defined less in terms of social stereotypes and more in terms of variations within the various social groupings. Certainly there is need of a *lingua franca* for the ordinary transactions of social life, and English needs to be learnt, but not as compensation for being able to speak Italian or other languages. It could even happen that monolingual English-speaking children might come to recognise the lack of another language as a deficit. This would be a momentous change in educational values, and one devoutly to be wished.

There is need, then, to get the idea of compensatory education into better perspective in the context of a multicultural society. There are handicaps that some children suffer in any cultural group, and education should address itself strongly to their amelioration, but many cultural differences between groups and between the mainstream cutlure should not be unthinkingly accepted as deficits. On the contrary they should be regarded as a source of enrichment of Australian society. For this an individual approach in the schools is needed. Indeed the presence of migrant children in our schools may provide an incentive to teachers to use individual methods. Certainly it will provide a severe test of their capacity to do so.

In Chapter 1, Professor Watts, after reviewing a wide range of general influences playing upon children, concludes as follows:

> In this review, we are thus brought to the conclusion that we must look at specific motives, values, attitudes, expectations and self-concepts as learned characteristics, and seek to understand individual differences in the light of each child's idiosyncratic experiences created in part by himself, in part by his socialising environment, and in part by his perceptions and interpretations of that socialising environment.

This statement could well be the guideline for compensatory education. There is certainly a need for additional financial assistance to schools where the need for individual attention to students is even more pressing than among favoured children; there is need for more pre-service and in-service programmes to assist teachers with special facets of teaching children who diverge in unfamiliar ways from other children; there is need for more curriculum development, some schemes dealing with broad issues that could be useful nationally, some with the more domestic details of school-based programmes; there is need to encourage more innovation; there is need to encourage more research and evaluation, and there is an urgent need to improve conditions for isolated children; but more fundamentally, there is the need to train all teachers to approach their task as assisting unique, individual children to profit from schooling, and to provide the conditions for them to attempt it realistically.

We can conveniently end this section with a check-list of common characteristics of special programmes for the educationally disadvantaged. These are proposed in the Sixty-Sixth Yearbook of the influential American National Society for the Study of Education:

1. Well-defined and explicitly stated educational goals
2. Indigenous and innovative curriculums and instructional practices
3. Recognition of the worth and dignity of the individual pupil regardless of his socioeconomic background, vocabulary, personal habits, or values
4. Meaningful and significant inservice educational activities for teachers who are temperamentally suited for their tasks
5. Effective utilization of educational specialists, such as counselors, school psychologists, and school nurses, to supplement the work of classroom teachers
6. Decentralization of administrative control
7. Active participation of local neighborhood leaders

8. Close co-operation between school, home, and civic and governmental agencies
9. Cultural activities for the pupils that supplement their school and home environments and experiences—trips to museums, art galleries, concerts, public libraries, downtown department stores, universities and colleges, and other schools
10. Use of the school as a neighborhood cultural, social, and recreational center
11. A carefully conceived and professionally executed plan of evaluation of the total educational progress of each pupil
12. A 'Hawthorne effect' on both teachers and pupils[34]

This is a significant list, and each entry is worth careful attention, but the striking point is that it is relevant to education of any kind at any level.

References

1. Bassett, G.W. Crane, A.R. and Walker, W.G. 1963. *Headmasters for Better Schools*. University of Queensland Press: Brisbane.
2. Report of the Interim Committee for the Australian Schools Commission, 1973. *Schools in Australia*, Canberra (Karmel Report), p. 9.
3. Jones, A.W. 1968. 'Educational Opportunity in a Centralised System of Education,' in *Opportunity in Education*. The Australian College of Education: Melbourne, p. 134.
4. ———. 1974. 'Decision-Making in a State Education Department' in Jecks, D.A. (ed.), *Influences in Australian Education*. Carroll's: Perth, p. 41.
5. Karmel Report, p. 13.
6. Beare, Hedley, in association with Glenn, M. *et al.*, 1974, *A Plan for Education in New Towns and Cities*. Australian Publishing Service: Canberra.
7. Experiments are being conducted in various centres in Australia, e.g. The Association for Modern Education (A.M.E.) School and the School Without Walls in Canberra.
8. Caldwell, Bettye M., 1970. 'Introduction', in Hellmuth, Jerome (ed.), *Compensatory Education: A National Debate, vol 3*. Brunner/Mazel: New York, p. iv.
9. Winschel, James F. 1970, 'In the Dark . . . Reflections on Compensatory Education, 1960–1970', in *ibid.*, p. 19.
10. Bloom, B.S., Davis, A. and Hess, R., 1965. *Compensatory Education for Cultural Deprivation*. Holt, Rinehart & Winston: New York.
11. Landers, J. 1963, 'The Higher Horizons Program in New York City', in U.S. Office of Education, *Programs for the Educationally Disadvantaged*. Government Printing Office: Washington.
12. Balson, M., 1965, 'Culturally Deprived Children in Victorian Schools'. *Teachers' Journal* 48, 9: 399–403.
13. Caldwell, *op. cit.*, pp. vi–vii.

14. Cirilleli, V.G., Granger, R.L. *et al.*, 1969. *The Impact of Head Start: An Evaluation of Head Start on Children's Cognitive and Affective Development*, vol. 1. Report to the U.S. Office of Economic Opportunity by Westinghouse Learning Corporation and Ohio University.
15. Jensen, A., 1969. 'How Much Can We Boost I.Q. and Scholastic Achievement?'. *Harvard Educational Review*, pp. 1–123.
16. Central Advisory Council for Education (England), 1959, *Fifteen to Eighteen*, vol. 1., H.M.S.O.: London (Crowther Report).
17. Committee on Higher Education, 1963. *Higher Education*. H.M.S.O.: London (Robbins Report).
18. Central Advisory Council for Education (England), 1963. *Half Our Future*. H.M.S.O.: London (Newsom Report).
19. Central Advisory Council for Education (England), 1967. *Children and Their Primary Schools* vols 1 and 2. H.M.S.O.: London (Plowden Report).
20. For example, Chazan, M., 1968. 'Compensatory Education: Defining the Problem', in *Compensatory Education—An Introduction*. Occasional Publication no. 1., Schools Council Research and Development Project in Compensatory Education, Dept of Education, University College of Swansea: Wales.
21. For example, Floud, J.E., Halsey, A.H. and Martin, F.M., 1957. *Social Class and Educational Opportunity*. Heinemann: London.
22. For example, Wiseman, S., 1968. 'Educational Deprivation and Disadvantage', in Butcher, H.J. (ed.), *Educational Research in Britain*. University of London Press: London.
23. For example, Blackstone, T., 1971. *A Fair Start*. Allan Lane, Penguin Press: London.
24. For example, Eysenck, H.J., 1969. 'The Rise of the Mediocracy', in Cox, C.B. and Dyson, A.E. (eds), *Black Paper Two*. Critical Quarterly Society: London.
25. For example, Bernstein, B., 1961. 'Social Class and Linguistic Development: A Theory of Social Learning', in Halsey, A.H., Floud, J. and Anderson, C.A. (eds), *Education, Economy and Society*. The Free Press, Glencoe: New York.
26. For example, Musgrove, F., 1963. *The Migratory Elite*. Heinemann: London.
27. For example, Halsey, A.H. (ed.), 1972. *Educational Priority*. H.M.S.O.: London. This is a report on research sponsored by the Department of Education and Science and the Social Science Research Council. It deals with problems and policies of the educational priority areas in England. See also refs 21 and 25 for research by Halsey.
28. For example, Lawton, D., 1968. *Social Class, Language and Education*, Routledge & Kegan Paul: London.
29. See Watts's critique of so-called cultural language deprivation in ch. 3.
30. See Karmel Report, app. E.
31. Ginsburg, H., 1972, *The Myth of the Deprived Child*, Prentice Hall: Englewood Cliffs, N.J.
32. Ibid., pp. 194–95.
33. Ibid., p. 233.
34. Chandler, B.J. and Bertolaet, F., 1967. 'Administrative Problems and Procedures in Compensatory Education', in *Sixty-sixth Yearbook of the National Society for the Study of Education*, pt 1, *The Educationally Retarded and Disadvantaged*, University of Chicago Press: Chicago p. 313.

5. School Organisation

Guidelines Relating to School Organisation

2.1   A school is likely to cater for the needs of individual children if it has a strong spirit of community.

2.2   Organisation should include effective internal procedures for planning the school's programme.

2.3   Schools should adopt an experimental approach to school and class organisation as there is no one best way of organising for individual teaching.

2.4   The school building, equipment and facilities should be used to best advantage, in harmony with a philosophy of catering for individual students.

2.5   The concept of discipline in education should be task-oriented; and the exercise of discipline should take account of differences in students' aptitude and interest in various tasks.

2.6   Organisation should be appropriately related to curriculum objectives.

2.7   Organisation should be appropriately related to teaching methods.

2.8   Organisation should be appropriately related to assessment procedures.

Introduction

School organisation cannot by itself ensure that individual differences are effectively catered for, but it is an essential factor in creating a suitable environment for effective action. Whether it is successful or not depends substantially on the nature of the actions of principals, staff and pupils, and the quality of the personal relationships between them. To claim that it is an enabling factor, allowing, but not ensuring, that objectives are achieved, is not to detract from its importance.

Although both the structure of an organisation and its mode of functioning must be in harmony if objectives are to be realised, structure

152

strongly influences the mode of functioning. The line of least resistance for the member of any institution is to accommodate himself to its structural pattern. Pursuing objectives that are incompatible with the organisation is an uphill task, and few are likely to manage it successfully. By the same token, a change in organisation can help to bring about a change in the mode of functioning, as when a new style of school building replaces a traditional one, and encourages a change in the behaviour pattern of those who work in it.

This examination of school organisation can be conveniently introduced by presenting two sharply contrasting descriptions, the first from a publication by Broudy, an American, the second from the 1967 English report on the primary school (Plowden Report)—

> . . . the school lives by rules that are supposed to take care of standard cases. Because the standard school systems are organized by grades, content must be organized into graded sequences. Each grade depends on the one preceding it to 'cover' prescribed bits of information or skills. The logistics of instruction require rules about attendance, time periods and arrangements through the building. In most schools, teachers are required to sign in and out; bulletins flow from the central office; reports are in transit in all directions, at all levels . . . School operation is so rule-ridden that the teachers' autonomy is restricted to trivialities . . . Why are rules so important to the system? Because it has no other principle of order.[1]

> A school is not merely a teaching shop, it must transmit values and attitudes. It is a community in which children learn to live first and foremost as children, and not as future adults . . . The school sets out deliberately to devise the right environment for children, to allow them to be themselves and to develop in the way and at the pace appropriate to them . . . It lays special stress on individual discovery, on first-hand experience and on opportunities for creative work. It insists that knowledge does not fall into neatly separate compartments, and that work and play are not opposite but complementary.[2]

Clearly the view of school organisation indicated in the second of these two quotations is more likely to be compatible with a programme designed to cater for individual differences. As a community, a school is much more likely to be concerned with co-operation among its diverse members than with framing rules to reduce differences to standard cases. In deliberately attempting to plan the right learning environment for children a school is much more likely to take account of the different needs of each than if it merely assigns them to grades with set tasks and standards. Its approach to curriculum, to teaching method, and to assessment is more likely to be flexible and more compatible with the objective of nurturing personal growth. These different features are elaborated in the following sections.

2.1 Fostering a Spirit of Community within the School

Getzels has described the functioning of an institution in terms of two dimensions that he calls *nomothetic* and *idiographic*.[3] His model is expressed thus:

Model Describing the Functioning of an Institution in Terms of Nomothetic and Idiographic Dimensions

(Nomothetic Dimension)

Social System

Institution ⟶ Role ⟶ Expectations ⟶ Observed Behaviour

Individual ⟶ Personality ⟶ Need Disposition

(Idiographic Dimension)

The term *nomothetic* refers to the institutional character of the organisation and includes such features as its formal structure, the rules that regulate it, and the external official and societal influences that help to determine the role expectations. The term *idiographic* refers to the personal elements which influence the particular way in which the institution functions. As can be seen from the model, the character of an institution is a product of these two interacting influences. The nature of the idiographic dimension is obviously of great importance in determining the climate of community within an organisation, as it is by the nature of the personal relations among members that a community is most obviously recognised. It is a commonplace observation that a number of school principals in similar positions will discharge their duties differently. The nomothetic dimension may be thus modified in actual practice by different styles of behaviour within the school.

The most significant personal relationships are those

1. between principal and members of staff
2. between members of staff and children
3. among members of staff
4. among children

For an institution to have a distinctive climate, as it would if it were a community, these different groups of relationships need to be compatible. Each of them is briefly commented on in the following sections.

Relationships between Principal and Staff

Perhaps the key relationship within a school, with an influence pervading all others, is that between principal and staff. If there is a recognition by the principal of individual differences among staff members, a friendly and co-operative attitude to them, it is likely that the same atmosphere will exist throughout the school. If this relationship is marked by tension and conflict and the arbitrary exercise of authority by the principal, this also is likely to be the pattern throughout the school. What, in fact, is the nature of this relationship in our schools?

In an intercultural study including teachers in England, the U.S.A., New Zealand and Australia in 1966,[4] Biddle found that there was greater social distance and hostility between Australian teachers and principals than among teachers in the other countries studied. This was so in spite of informality that exists between many principals and teachers with easy use of first names and other expressions of camaraderie. In a more recent study,[5] Campbell claims that this is less valid now, largely because those higher in the educational hierarchy have transferred much of their authority in classroom matters to teachers.

The situation that Campbell describes, although certainly lessening the likelihood of conflict between principal and teachers, does little to increase the prospects that schools will become communities of administrators, teachers and students. Co-operative relationships, of the kind that lead to joint endeavours, are needed, not just a friendly policy of non-intervention. In some illuminating verbatim statements of teachers questioned about these relationships with principals in the conduct of their teaching programmes, quoted by Campbell in his study, the lack of involvement by the principal in what is, after all, the heart of the school's purpose, is brought out clearly—

> Our head doesn't care what teaching style you use as long as you keep the children quiet.

> I would like to have much more free activity out the room gets in a mess, and the principal is frightened that the cleaner will quit.[6]

Both of these teachers reported that their relations with their principal were cordial. A courteous and friendly attitude of principals to teachers, both in and out of school, is certainly important, but it cannot be an effective substitute for that deeper sense of partnership that expresses itself in sharing with others the significant tasks of the institution, such as defining its objectives and planning its programme. This attitude to shared responsibility expresses humility in recognising the different talents of others, and a sincerity in accepting them. More than in his social contacts with members of staff, the principal's personal style is best judged in terms of the organisational arrangements he sets up to facilitate co-operative planning and co-operative action. These reflect his educational leadership, rather than his authority. We shall return to these nomothetic elements later.

Relationship between Teacher and Pupils

There is some evidence that teachers in Australian schools are more authoritarian in their relationships with children than at least some other groups of teachers studied. Professor Bush, a visitor to Australia from Stanford University, has written as follows:

> The teaching and learning roles are more clearly defined in the Australian than in the American secondary school. Relationships between teachers and pupils in Australia are, on the whole, characterized by greater social distance and greater formality. Teachers are more the directors and pupils the followers.[7]

Adams's research evidence points in a similar direction. Using data gathered in the intercultural study already referred to, he concluded that Australian teachers stress teacher-made rules more than do their counterparts in the other countries. Australians, least of all the teachers studied, emphasise permissiveness of control and discussion as an interactional style. In summary he writes as follows:

> Australians de-emphasize personal relations, free communication, the use of undifferentiated groups, and permissiveness.[8]

To many Australian teachers, talk of schools as communities, pervaded by a spirit of mutual respect, is unrealistic. Maintaining order, they claim, is difficult enough, and the difficulty is increasing. Particularly is this so in secondary schools, where students are inevitably affected by the earlier entry into adult life indicated by lowered ages for voting and for drinking in public bars, and by the widespread slackening of parental control. Undoubtedly, in some schools, or with some groups of children, the teacher can exercise little more than a custodial function. Some problems may well be insoluble, at least with educational methods, but they do not negate, as a realistic objective in most schools, the creation of a constructive relationship between teachers and pupils, based on a recognition by teachers of the child's individuality, an insight into the influence shaping it (as outlined particularly in Chapter 2), and an attitude of acceptance of it. The need to understand children in order to teach them has never been greater. The use of arbitrary authority has never been defensible in an educational programme, and it is likely to be increasingly self-defeating in the future.

The relationship deemed necessary is not merely a sentimental one. Teachers and children are brought together for a serious purpose, and achieving this must be accepted as a realistic criterion of success. But teaching and learning have an influential affective component, and are unlikely to be successful if this is neglected. The child needs a sense of security in learning, freedom from fear of failure, satisfaction in achievement, and the constructive stimulus of those whose vision of the world is larger than his own. The relationship between teacher and child must be a personal one if the individuality of the student is to be taken seriously. It must express the teacher's informed judgement about the child's abilities, interests, needs and problems, and a sincere desire to deal with them in the child's best interests. The possibility of such a relationship is not dependent only on the teacher's willingness to play this role, but on the organisational arrangements which allow him to do it. A teacher who is committed to a class-teaching arrangement, or is otherwise overwhelmed by children in the mass, is unlikely to be able to deal with other than standard cases. The relevance of methods and other aspects of school organisation is made clearer in later sections.

Relationships among Teachers

A useful research study that should be conducted is an eavesdropping project on conversations among teachers in and out of school. At present 'bugging' is out of favour, so it would probably be necessary to use a 'fifth column' research design, or somehow cajole teachers into reporting with unusual candour.

One topic of perennial interest, at least in the schools of yesterday, was that of school inspectors and their various idiosyncrasies. An amusing example of conversation on this topic is to be found in the somewhat cynical account of the public school system in New South Wales in the earlier part of this century given by Brian James. The setting is Manly beach where teachers regularly foregathered in the long summer holiday and indulged in the 'sweet regaining of their self-esteem'—

I said to him; 'The last inspector promised me my mark . . .'
'I went right to head office, and I told him straight . . .'
'I hit the roof when he said that . . .'
'I went off like a packet of crackers . . .'
'Wait till I tell you about old Greenway—you remember old Greenway?—Can't teach for nuts—and he had the hide to say . . .'

'Psychology—just a stunt if you ask me . . .'
'Should have seen my garden . . .'
'Best concert they ever had . . .'
'I got no credit for the physical display at all—best ever seen in . . .'
It went on endlessly in the same old tones of grievance and triumph.[9]

My own memory of staff room conversations yields little of serious substance. A vivid memory is of a science teacher on a high school staff who claimed to have an absolutely foolproof system of making money at horse-racing. He never actually put the system to the acid test, but each Monday morning he would report on the exact financial transactions that would have taken place had he actually invested the money according to the system. Later in the week the topic would again come to the fore with the plans for the forthcoming Saturday's racing. Other memories are less mercenary, but none the less trivial. Relationships among the school colleagues that I remember were cordial, but banal.

Also in anecdotal vein, but by way of contrast, I recall a group of teachers in an American elementary school, who, working as a team, filled every available hour of their free time with sober exchanges about methods, plans, problems and successes relating to the children in their team. Their industry and commitment were admirable, but there was a hint of undue solemnity in their relations. To an Australian, they seemed to take themselves a little too seriously.

Neither the memory of experiences within one's own country or isolated observations in another is an adequate guide in examining the significance of staff relations in a school, but they are suggestive. Fellowship among staff is a necessary ingredient in a school that can fairly be called a community, but it needs also a deeper concern with individual differences than is involved in the exchanges of trivial conversation.

In succeeding sections there are many proposals regarding the conduct of a school, in its day-to-day practices as well as in its longer-range planning—all dictated by the facts of individual differences among children. It is in active participation in these by teachers that professional satisfaction is found and more mature relationships develop based on shared responsibility. Involvement in decision making and in innovative projects, collaboration in team teaching and other school programmes—these are the keys to collegial relationships within the staff.

Relationships among Students

Bringing children together in a school provides varied opportunities for them to be influenced by each other, for good or ill. Much of this social process occurs in informal situations, but, of course, situations also are contrived. Socialisation is a normative process, and is affected, if not directed, by rules, expectations, exhortations, codes, traditions, and other kinds of constraining or facilitating influences. These influences may be imposed by an authority external to the group, or may arise within the group itself.

Much has been written of peer group influence, particularly among high school students. Riesman uses the term "other-direction" to express the idea of motivation by social approval—particularly by peers.[10] He views this with concern, particularly when it becomes the dominant motivational style. Excessive dependence on others for approval makes these others the arbiters of standards and styles of behaviour and increases the vulnerability of the individual. Other-direction clearly expresses a convergence of individual differences towards group norms; it could lead to a complete denial of individuality. Only a superficial type of community is likely to emerge under such conditions of social influence. Its coherence is obtained at the price of individuality, and because of this, it is likely to become what Riesman calls a 'lonely crowd'. Peer group approval is a significant factor to consider in any account of relationships among students in a school, but it would be folly to place great reliance on it, either as a means of social control, or of mobilising the creative powers of the group.

A sense of community among children requires a degree of like-mindedness, but this need not lead to the suppression of individuality. Individuality may express itself in competitive behaviour or in withdrawal (in colloquial terms, 'doing one's own thing'), but it may also enrich a task undertaken in common with others. It is in this mobilisation of difference that true community exists. The community so created gives security to its members, while, at the same time, freeing them for their own adventures in ideas and actions. It encourages toleration of the personal idiosyncrasies of fellow students so apparent in day-to-day relationships and also of the racial and cultural differences among those more remote. It strengthens the possibility that young people growing up will better understand the meaning of justice, and practice it, since this also is based on respect for individuality. Creating this kind of school community is the supreme task of school organisation.

A very important relationship among schoolchildren is that between the sexes. Possibly at no time has the need been greater for a wholesome relationship between the sexes. Traditional morality and social custom, which previously regulated these relationships, have weakened and have not been replaced by effective substitutes. Sex is openly exploited commercially, and competition between the sexes and charges of inequality are common. One of the most basic of individual differences thus seems in modern society to be among the least satisfactorily managed.

In schools there is controversy about coeducation and sex education, each being an attempt in educational terms to deal with male-female differences. Advocates of coeducation claim that it is a more natural arrangement, and is likely to lead to better relationships between the sexes. Segregation, they claim, is unnatural, and is more likely to lead to social maladjustment. Opponents claim that each sex has its own rhythm of development, and is best served by an educational programme designed specially for it. In fact, it is coeducation that is most commonly practised at all school levels, and many schools that traditionally have been segregated are adopting coeducation in some form or other. There is little research evidence regarding the merits of coeducation, but it is hardly reasonable to claim that merely bringing boys and girls together in the same school is likely in itself to increase understanding and respect between the sexes. What it can do is to provide the opportunity to plan a particular kind of educational programme to lead towards this objective. The key to the advantage of coeducation, then, is in the kind of school community that is created, and its success in creating attitudes of respect between boys and girls. In this point the virtues of coeducation are not differently derived from those of other kinds of heterogeneity, whether planned or unplanned, that might be found in a school. The attitudes engendered among children with regard to differences in scholastic aptitude, to physical handicap, to language differences, to differences in skin colour, and the like, depend on the advantages taken of the situation, not simply on the existence of heterogeneity. Coeducation provides the opportunity for a significant experience in sex education, namely the association of the sexes in the kind of school community that encourages a balanced and constructive relationship between them. How successful it will be ultimately in this task depends a great deal on the kind of influence that children are exposed to outside the school. But this is true of any task that the school attempts.

Nomothetic Characteristics of the School As a Community

The foregoing discussion of the school as a community has been in terms of the personal relationships among its members, but structural features of the institution also are clearly relevant. As has been already stated, the mode of functioning of an organisation is likely to be influenced by its structure, even though considerable variation within a given structure is possible in line with differences in idiographic characteristics.

The typical form of organisation in schools is bureaucratic, similar to that usually found in other organisations in commerce, industry, and service organisations, including government services. Writing of the American scene, Williamson underlines this point—

> It is no accident that the bureaucratic substance of society's mandate in turn made bureaucracy the logical organizational form of the schools. The principal goals of schooling could be quite logically considered in stable product terms—graduates who had certain commonly shared knowledge, abilities, and attitudes which in theory at least, could be prescribed before the process of schooling began. This fact, coupled with the size of the educational establishment and the relative stability of the needs of society, made bureaucracy as inevitable for schooling as it was for other institutions.[11]

The main characteristics of this type of organisation are as follows:

1. A hierarchy of authority
2. A division of labour among members
3. A system of rules governing the duties and rights of members
4. A system of routine procedures for dealing with the tasks of the organisation
5. Impersonality in interpersonal relations
6. Selection and promotion based on merit

These provisions do facilitate efficient operation in an organisation and protect it from corrupt practices, and to the extent that an educational institution has similar needs to other organisations, no doubt they are beneficial to it also. But with a different view of the educational task than that expressed in the quotation above, namely catering for individual differences rather than producing a standard product, major organisational differences are needed from those primarily concerned with producing or distributing goods, or administering services of a routine kind. A brief examination of the six features of bureaucratic organisation listed will help to bring out these differences more clearly, and to point the way to a more systematic description of an alternative organisational type more appropriate to a collegial or community model.

Hierarchy of Authority. The hierarchy of authority in an organisation is based typically on the wide range of competence among members, extending from those with high level managerial skills, through middle range executives, to supervisors and operatives, each accepting different levels of responsibility.

In a school this hierarchy is much less appropriate. With modern standards of professional training, both pre-service and in-service, the range of competence from principal to staff is reduced and the need for intermediate positions is less relevant. The principal has important managerial tasks which are peripheral to the main concern of the school, namely its educational programme, but his primary responsibility is as educational leader. As such he works with the staff well-qualified in broadly the same field as his own. Indeed some of them are likely to have special gifts not shared by the principal. His administrative responsibility on the educational side is thus most appropriately that of giving leadership by co-operating with members of staff and mobilising their different talents for effective action. If a staff becomes large, the difficulty of doing this by direct contact increases, and the appointment of intermediate staff (deputies, subject masters and the like) is commonly resorted to. Under these circumstances, hierarchical structure becomes more apparent, and a bureaucratic mode of functioning is more likely to occur.

This is one reason why schools should not be allowed to grow into large institutions. Where this does occur (and there are good economic arguments for it, particularly in the case of high schools) the chief organisational problem is to retain a co-operative mode of functioning, while providing the additional administrative assistance needed, including support staff with skills different from those of teachers. Professionals do not fit easily into bureaucratic organisations, and when the professional task is the creative kind that teaching should be, the problem is greater.

Division of Labour. The division of labour in the bureaucratic model is to cope with the appropriate segments of the main complex tasks of the organisation. It is seen most clearly in the production of an industrial plant where operatives perform reduced contributory tasks to a total process.

Schools, too, have made use of a division of labour with teachers engaging in self-contained tasks teaching a class or a subject, administrative staff with explicitly defined duties (often embodied in regulations or salary agreements), and other specialist support staff such as counsellors, librarians, remedial teachers, etc. The division, however, is not directly comparable to the discrete kind that one finds in many types of mass production in industry. Each is working with a complete process in a particular way, teaching, administering, counselling, etc. Moreover, because there has been this growth of specialist services in schools with the possible dislocation to the child's integrated view of the process of schooling, a countermove to co-ordinate more closely the different contributions of specialists is occurring. Decision making is more frequently approached by consultation and group action rather than by isolated action by those in authority, and programmes of teaching are more frequently being planned as co-operative ventures by groups of teachers combining their individual talents for more effective action. The resultant organisation is very different from the division of labour of the traditional bureaucracy.

No doubt traditional bureaucracies are also restless in this time of change and are concerned about the need to re-examine objectives and review their procedures. In doing so, no doubt many features of the search for self-renewal in educational institutions will be relevant to them also. But the character of educational institutions is inherently unique in that its product and its processes are but different forms of the one objective.

Rules Governing the Duties and Rights of Members. A stable organisation with explicit objectives can work effectively according to a routine. The work pattern can be expressed as a set of rules to be followed.

Schools, too, have made considerable use of rules, applied to both staff and students. A number of historical factors help to explain this. The schools were part of a wider system of schools, and were obliged to conform to consistent practices. Being undertrained, most teachers found it essential to follow prescribed syllabuses and methods of teaching. The role of the school in a stable society was itself stable, and could be standardised.

All these conditions have changed. Modern systems of education have recognised the value of encouraging initiative at the level of individual institutions. Thus the responsibility of the school principal has been strengthened, making fewer rules necessary aimed at keeping institutions in line with each other. The upgrading of teachers' education has increased both their desire to exercise personal judgement and their capacity to do it effectively. Students also have different expectations regarding the use of authority, particularly in the secondary school, and are less amenable to conform to rules, particularly those directed at their personal conduct. This point is elaborated further in a section dealing with discipline. Finally, and perhaps most significantly, the society in which the school functions is unstable, and the school is engaged in a restless search for a proper role. Under such conditions firm rules make innovation difficult. When a school is substantially free to plan and carry out its own programme; when teachers are well prepared and are able to participate in the task of planning in a sophisticated way; when students are more vocal about their own education, and when social changes are so pervasive that the school feels obliged to reconsider its whole *modus operandi*, rules are inadequate to give the organisation the functional quality that it needs.

Rather it needs to strive to clarify its objectives, to express them in realistic operational terms, to experiment with procedures that appear to lead effectively towards their realisation, and to keep the whole procedure under critical review. The reliance of a bureaucracy on a fixed set of prescriptions is thus largely irrelevant to a modern school grappling with the difficult problems of catering for individual differences and of keeping a sense of direction in a changing social milieu. The discipline required under such circumstances is that of critical inquiry rather than conformity. When this more difficult test is applied, it does not mean that everything that has become traditional is discarded. Rather its value is reassessed, and it may, of course, be reaffirmed.

Routine Procedures. The comments made about rules are relevant also to routine procedures. Standardisation and automation have contributed greatly to the success of modern industry, but there are few lessons to be learnt from them in conducting an educational institution, if this institution is to provide a community life for its members. Routine procedures that support the main teaching function should, of course, be as efficient as possible, but if allowed to intrude too much they tend to create a rigidity that is ultimately self-defeating. There have been moves also to routinise the teaching function by means of programmed teaching systems, particularly in America. These 'teacher-proof' packages can be valuable if used judiciously, but alone they cannot create a suitable environment for learning.

An institution seeking a mode of operation that assists it in becoming as educative community, sensitive to the separate needs of its members, needs to look more to methods of obtaining flexibility than routine.

Impersonality. The stress on impersonality within a bureaucratic organisation is connected with the idea that efficiency is deemed to depend on careful planning, standardised techniques and the strict following of job specifications, rather than on personal relations. It is the system that is efficient and its members serve it by fitting into it. The control of the human factor also protects an organisation against malpractices such as nepotism and the abuse of a person's position for personal advantage. Much has been written about the 'organisation man' at the higher level of company management who identifies himself emotionally with the company and its demands, often at the cost of his personal judgement.

Favouritism is, of course, out of place in schools, but it cannot be corrected by impersonality. A school is centrally concerned with social interaction among its members, both adults and children. This has been already discussed in connection with the elucidation of the idiographic element in organisation, and there is no need to deal with it at this point.

Selection and Promotion. In a school or other organisation there would be few dissentients to the view that selection and promotion should be based on merit rather then on seniority alone. The question of promotion has been something of a *cause célèbre* among teachers for decades, and the assessment role of inspectors has been subjected to a prolonged and often bitter criticism. It has been attacked on a number of counts— intensification of uniform practices in schools, capriciousness in terms of the whims of particular inspectors, inaccuracies and misjudgements through inadequate information, and, perhaps most serious of all, its arousal of a competitive spirit among teachers.

The practice of inspection has undergone many changes aimed at reducing its frequency, limiting its application to aspirants for promotion, delegating it to school principals, altering classification schemes which unduly highlight relative seniority of teachers, and revising the classification of schools and the structure of salary scales to reduce the competition for scarce positions.

The problem is a difficult one. No system can or should avoid the task of evaluating its members and its institutions and of recognising special industry or merit when it occurs. But the effectiveness of a system that is permeated with a narrow spirit of accountability is likely to be constrained in its programme by excessive caution.

Issues likely to be critical in moving towards a satisfactory solution are the criteria that are used in assessment and the use of schemes that are unobtrusive, leaving the initiative for seeking promotion to those concerned. If teachers consider that they are being assessed on realistic criteria that take adequate account of the circumstances in which they are working, and of their own interpretation of appropriate curricula and methods, they are more likely to accept evaluation as a professional task. If, also, the scheme is such that they are in a position to decide whether to seek promotion and by so doing to know that the judgement of those with whom they work day by day is taken seriously into account, the divisive influence of promotion within a school is likely to be significantly reduced.

The Dynamics of Bureaucracy in School Organisation

Pusey,[12] in his study of Tasmanian secondary education, has drawn a graphic picture of the dislocation to community spirit within a school when a formal authority structure is allowed to predominate. He calls it a 'disabling pattern'. It arises, he claims, from the reaction of students, teachers and principals to formal authority. This reaction may be one of rebellion (and some choose this), or ingratiation (and some choose this), or withdrawal. Withdrawal is the most common response, and it is this reaction that is at the heart of the disabling pattern. The form that this withdrawal takes among students, teachers and principals is described in detail by Pusey, and interested readers are referred to his book for a full account. Only a brief elaboration is given here.

First, the key relationship between teacher and student. The authority of the teacher is potentially threatening to students—particularly to adolescent students because of their burgeoning sense of selfhood. He is empowered to comment on and evaluate their performance, their personal style, and virtually the whole gamut of their feelings—all this publicly, in the presence of their peers. By withdrawing they set up a psychological barrier between themselves and the teacher, enabling them to keep their personal life more to themselves, or to share it with fellow students and adults whom they regard differently. This act of increasing the social distance from the teacher, reinforced by collective sharing with fellow students, helps to reduce their sense of insecurity. More subtly, they reduce anxiety from the pressure on them to disclose their inner feelings and to display their initiative, by making teachers structure each required task in detail. They thus ensure that requirements are explicit, relieving them of the uncertainty of having to act creatively. The price paid for this manoeuvre is high for both teacher and students. The teacher is alienated from his students in all but superficial relationships, and his capacity to influence them personally and emotionally is reduced. This is particularly apparent in school tasks involving value judgements in aesthetic subjects such as literature and the arts, and in social and moral judgements in the social sciences, but it affects attitudes and motivation in all subjects. The students are alienated from the teacher also in a significant sense, de-emphasising their own personal style in their involvement with school tasks, thus lessening their relevance. For psychic support they turn more to the culture of their peers.

Second, the relationship between teachers and principal. Just as the authority of teachers is potentially threatening to students, so the authority of the principal is potentially threatening to teachers. No matter how much emphasis is placed on the technical features of teaching, it is accepted, tacitly at least, by both teachers and principal that the quality of the teacher's performance depends essentially on personal factors such as confidence, sensitivity, concern, verbal competence, etc. His performance is an intimate reflection of his worth as a person. The principal's authority over the teacher thus is not merely official, but also personal. Any evaluation that he makes of the teacher, although made professionally, is tantamount to a personal judgement. This relationship is not mutual; the teacher cannot evaluate the principal, at least publicly. Thus, it is the teacher's self-esteem that is at risk. The subtlety of this relationship is unlikely to be seen by many principals who have learnt their job mainly by observing their superiors in climbing the promotion ladder. They see their responsibility as all-embracing. It is their school; they must *run* it; they must be accountable for *all* the activities of staff and students, even though many would be clearly beyond the range of their control. The bureaucratic model on which the principal operates encourages the withdrawal syndrome among the staff. They put a psychological barrier of impersonality between themselves and him. They resolve the uncertainties of their relationship by influencing the principal to make his policies explicit. To the exhortation that they are professional people, and should show initiative themselves, their likely response is; 'But it is the principal that is responsible'. No real leadership is possible under these conditions. With the multiplication of rules, the task of enforcing them is thrown more and more on to the principal. To the teachers, the 'good' principal is one who backs them up. The 'weak' principal is one who is prepared to see the student's side of the case as well. So the principal is alienated from his students as well as from his staff. His role becomes more and more settled as that of disciplinarian. The 'good name' of the school becomes a dominant concern, taking precedence over its quality as a satisfying community for its members.

Third, the disabling pattern is reinforced by the principal's own insecurity in relationships with his superiors. The pervasive influence of 'head office', although often critised, is inwardly accepted as a prop to his own authority, and as protection against the burden of personal responsibility. The injunction laid on him by well-meaning superiors to accept more autonomy for his school carries with it the threat of greater accountability, and the uncertainty of having to measure up to unknown demands of his qualities of leadership. The withdrawal reaction and the protective mechanism of formalising external controls are fairly predictable outcomes, reinforcing the whole disabling pattern of principal-staff-student relationships. An unfortunate by-product, weakening organisational effectiveness still further, is the separation of the school from the community. The pervasiveness of authority at all levels, the reliance on routine and rules, and the general conservatism of outlook, present a forbidding front to the community. Community participation in the life of the school is one more uncertainty for the school authorities that is best kept under control. The artificiality of much school experience is thereby intensified.

Whatever the virtues of bureaucratic organisation may be in maintaining efficiency in an institution, it is clear that it has serious defects in an educational institution which is seeking to create a stimulating and supportive community environment for its members. The human side of organisation may be peripheral in an institution engaged in technological processes (although the prevalence of industrial unrest casts doubt upon this), but in a school it is quite central, being both process and product. It is thus essential that the 'disabling pattern' described above be overcome if a suitable environment is to be achieved for the handling of individual differences.

The Concept of Community Defined

The argument advanced to elucidate the concept of community has been somewhat negative in form, in that it has preceeded from an analysis of the problems that bureaucratic educational institutions encounter when they try to take seriously the task of treating their students as persons. It is the history of school organisation that has dictated this approach. But the concept of a school community is positive in its own right, and can be justified by its own distinct qualities. Structurally it could be described thus:

1. *A low formal authority gradient*, i.e. a minimum of positions formally authorised by law or by delegation. From this it would follow that many of the organisational tasks of the institution would be shared on some agreed basis, without regard to official rank. For members of the organisation temporarily holding positions of special responsibility, recognition might be given in terms of work-load, financial incentive, etc. A position which is at present locked into the formal hierarchy of positions in many secondary schools is that of subject master or departmental head. This could well be a leadership position determined by domestic action within the school, and change from time to time. In the same way, although with greater difficulty, the deputy headships and headships of schools might be held for specified limited periods. Salary schemes would have to be substantially revised to accommodate such arrangements.
2. *Collaborative decision-making procedures.* These would need to be open, and involve those directly affected by discussions, including students as well as staff and principal.
3. *Effective communication networks.* These should effectively link principal, staff and students within the school, and parents and other members of its community outside.

4. *Effective pastoral care schemes*, particularly for students and inexperienced members of staff.
5. *Suitable social arrangements*, particularly allowing easy meeting of principal, staff and students within the school.

Functionally, it could be described thus:

1. *The use of formal authority at a minimum.*
2. *Attitudes of trust, mutual respect, and warmth among members.*
3. *Staff discipline based mainly on their sense of professionalism.* This would involve the recognition of charismatic leadership and experience among their own members as well as among those holding positions of formal authority, a tolerance of differences in outlook, and acceptance of the task of initiating new members of the profession in a constructive way.
4. *Co-operative attitudes among staff members.* These would arise from a sense of corporate responsibility for the pursuit of broadly similar educational values, particularly those dealing with inquiry and its liberating effect on the lives on individual children, with aesthetic experience and with the sensitising of children to the humane conduct of social life.
5. *Student discipline based mainly on active involvement in the life of the school.* This would involve a sense of relevance in the curriculum followed, a feeling of security in personal relationships with principal and staff, and a tolerant attitude to differences in ability, interests and physical appearance among fellow students.

Ben Morris speaks of the educational enterprise as 'essentially commerce between persons', and 'as an adventure in mutuality';[13] and this is as good a way as any to express the concept of an educational community.

2.2 Establishing Effective Planning Procedures for the School Programme

In the preceding section the importance of co-operative planning to help create an open, harmonious school climate was stressed. Its importance in directly improving the effectiveness of the school's programme also needs to be stressed.

The task of relating the goals of an institution to the activities of its members is very complex. Institutions serve outside interests as well as those of its members, and among its members, needs and interests vary widely. Mobilising all these diverse elements into an effective whole is difficult, and evidence of its failure is common. Obvious examples are the lack of correspondence between the stated goals of the institution and the actual practices of individual teachers, disharmony between the needs and interests of students and the objectives set by teachers, and disharmony between home and school.

An essential feature of successful planning for a school, with its varied members, is provision for frequent and close consultation. If this is neglected, misunderstandings and antagonisms are likely to occur. The alternative to consultation is the use of authority, and this limits the communication network, and reduces the range of options that might be considered. When authority is accepted as the basis for organisational structure in a school, divisions between principal and staff, and between staff and students are likely to occur.

In initiating and implementing a plan there is both a rational and affective component. Ideas and skills have to be understood to be mastered, but they have also to be accepted and responded to. Both the rational and affective components are better served by collaborative methods than by the use of authority. Consultation provides the opportunity for the examination of ideas and for presenting different perceptions of them and clearing up misconceptions. It also provides the opportunity for examining different value judgements about the ideas, for one person to be influenced by another, and for attitudes to be changed or reinforced. The plan that is subjected to scrutiny is thus more likely to be understood and accepted by all than one dictated by a single person or small group. The actual arrangements made for consultation will vary in different institutions and according to different groups involved.

The Staff Conference

The most obvious method of liaison of principal and staff is the staff conference. For this to be effective it must be accepted as a decision-making body, each member having an equal chance to influence the decision. Decisions arrived at in this way are likely to be as soundly based as directives given by a principal, or other person in authority. The principal as educational leader has every opportunity to advance his own ideas, and in the process of deliberation proposals can be modified, expanded or enriched by the contributions of others and by reference to outside authorities by way of books, advice from inspectors and advisory teachers, or the report of a staff member fresh from an in-service conference at a teacher's centre, and through other influences. This reconstruction of ideas through discussion is a creative experience and encourages each participant to believe that the idea is a personal possession. It sensitises him to new practices, and influences his attitudes and his feeling of identification with the proposals.

Increasingly it is being recognised that the individual school is an effective unit for introducing new ideas or carrying out a particular type of programme. Particularly is this so in attempting to devise improved ways of catering for individual differences because of the significance of the particular setting (in school, home and locality) in which the differences are expressed.

The use of staff conferences differs, of course, according to the size of the school concerned. Procedures may be less formal with a small staff, but the same confidence in the role of consultation must exist, even though there is no formal observance of committee procedure with its formal resolutions, points of order, minutes, etc. For a large staff to discuss a proposal and reach a decision, it is virtually essential that more formal methods be used. With a large staff there is need also for sectional meetings for special purposes.

Liaison with Pupils

But do democratic planning procedures among the staff lead inevitably to democratic treatment of students? It would be surprising indeed if a staff that attempted to deal with its own problems with due regard to the participation of all concerned were to be authoritarian in its relations with students.

But this should not be taken too much for granted. Planning is needed to ensure that each child is playing an active part in the conduct of the school, not necessarily in formal committees, but in less official ways such as assuming responsibility for particular tasks in the classroom, helping to organise a club or a class project, caring for animals, or looking after equipment. Even the youngest children can understand the idea of democracy in schemes of social control in which they have a chance to participate.

Older children in secondary school are more likely to seek some formal scheme of self-government run on democratic lines. The prefect system, a legacy from nineteenth century English schools, has been widely used as a form of liaison between teachers and students. Recently, it has come under criticism in failing to provide the great majority of students with an opportunity to participate, and at times, in being too authoritarian in spirit. The elected school council seems the obvious alternative, but it, too, has its problems. Whereas the prefect system can produce role conflict among prefects in their attempt to reach a satisfactory relationship to staff members on one hand and their fellow students on the other, the student council may even widen the social distance between staff and students by attempting to define and maintain its own sphere of influence. Moreover, it may fall victim to

the ills that often afflict adult systems based on universal franchise—
apathy among the silent majority, and control by a non-representative
minority. Such a situation is more likely to lead to confrontation rather
than co-operation.

There is thus a great need for experimentation in schemes that more
effectively link staff and students in co-operative planning. This applies
to younger children as well as to adolescents. There is need also, as
has been discussed, for better communication between the school and
its community.

2.3 Experimenting with Schemes of Class and School Organisation Designed to Cater for Individual Differences

The need to experiment suggests that there is no settled view about
how best to organise children in a school to achieve greatest effectiveness
in teaching and learning, and this, in fact, is so, in spite of the fairly
common view that existing practice, being established and familiar, is
necessarily satisfactory. A degree of stability is of course needed, if
only to allow an innovation to be adequately tested, but an uncritical
view that a new scheme is a panacea for all ills, blinds its supporters
to both a balanced appreciation of it, and to the advantages of
alternatives.

It may be objected that one should not experiment with children;
and this is true if experimentation is ill-considered. But a carefully
planned experiment is quite different from trial and error. It is either
based on research, (or on the opinions of those familiar with research),
or it is a reasonable application of established generalisations, or is
guided by explicit objectives. In many cases also it has a substantial
area of common ground with existing practices.

At present there is vigorous support in primary education for an
informal type of organisation which allows considerable opportunity for
independent learning by children. This open style of organisation is
perhaps the boldest step yet taken to reach a satisfactory solution to
the problem of catering for individual differences among primary school
students, but it, too, should be regarded as experimental, and is better
served by close examination than by uncritical advocacy. The same may
be said of the main innovations in secondary school organisation.

Although there is not complete agreement about the form that school
organisation should take, few would question that it has a vital influence
on the teaching programme. Structural features such as the grouping
of children in classes, or other teaching groups, and the way in which
they progress through the school, restrict or facilitate what a teacher
can do, and how well he can pursue the objectives of the curriculum.

So, too, do the architectural planning of the building and other physical features. School architecture is typically conservative, for economic and other reasons, and tends to lag behind educational practice. Ideally organisational structure (including architectural layout) and function complement each other, but in practice they are often out of step.

As has been already stated, one of the significant features of the modern ferment in education is that the individual school is being accepted as an important functional unit in achieving more effective education. Principals are being given more authority in the conduct of their schools and encouraged to co-operate with their staff and parents in planning the school's programme. It is thus more likely that all aspects of a school's life—the strengths and limitations of staff, the needs of students, community resources, the building and its facilities, and school organisation—will be treated as a whole, and effectively co-ordinated. In any such plan the varied nature of the student body is a major consideration.

Homogeneous Grouping

The dominant method in schools to cope with individual differences has been the grading of students. Classifying and grouping students according to various criteria (age, social maturity, intelligence, achievement) has been considered the best way to make the task of teaching them more manageable. Thus it could be said that the major method of dealing with individual differences in schools has been to try to reduce or eliminate them by homogeneous grading.

Viewed in the perspective of educational systems this is expressed in the differentiation among institutions catering for different groups. Examples are the divisions of pre-school, infants, primary and secondary, various types of special schools, academic secondary schools, technical schools, agricultural schools, matriculation colleges, boys schools, girls schools, religious schools, and many others.

Viewed in the perspective of organisation within schools, it has usually taken the form of grading of students into sides or sections of the school, or into classes. This grading of students has had as its correlate the grading of tasks, thereby matching the skills and knowledge to be taught to the capacity of the students to deal with them. This attempt at educational engineering has been taken even further by the attempt to match the teachers' knowledge, interests, and personality, to the needs of students. The resultant organisational concept is of groups of students undertaking appropriately graded tasks with the help of appropriately qualified staff, and moving upwards step by step as the work of each grade is mastered. In metaphorical terms school organisation could thus be described as a ladder, with climbers occupying its rungs at various levels. Seen in motion, some groups move rapidly step by step, others slowly; some have only a precarious footing; and some give up before reaching the top. Whether the ladder is conceived in sociological terms as a ladder of opportunity from the 'gutter to the university', or in biblical terms, as a 'ladder between earth and heaven', the lock-step progress is the same.

This concept of grading can be seen most clearly in the primary school. Indeed it has been common practice in many school systems to refer to teaching groups as *grades*, and for curricula to be set out in terms of grade requirements. It has also been common for teachers to consider themselves as specialists in the teaching of particular grades, either because of considerable experience with the syllabuses concerned or because of an affinity with the age group concerned.

In the secondary school there has been as marked a use of homogeneous grouping in school organisation, but it has taken a somewhat different course. Since the creation of public systems of education in the nineteenth century, the primary school has been a school for popular education, that is, a school for all children. The secondary school, by contrast, was selective in its origins, and it has become a popular institution only in response to democratic influences of the twentieth century. The main method that it has used to deal with the great range of talent, temperament and aspiration of this new population has been the familiar one of homogeneous grouping, either vertically into streams that move through similar curricula at varying speeds, or horizontally by interest or ability groups based on such criteria as preparation for higher studies and various types of vocational training, or a combination of both. A well-known example of the division of a total secondary school population is that presented in the *Norwood Report* in England. Produced during the last years of World War II, this report provided a blueprint for the post-war reorganisation of secondary education in that country. The scheme proposed was a division of students into three different types of course, to be provided in separate schools or in separate streams within a single school. The criteria are worth quoting in full—

> First there would be a curriculum of which the most characteristic feature is that it treats the various fields of knowledge as suitable for coherent and systematic study for their own sake apart from immediate considerations of occupation, though at a later stage grasp of the matter and experience of the methods belonging to those fields may determine the area of choice of employment and may contribute to success in the employment chosen.

The second type of curriculum would be closely, though not wholly, directed to the special data and skills associated with a particular kind of occupation; its outlook and its methods would always be bounded by a near horizon clearly envisaged. It would thus be closely related to industry, trades and commerce in all their diversity.

In the third type of curriculum a balanced training of mind and body and a correlated approach to humanities, Natural Science and the arts would provide an equipment varied enough to enable pupils to take up the work of life: its purpose would not be to prepare for a particular job or profession and its treatment would make a direct appeal to interests which it would awaken by practical touch with affairs.[14]

Time has shown that the adolescent population of England cannot be divided neatly into these three groups, but the underlying idea of the Norwood categories, particularly the distinction between an academic type of student (studying subjects 'for their own sake') and a practical, vocationally oriented student, has continued in many places in the post-war period, and is still influential as a rationale for secondary school curriculum organisation. The role of secondary education in preparing students for higher study has ensured the survival of the academic type of course with its emphasis on the study of basic disciplines, and students pursuing this curriculum have been grouped accordingly. For others continuing in secondary education, either because of community expectations of higher educational standards, increased entry qualifications for many kinds of work, reduced prospects of employment, or simply obligation under school attendance laws, a variety of schemes have been tried, stressing what Norwood calls 'the near horizon', that is, relevance to the student's immediate future.

It is not appropriate at this point to discuss the concept of relevance in curriculum. This is done in a later section. It is mentioned here only as an important example of a basis for grouping students. The most common interpretation of relevance has been in terms of vocational courses stressing technical, business or trade courses, citizenship courses, home and family studies, or environmental studies of different kinds.

No matter on what basis homogeneity of groups within a school is planned, it seems clear that it is not the panacea for dealing with individual differences that its common use might suggest. This judgement is made on the following counts:

1. However homogeneous grouping is done, it can only be approximate. In most cases it is really reduced variability rather than homogeneity. To treat each member of such a group as identical is not efficient, and may be harmful.

2. So-called homogeneous groups are likely to be unstable, as the common element used to form them almost certainly has different antecedents in different children, and alters as these antecedents change. This fact has been emphasised in Chapter 1. For example, two children judged to be equal in reading, may be the product of quite different influences. A change in the performance of one may occur because of altered home circumstances, and the other through the pupil's improved health.

Differential responses to particular learning experiences, altered home or school circumstances, shifts in motivation, specific remedial teaching, and many other influences are constantly at work, and combine in unique patterns in particular cases. The pace also at which changes may occur in similar variables in different children is by no means constant. Thus quantitative and qualitative changes are compounded.

To maintain a homogeneous group in such circumstances requires constant readjustments. To do it effectively calls for continuing alertness and a high degree of diagnostic skill. It is much more likely in practice, once a group has been formed, to convince oneself that it remains stable, and to treat it accordingly.

3. Any form of homogeneous grouping, being done on the basis of limited criteria, must necessarily also create diversity. One may group by age, and by so doing create diversity with respect to social maturity, reading achievement, physical skill, linguistic ability, interest, and endless other variables. Whatever is done expresses some scale of priority, and some element of compromise. In choosing one basis for grouping we necessarily neglect or reject others. This, of course, may be justifiable, but too often it is done as a matter of routine, without proper regard for what is neglected.

Heterogeneous Grouping

However homogeneous grouping is done, and however sensitively readjustments are made as changes occur in students, by the very nature of the process the individual cannot be the centre of interest. We deal with his reading or spelling, his interests and his aptitudes, by relating these to those of other children, or as qualities of the abstract 'child', but the person as a complex entity eludes us.

Thus, not surprisingly, the search for forms of organisation that do cater better for individual children leads to a greater acceptance of heterogeneity in grouping. This is regarded by some as an acceptable condition for individualisation of teaching, by others as a positive advantage.

Schemes that favour heterogeneity tend to make capital out of individual differences by encouraging productive interaction between the members of the group. For example, young children may be deliberately arranged in mixed age groups so that the older ones may help the younger, and the younger learn from the older; schools may deliberately adopt coeducation to make it easier to encourage an attitude of mutual respect between the sexes; racial or social groups may be deliberately mixed to increase the chance of fostering more tolerant understanding.

The first example, mixed age grouping, occurs naturally in small rural schools, but it has also been experimented with in larger schools, particularly in England, where it is referred to as *vertical* or *family grouping*. The span of years adopted might vary from that of adjoining age groups, e.g. 5-year-olds and 6-year-olds, to a spread of three or four years. With this latter arrangement, say with infants from 5 to 7 or 8, a class becomes a school within a school. Some new 5-year-olds join it, once or twice a year; some 7-year-olds or 8-year-olds 'graduate' to older groups. The family atmosphere in such classes has been very favourably commented on, particular stress being laid on the sense of security provided for new students by the presence of older children, often older brothers and sisters, and on the constructive social attitudes of older children to younger. This attitude is expressed in the following quotation:

'We have been struck by the atmosphere of happiness, confidence and serenity which characteristically pervades classroom after classroom of family-grouped children. Such an atmosphere does not belong exclusively to family-grouped classes, of course, but it is the regularity with which it occurs in them that makes it too marked to be coincidental.'[15]

Mixed age grouping is a fairly obvious form of contrived heterogeneity in teaching groups, and of course many other ways of achieving heterogeneity are possible. The search for effective solutions along these lines is likely to be determined by the teacher's own philosophy about human differences, and by his belief in the efficacy of learning through experience.

Schemes that merely accept heterogeneity as a suitable situation for learning, rather than stress it as an intrinsic advantage, are attuned more sensitively to individual methods of teaching and learning. When a teacher knows that a group is heterogeneous, there can be no pretence that the children in it can be taught the same things at the same pace. What form individualisation will take cannot be discussed here in detail, but in general it is obvious that the methods used will depend a great deal on the school's approach to the curriculum.

If this involves a fair measure of prescription, stress is likely to be laid on methods that vary the pace of learning; if it is more permissive and open, the methods will provide for differentiation of tasks, as well as variation in the pace at which they are completed.

2.4 Using the School Building, Equipment and Facilities to Best Advantage

We may usefully distinguish between the structural features of a school building and the functions that go on in it.

It would be expected that these would be in harmony, the building being designed to facilitate the functions, and the occupants making use of the facilities in the way they were intended. A modern supermarket is a good example of a building where layout and function are effectively related.

In practice, however, with schools as with other buildings, structure and function can easily get out of step. This may occur as functions change but have to be carried on in an outdated building, or, less frequently, when a new type of building is not taken advantage of because of the different habits, expectations, and skills of those who work in it.

Ideas in education change very slowly, or are adopted very slowly; but even so, buildings generally change even more slowly. Thus the problem of dysfunction due to ageing buildings is inherent. It would be fair to state that at any given time the majority of school buildings are out-of-date, and that only a relatively small number of recently built schools reflect modern ideas on educational practice. Thus, a major practical problem for schools is to make the best use of existing facilities.

The need for major change in school design has only recently become apparent. The conventional school consists basically of a number of self-contained classrooms, some specialised laboratory type rooms (particularly in secondary schools), assembly hall (in some schools), accommodation for staff, and various offices. This type of building has served education well. The innovations that have occurred have been accommodated within it without too much dislocation, mainly because the basic organisation of students into classes has not been questioned. The need for individualisation of teaching was recognised, but in the main was subordinated to the dominant philosophy of mass education by the use of prescribed curricula and didactic teaching methods. Where individual methods were practised, they were restricted to the self-contained classroom.

The realisation that an effective scheme to deal with individual differences requires a substantially different approach to school organisation and to the school plant has been a slow growth, and is only now being accepted. The resultant shift in thought about school architecture and facilities is the most striking that has occurred for at least a century. The general features of this pattern are these:

1. *Flexible teaching space.* Spatial arrangements are designed to provide for groups of varying sizes. Spaces can be rearranged by the use of folding doors, movable screens and similar devices. These not only meet the needs of a programme that may vary during a day or week, but cater also for more permanent changes that occur through innovations in method, curriculum and organisation. The easy removal and relocation of fixed partitions is another useful feature of modern planning where the future use of a building cannot be known in advance.

2. *Movable furniture.* With a flexible spatial arrangement in school buildings, furniture must be movable to suit the different arrangements for teaching. Accordingly chairs, tables, bookshelves, racks, cupboards, display boards and other furniture are designed for easy handling and rearrangement. Floor surfaces are treated in a way that allows easy movement, and also keeps down the noise level. Hard-wearing carpet is most commonly used.

3. *Open design.* The general design is open, to assist ease of movement of staff and students throughout the building and co-operation among staff. Fixed internal walls and corridors are kept to a minimum. There is provision for privacy, but the dominant features are openness and visibility.

4. *Special activity areas.* Areas for special activities are provided in conformity with a view of curriculum as independent, active participation by students in school tasks. In primary schools these might include provision for pottery, carpentry and modelling, sewing, cooking, painting, music, physical education, library, care of birds, fish and animals, mathematics, science, and many others. In secondary schools more elaborate provision is made for specialised laboratories.

5. *Provision for the housing and operation of equipment.* Independent learning by students has been facilitated by the production of easy-to-use, miniaturised, and relatively inexpensive electronic equipment, and of illustrative and structured materials in various subjects that can be used by children on an individual basis with a minimum of instruction and supervision by teachers.

These five features, expressed in architectural terms, do not lead inevitably to a single, unique design. Many variations are possible and desirable to meet different situations. If education is approached in an innovative spirit, it should be reflected in school architecture. Standardised plans and construction may be economical, but they do not help materially in the search for harmony between structure and function. Whatever the variations, the modern school building is a generic type expressing a philosophy characterised by respect for individual differences among students, and inquiry, self-reliance and activity in the learning process. This represents a substantial shift in design from the school embodying a philosophy of essentialism in curriculum and reception learning as the chief guide to teaching method, and is likely to guide school design in the foreseeable future. The need to use a building effectively applies both to new schools and to conventional schools. Clearly the task of teaching in a way that takes account of individual differences is more difficult in a conventional school, but the critical factors in success are the conviction of those who work in the building of the value of individual methods, and their ingenuity in using and adapting the facilities that are there. It is by no means uncommon to see an old building being used effectively, and a modern open plan building being used traditionally.

At the primary level some practicable steps that might be taken to make an old building more suitable for a modern approach to teaching are as follows:

1. Converting the conventional classroom into a workroom. Ordinarily it is set up more like a small theatre. This would involve such steps as these:
   (a) Making all fixed furniture movable, and relocating it in a position that increases the open floor space. Ideally this would be achieved with replacement furniture, but existing furniture can usually be altered. Not all of it need necessarily be retained. It is not really necessary to have a seat and a desk for each child.
   (b) Increasing the flat surfaces available to the children for various activities.
   (c) Adding to display areas on walls for children's work.
   (d) Altering the floor surface to reduce noise and improve comfort. The most acceptable treatment is carpeting with a durable material.
   (e) Brightening the general appearance of walls and furniture with paint or wallpaper. This does not directly contribute to individual methods, but it is indicative of the type of learning environment in which they occur.
2. Using space outside the classroom for special activity areas. This space might include corridors, spare rooms, library, assembly hall, verandahs, basements, sheds, and protected outdoor space. If an

additional building can be added to the existing school plant, so much the better. Use can also be made of the playground for a variety of purposes, and of the accessible neighbourhood.

At the secondary level schools usually have specialised rooms such as library, science laboratories, assembly hall, home science, typing, manual arts (usually workwork), art, music rooms (less frequently) and language laboratories (less frequently). Special rooms for subjects such as social sciences, English and mathematics are rather uncommon. Although these subjects require equipment and can be taught by activity methods quite as well as subjects that are more obviously practical, they are usually taught in characterless rooms with little more than basic furniture and a blackboard. Such rooms are ill-adapted for individual teaching. The extension of the concept of a laboratory for these subjects is clearly merited, and the conversion of existing rooms could easily be done.

The use of specialised rooms entails considerable movement of students about the school, but this is inherent in any form of organisation that tries to maximise for each student the availability of necessarily limited resources such as specialised rooms and equipment. It is not necessarily a disadvantage.

2.5 Developing a Scheme of Discipline That Takes Account of Individual Differences

Discipline is an important element in any scheme of education. It readily becomes an issue among parents and teachers alike in their assessment of new practices, particularly those who in attempting to cater for individual differences are disposed to relax some of the conventional constraints on children. The charge of soft pedagogy is an easy one to make, and is often applied as a brake on innovative practices.

This topic could be discussed quite appropriately in other sections of these guidelines, particularly in connection with methods of teaching. However, it has been thought best to deal with it as an aspect of school organisation, because it does have relevance to the school as a whole through general rules and conventions, and through the need for consistency among individual members of staff.

At first glance, it might appear that discipline and individuality are incompatible, one stressing the subjection of the student's behaviour to a common code, the other appearing to allow his right to his own. But this is an inadequate view, both of discipline and of individuality.

Discipline is a form of behaviour, and as such has to be learnt. It is thus subject to the variety of learning situations that the existence of individual differences dictates. Accordingly, the scope, mode, degree and timing of discipline need to be geared to the individual learner even when the same end-product is aimed at. Conversely individuality is achieved, not by rejecting discipline, but by voluntarily accepting it. The commonly held view that individuality is doing what one likes hides the important fact that achievement in a task is only possible if the discipline involved in achieving it is accepted.

A suitable definition of discipline is the *observance of the requirements of a task*. Each person has to learn what these are, and accept and master them if he is to succeed in that task. It may be learning to swim, to play a musical instrument, to lay bricks, grow flowers, do addition sums or quadratic equations, read, speak a foreign language or one's own, plan one's time, play a team game, observe social conventions, drive a car, and operate it safely and effectively on the road, seek and retain good health, or any other task. Each task has its methods or rules that the learner inescapably has to observe.

How successfully the learner does this depends on his insight into the nature of the task, his command of the skills that may be involved in performing it with precision, his motivation to succeed in it, and the assistance and encouragement he receives from others. Since each of these may vary greatly in different pupils, it is clear that discipline among children must itself be a variable product, being achieved by individual pupils at different times for different tasks, and with marked differences between individuals. The three components of discipline—the intellectual, psychomotor, and affective—merit further elaboration.

The Intellectual Component of Discipline

In academic discourse this is the most familiar feature of the concept of discipline. In fact an ordered body of knowledge is commonly referred to as a discipline. The discipline involved derives from the web of relationships that gives a particular body of knowledge its structure. Anyone who seeks to comprehend this structure must understand these relationships.

A person's ability to do this is determined by many factors, including his capacity for relational type thinking, his experience in such thinking, and the level of complexity and abstraction involved in the relationships. A student's capacity for intellectual discipline is thus significantly influenced by these factors.

In the planning of tasks for students the intellectual component is obviously of great importance. Obviously there can be no intellectual discipline for a student confronted with a task beyond his comprehension, and it is thus essential to try to adjust the form in which subjects are presented to make them more comprehensible to each student. These are matters more appropriate to a discussion of the curriculum, and they will be taken up there. In the present context it is only necessary to point out that comprehensibility of subjects is likely to be increased for a greater number of students by taking steps that reduce complexity by analysis, that make abstraction more meaningful by application and illustration, that vary the pace of presentation, and that allow for the repetition of complex operations.

It is true also that there is little or no intellectual discipline in tasks that are too easy, where the structure of relations is self-evident. The critical educational question about intellectual discipline is whether a student is working at an appropriate level, assuming that methods of presentation are suitable, and that there are effective degrees of student involvement through interest and other forms of motivation. Discipline is affected adversely if levels of difficulty are lower than necessary, resulting from the teacher's over-emphasis on the needs of the slower learning students in a group, by his assumption of too dominant a role in the process of explanation, or from the students' lowered concentration and effort through defects in the general conditions of learning.

It is a matter for serious concern if levels of intellectual discipline in an educational programme are needlessly low. Popular education, on the scale now provided, is enormously expensive, and it is reasonable to expect that there will be a clear benefit from it in the community's increased capacity for intelligent thought and judgement, even though these may not be the only outcomes sought. However schools are conducted, if intellectual discipline is not achieved, they are to this extent defective.

The Psychomotor Component of Discipline

Many tasks call for precision and co-ordination of movement, and for these, discipline involves sustained practice. Countless school tasks have this element of skill, and acceptance of the training necessary is essential for mastery of them. Obvious examples are those in which bodily movement is prominent: writing, drawing, painting, modelling, mapping, dancing, running, catching, throwing, playing a musical instrument, and so on. Less obvious, but equally important, are skills in which bodily movement is less prominent, but which also require habituation through sustained effort and practice. Examples are speech, either in a foreign language or one's own, inquiry skills in which a methodology is established through usage that assists a person in tackling problems, and social skills involving conventions and practices which are strengthened by repetition.

High standards of performance, whether it be in a cricket shot, the rendering of a musical score, the fashioning of a pot in clay, the acting out of a dramatic role, the carrying out of a social studies project, solving a mathematical problem involving computation, or the observance of conventional manners all require discipline in this sense.

The Affective Component of Discipline

In common usage the affective component of discipline is the most familiar. In fact, the striving involved in carrying out a task is often virtually identified with discipline. For some this carries the overtone that the striving should necessarily be sustained by external influences and that the effort be coerced to some degree. Undoubtedly the concept of discipline does raise the question of the source of control involved, and this aspect will be examined. But it is an important matter of principle to recognise that to accept the requirements of a task because of intrinsic interest in it is evidence of discipline just as definitely as when the locus of control is external.

It has already been made clear in previous chapters that the capacity of individual children for intrinsic interest in various tasks differs greatly according to the variety of their experiences in home and community, and according to their perception of the relevance of these tasks to themselves. In particular, the reaction of children to the contrived environment of the school in which specific values may be stressed will differ also according to their common ground with values known to them and accepted by them. Mature intellectual values such as the importance of objective inquiry, social values such as toleration of differences, fairness, truthfulness, responsibility, compassion, and aesthetic values which underlie the arts, all of which are of special importance in the civilising work of a school, will be reacted to very differently by children according to their familiarity with them, and the reinforcement or rejection of them in out-of-school experiences.

The School Programme as a Major Determinant of Discipline

The cognitive, psychomotor, and affective elements of discipline merge in the school's educational programme, and the pursuit of self-discipline among pupils and the key to problems of indiscipline should be first sought there. Catering for individual differences through the curriculum and the management of learning contributes directly to the encouragement of self-discipline; disregard for these differences by prescribing unsuitable curricula and a uniform pace of learning for all, by emphasising didactic teaching methods and group testing, and by employing homogeneous grouping as the criterion in the formation of classes militate against the development of self-discipline.

Measures that stress concern for individual differences lead inevitably to informality in the conduct of schools, and this may appear to encourage permissiveness. Modern schooling is criticised for its condoning or encouraging of indiscipline more often than on other counts. No doubt many schools are poorly managed, whatever their philosophy of education may be, but in terms of principle, effective provision for individual differences is more likely to promote discipline than to weaken it.

The social environment of the educational programme also has a strong regulatory influence on children's acceptance of discipline. An authoritarian climate stresses coercive discipline; a relaxed, supportive atmosphere fosters voluntary participation. Both are largely the product of the relationship between the teacher and his pupils, and of the social milieu that he encourages among his pupils. Piaget has described well the importance of the peer group influence in a classroom as a stimulus to learning—

> . . . the children are individually aware that parallel to their classroom discipline . . . there exists a whole system of mutual aid based upon a 'special understanding' as well as a sense . . . of justice . . .
> In this respect the co-operation among the children themselves has an importance as great as that of adult action. From the intellectual point of view it is such co-operation that is most apt to encourage real exchange of thought and discussion, i.e., all the forms of behaviour capable of developing the critical attitude of mind, objectivity and discussive reflection. From the moral point of view, it results in a real exercise in the principles of behaviour, and not solely in the submission to external restraint.[16]

Thus, the major areas of a school regime, namely the educational programme and the quality of the social relationships of the school community, are open to management in ways that substantially influence the nature and incidence of discipline. There is no doubt that many disciplinary problems in schools are actually created or exacerbated by the way in which the educational programme is planned and carried out, and by the low level of school spirit engendered. Poor discipline in a school may be the direct result of an unsuitable educational programme or a badly managed one, or of a low level of student morale.

In placing this emphasis on the quality of the educational experiences created for children in schools, authority of other people as a source of discipline is not being rejected or avoided. But the emphasis is being put on the inherent authority that derives from the requirements of tasks in terms of insight, practice and sustained attention rather than on rules and the authority of one person over another. The use of inherent authority is important in its own right because of its obvious relevance to the encouragement of self-discipline, and it is important also because of its effect in reducing, if not eliminating, the need for arbitrarily imposed authority.

Discipline As Imposed Authority

It would take us too far away from our central concern with individual differences to try to deal comprehensively with the many issues that arise in considering the school's authority over the conduct of pupils beyond the limits of the educational programme. Complex sociological and moral questions are involved. This brief treatment attempts no more than to try to relate some of these wider influences to the central theme of individual differences. It is acknowledged that many serious questions that perplex school authorities are left unanswered.

Three major sources of authority in schools, outside that of the educational programme itself, can be identified:

1. School rules, routines, and traditions
2. Adult social norms and conventions regarding the conduct of children with which the school aligns itself
3. The authority of teachers

School Rules, Routines and Traditions

Some of these are related directly to the educational programme, specifying, for example, the timetable of lessons and the procedures to be observed in using facilities such as the library. Others are broader in their application, regulating the pupil's dress and conduct during school hours, and, in some cases, while travelling to and from school. Others are even more wide-ranging, reaching out to the students' life beyond the school, and into adult life through 'old boy' and 'old girl' traditions.

Rules and procedures associated with the educational programme obviously need to be reviewed in the light of changed objectives in that programme. The way in which the school day is scheduled, talking by students in class, and the movement of students within the classroom and to and from it are obvious examples. The purpose of rules is to facilitate learning and to safeguard the rights of all concerned. However, formal and informal structures and procedures, once established, tend to become functionally autonomous, and hence self-perpetuating. They tend to assume an arbitrary character and become harder to justify on rational grounds.

An institution's critical approach to its own rules is a good indication of its capacity for progressive development. The positive case for them needs to be examined and made explicit from time to time, and made clear to those to whom they apply.

It would be naive to suggest that once the rational nexus between rules and the educational programme has been established all disciplinary problems would disappear. Some children reject school for various reasons over which the school has little or no control, and the compatibility of its rules with its educational programme is not by itself a guarantee that rules will be accepted. It does, however, offer the best chance possible. It must be accepted that for some children, at least some of the time, the school can play only a restrictive, custodial function, not an educational one. This may be called by some the exercise of discipline, but it is not a role that the school should be asked to play, being incompatible with the relationship of trust and mutual respect that there should be between teacher and student.

Rules that regulate the conduct of children present special difficulty because their sanction is conventional, and less obviously rational. School uniforms and the length of boys' hair are good examples. Where disciplinary problems arise in connection with these matters, they are often presented as a clash between the authority of the school and the individual rights of students. In fact, however, they more accurately express a clash between the conventions of school and the pressures towards conformity in the student subculture. The disciplinary problem thus derives from the collision of two interpretations of social conformity, one existing and well established, the other *avant garde*. A school may tackle disciplinary problems of this kind by changing the rules. In the case of hair-style this occurred. Long hair is no longer regarded as a threat to discipline. In fact it hardly causes a comment of any kind; and there is some evidence that there is already a trend towards shorter hair. The wearing of school uniforms is still controversial. Changing the rules of an institution to legalise the actions of those that infringe them is hardly a satisfactory general recipe for the upholding of discipline. But the example does underline the need for rules to be flexible when dealing with conventional behaviour. It is important to eliminate what is arbitrary in the administration of rules if discipline is to be achieved without coercion.

Adult Social Norms

The role of the school in dealing with the general conduct of children is somewhat ambiguous. Its primary responsibility is with an instructional programme, but it cannot escape some involvement with wider social and moral aspects of the student's general behaviour. Some educationists place great stress on this wider responsibility, and would include positive moral and social training in the school's programme. Others consider that the home is responsible for these, and that the school should become involved only marginally when the general behaviour of students impedes the educational programme. There is, however, an increasing tendency for the schools to be asked to accept greater responsibility for the social and moral training of children. The pressures towards establishing religious programmes, sex education and health education, including instruction about drugs, alcohol and tobacco, are good examples. This is brought about partly by the decline in the influence of the family, and partly by the rather pathetic belief that social abuses in society can be rectified by teaching the children a different code of behaviour from that practised by the adults.

Whatever share of responsibility the school does accept for these broader objectives, it is hampered in its work by the separation between home and school that typically exists, as has been pointed out in the guidelines dealing with environmental influence. Whereas, as has been shown in Chapter 1, each child's need is distinctive, the school is put in the position of trying to exert an influence in this most personal of educational tasks, through a generalised code, which is sometimes described (usually slightingly) as middle-class morality.

In the senior secondary school where the age gap between student and adult is so narrow, the problem is particularly difficult. The right of each student to the role of adult responsibility (however this is interpreted by the person) is hard to deny, yet to admit it in practice may threaten the institutional code. One type of solution to this problem is to capitalise on the maturity of senior students by enlisting their support as allies with adult authority. Another is to create a separate senior school where rules are tailored to the maturity of the students, more in keeping with an adult community.

At all levels of education the influence of the adult world is pervasive, however selectively the school may try to interpret community values and practices. If adults condone behaviour in society, which, if it occurs in school, is called indiscipline, the school is placed in the impossible position of trying to create what is virtually a counter-culture. Whatever success the school may have in this general area of social and moral behaviour is likely to be achieved not through rules which neither adequately reflect the pluralism within the community or have the sanctions of adult society, but through diagnosis and counselling of individual students. For this the school needs to have a psychological rather than a moralistic orientation, and it needs more resources in counsellors and social workers than at present exist to mount such a clinical programme.

The Authority of Teachers

It is a commonplace view that some teachers are 'better' disciplinarians than others. What is not so obvious is that in making such a judgement, a particular kind of learning environment is assumed, and that the teacher's disciplinary power is being assessed in terms of this situation.

The most common assumptions are that a whole class is being taught together, that each student is aiming at a uniform standard of achievement in a set task, that the students' attention is stimulated and sustained more by promises or threats on the part of the teacher than by the students' intrinsic interest in the task, and that the teacher's relationship with the students is formal rather than relaxed and friendly. In such a situation the teacher's discipline is an external factor, not functionally related to the learning task being undertaken. It derives from the personality of the teacher, particularly in the display of aggressive qualities, and from a formal code of sanctions approved in the school, which may be invoked directly by the teacher, or indirectly, by reference to his superiors. A 'strong' disciplinarian is able to maintain control mainly through personal qualities alone; a 'weak' disciplinarian has greater need of the support system of the formal code and of superiors with the power to enforce it.

If different assumptions are made about the characteristics of the teaching situation, the disciplinary role of the teacher also changes. If teaching is individualised, or carried on in functional groups, and if the curriculum is interpreted as activities to be engaged in rather than as facts to be memorised, and if there is scope for choice by students, the difficulty of keeping a whole class in step is removed or reduced, intrinsic interest is likely to be greater, the teacher's contact with individual students is likely to be more personal, and the learning environment, in becoming more informal (although not casual), becomes more relaxed. In these circumstances discipline has a good chance of becoming inherent, that is based on the experiences themselves, rather than being imposed as an external constraint. The authority of the teacher in such a situation derives from the respect he gains from students because of his expertise and maturity, his concern for their progress, his care in diagnosing their difficulties and giving appropriate help, the trouble taken to plan an interesting programme of work, the warmth of his relationship with them, his confident manner, his tolerance of differences and particularly of slow learners, the depth of his own knowledge, yet his readiness to admit its limitations, and his infectious enthusiasm for the school tasks in hand.

It is realised that this is a somewhat idealised picture, and that in the real world of the classroom, conditions of work are often different from this. The blackboard-jungle image is by no means fictitious in some schools, and in these, an educational interpretation of discipline and authority may seem rather unreal. But to admit this is not to imply that such an interpretation is false or useless, but rather that it is not likely to be effective in all circumstances. Some of these circumstances are not within the teacher's control; but some are, and it is of great importance that he try to approach these through professional insight and a constructive attitude to the development of his students, rather than through restriction enforced by aggression, whether exercised verbally or physically. After all, the cultivation of discipline as the methodology of coercion is hardly a professional accomplishment.

Concluding Comment

We could end this section appropriately where it began. Discipline and individualty are not incompatible. On the contrary, discipline is one of its most mature expressions. For teachers and others who need to create a disciplined situation in which children develop, and to strengthen the child's capacity for self-discipline by practice in the exercise of responsibility, an understanding of his needs, interests and limitations is essential, as also is an insight into the kind of learning environment that best stimulates and accommodates individual differences among children. No doubt modern education is defective, as its critics claim, in its exercise of discipline, but it is not because of its failure to coerce pupils into various forms of obedient and submissive behaviour (which the critics usually mean), but rather because of its failure to create conditions of learning in schools which strengthen self-discipline expressed as interest, effort, initiative, a striving for high standards of achievement, sensitivity to humane feeling, and concern for others.

2.6 Relating School Organisation Appropriately to Curriculum Objectives

The implications of individual differences for school curricula are dealt with in detail in a later section of these guidelines. Here only the relevance of the school's organisation to curricula need be discussed. This, however, is of considerable significance, as organisation and curricula are very closely related, and curriculum objectives are hardly likely to be achieved unless the supporting organisation is compatible.

In primary schools the grade structure virtually determines major features of the curriculum, particularly the scope of what is taught and the sequence followed. The official structure of the day and week direct the rhythm of work by both teachers and students. The physical provisions of rooms and special facilities regulate the way in which activities are carried on, and hence influence the quality of the curriculum. The assessment system, particularly when applied on a school-wide basis for the purpose of establishing standards of achievement, also has a substantial effect on the curriculum objectives followed by teachers. Even more pervasive in its influence is the general philosophy of the school, which sets the seal on what is valued in children's activities and achievements.

In secondary schools organisation is even more closely associated with curriculum in that the basic arrangement of classes and courses, the deployment of staff, the timetable, the allocation of classroom and laboratories, and the examination system virtually mirror what is taught.

Since the curriculum is the heart of school experiences for children, it is obvious that the organisation of the school should endeavour to create the best conditions for its objectives to be realised. In fact organisation is not always responsive to the spirit of the curriculum, sometimes hindering rather than helping it, or being in various ways less supportive than it might be. Often the organisation of a school has been determined by past policies, and this has settled into a familiar and comfortable routine that tends to be self-perpetuating, even though now dysfunctional.

In defining the curriculum, educationists have usually stressed planned and intended outcomes. Typical of such definitions is the following by Neagley and Evans: 'Curriculum is all of the planned experiences provided by the school to assist the pupils in attaining the designated learning outcomes to the best of their abilities.'[17] But there may also be a hidden curriculum, not planned, and not even explicitly recognised, consisting of children's experiences at school that arise from organisational features, attitudes expressed or implied by teachers, situations that exist although not part of the official programme of the school, contacts with other children that occur informally, and so on. These may be beneficial or harmful. Stenhouse, discussing the curriculum in English schools, relates a case where the organisation was obviously harmful—

> . . . I taught in a school in which certain bottom stream classes were allocated to an old elementary school half a mile away which served as an annex. Teachers arrived late, there were no labs or workshops, the main aim of the teachers was to keep the students quiet. And out there they could not contaminate the main school. Nobody wanted to talk about it, but it was a substantial factor in any analysis of the curriculum offered to those children.[18]

Clearly, it is the whole learning environment that determines the curriculum as it is experienced by children, and all the factors that help to create this environment, whether directly or obliquely, need to be kept in mind. If regard for individual differences is the guiding criterion in planning educational experiences, the impact on traditional organisation patterns is likely to be considerable. In primary schools the grade concept of curriculum would have to be substantially modified or given up, and a different arrangement adopted more compatible with the differential pace of students' learning and choice of tasks. Changes in other features of organisation aligned with the grade concept would also be necessary.

In the secondary school the implications would be even more challenging because of the external constraints from tertiary institutions and employing authorities. The organisation of most large secondary schools could be likened to a system of races or channels through which the students have to pass. The small number of alternative curricula that typically have been offered has been obviously inadequate. They have neither satisfied the wide range of students' interests, motivation, abilities and experience, nor the varied requirements of outside bodies such as employers and tertiary institutions.

If the problem of catering for the needs of individual pupils is to be taken seriously schools will have to grapple with the task of attempting to create their own curricula, rather than simply dispensing those prepared by others. This should not be taken to mean that curriculum schemes prepared by outside bodies should be disregarded. On the contrary, the well-conceived and well-researched .curriculum schemes that are now replacing the earlier 'armchair', prescriptive syllabuses, can be very valuable in their philosophical approach, their proposals for themes, tasks, and materials, and their guidelines for methodology and evaluation. But the responsibility for interpreting and applying them in particular circumstances must be accepted by each school. This school version of the curriculum can be authentic reconstruction, even though it is basically complementary. Planning this school-based version is a major task of leadership for the principal. It is also demanding for teachers, requiring much more initiative and effort then the pursuit of routine practices. It is probably the severest test of their professionalism, as well as its greatest opportunity. Whannell, in a study of Queensland state high schools,[19] found that of a number of different areas where decisions had to be made in a school, the two, 'Particular Instructional Policy' and 'Introduction of New Instructional Methods', were most favoured as ones in which teachers might wish to participate actively. This is promising for the prospect of school-based curriculum development, although the proportion in favour was not much above half those teachers consulted. There is, of course, nothing to suggest from these figures what the situation might be in other Australian States, or whether primary teachers would have similar attitudes, or, more importantly, how such attitudes might be strengthened or weakened by rewarding or unrewarding experiences.

School-based curriculum development in its modern sense is an experimental area for which there are few precedents. Accordingly it is easier to state its requirements in terms of tasks to be done than procedures to be followed. The procedures may, in fact, prove to be very difficult to work out, as they require a great deal more time for planning than principals and teachers have to spare, at least under present circumstances. The task of making more time available is not easy. It might be achieved, for example, by lengthening the school day, or by developing a form of organisation involving more independent work by students without the necessity for scheduling all their time in situations involving direct teaching or supervision, or by a more generous staffing policy, or by allowing teacher aides to supervise.

None of these at present would be regarded favourably by teachers or administrators. It is quite clear, however, that the securing of more time for planning during regular school time for both principal and staff is a key factor in the success of the policy of autonomy for schools, and, in particular, of school-based curriculum development.

The main tasks that school-based curriculum development involves are listed below and subsequently commented on:

1. Interpreting curriculum objectives
2. Formulating programmes
3. Marshalling resources, both inside and outside the school
4. Implementing programmes
5. Reviewing and evaluating objectives and procedures

These tasks are listed sequentially, and appear to have a natural order. In practice the order may vary from school to school. In one school interest in curriculum development may arise from a concern about resources, and spread from this to programmes and objectives. In another the task of considering objectives (which is usually not immediately popular with teachers) may become realistic only when an attempt to evaluate the school's programme is made. The discussion of tasks concludes with a summary of procedures for attempting these tasks.

Interpreting Curriculum Objectives

The term *interpreting* has been used as being more appropriate than *formulating*. It is unlikely (and probably undesirable) that individual schools will formulate objectives for their programmes independently of the wider professional and social community to which the school belongs. Objectives, in some form or other, arise outside the school, usually in curriculum schemes formulated by state departments of education or independent research groups. The task of each school is to interpret them in the particular setting where they are to be applied.

This process of interpretation can be tackled in various levels of comprehensiveness and sophistication, and can be a genuinely creative task. Teachers are usually most disposed to deal with instructional objectives relating to matters of day-to-day concern, but wider issues about purposes and priorities are never very far away. These may be related to the balance among subjects, the integration of subjects, and consistency in the school's guiding philosophy. The history of the curriculum movement, particularly in its more recent scientific phase, has been one of separate subject development, with little thought to the consequent problems of fragmented school experience for children. Each school must try to overcome this defect when considering its own objectives. The unique culture of a school is created by many influences both internal and external, but the coherence of its educational programme is a major factor in it. Undoubtedly some of the most serious issues of interpretation of curriculum objectives for a school are those concerned with the overall impact of its programmes.

Deliberation about objectives, whether directed towards specific projects or towards schoolwide programmes, should involve interested outside specialists such as advisory teachers and inspectors, and parents and other members of the community. Drawing parents into discussion about school objectives has many practical difficulties, although there is no doubt that many parents do have positive views about the school's curriculum. Whether this kind of discussion is engaged in as a genuine source of advice, or as a communication strategy, it is a significant element in the deliberation process about objectives. Discussions should also involve students, the particular steps taken varying according to the maturity of the students. It seems inconceivable that school programmes should be established and implemented without an attempt to seek the advice of the parents and students for whom they are planned, or without any attempt to explain their purpose to them. Yet it is not uncommon. Many students leave secondary school not only dissatisfied with their school experience, but quite ignorant of what the teachers were trying to do for them.

The need for deliberation about objectives within a school is clear enough, even though the practical steps by which it can be organised may not be.

Formulating Programmes

A school's programme is not merely a list of topics or themes to be covered, but a statement of strategy through which objectives are to be pursued. It would, of course, include the scope and sequence of knowledge to be taught, but, more significantly, it would set out explicitly the type of learning activity planned. It is in this process of relating knowledge in the various curricula to the methods by which it is developed through teaching that the character of the curriculum is most clearly revealed.

Marshalling Resources

An important part of the strategy of curriculum development is the co-ordination of the necessary teaching resources. The most obvious source of these is in the school itself, and particularly in the library, resource centre, or laboratory. The planning of the curriculum so that full use is made of the library and its staff is a basic step in the strategy of school-based curriculum development. Not uncommonly the library is used as a supplement to the work of the classroom rather than as an integral part of it. Worse still, it is sometimes used quite separately from the curriculum.

But there are other resources available to the school. These may be facilities provided by education authorities, community institutions, or quite ordinary resources such as the natural environment, public institutions, factories, farms and mines, all of which are potentially useful for educational purposes. Facilitating their use by securing authorisation, planning transport for excursions, arranging guided tours and visiting speakers is a significant aid to effective planning. If arrangements of this kind are difficult for teachers, the resources are unlikely to be used.

Implementing Programmes

The problems of making a curriculum work effectively are much the same whether it is school-based or prescribed from outside, except perhaps that the will to succeed with a curriculum of one's own devising is likely to be stronger. Some likely problems encountered by teachers are:

1. Misjudging the interest or competence of the students
2. Misjudging the time needed for particular projects
3. Breakdowns in the availability of materials (films not arriving on time, excursions having to be postponed, etc.)

4. Realisation of personal inadequacies in background knowledge, in skills in using equipment or methods, etc.
5. Breakdown of co-operative arrangements with other teachers
6. Timetable problems

Undoubtedly, teachers could add to this list.

Reviewing and Evaluating Objectives and Procedures

Progress in implementing a curriculum needs to be kept under review, and it is to be expected that the incentive to do so would be strong when objectives and procedures are worked out at the local level.

Evaluation studies in education are notoriously difficult because of the problems of measuring intangible variables, and also because of the difficulty of separating effects of the teacher's influence on children from other influences, both inside the school and outside it.

However it is important that a critical attitude towards planning be maintained, even if the form of the evaluation is no more than a systematic description of events, processes and outcomes. To see clearly what is happening as the planned curriculum is progressively introduced is valuable, in spite of the fact that an accurate analysis of the underlying causes is not possible.

Evaluation should be used with discretion. It should certainly be an antidote to complacency, but it should not be allowed to unsettle an institution. Plans need time to be effective. Both staff and students need to become familiar with new curricula before a reasonable judgement can be made. Premature judgement on educational innovations is all too common, and often leads to the abandonment of promising new ventures.

Procedures for Attempting These Tasks

The practical difficulty of creating the organisation for adequate planning in a school has already been noted. Essentially, it involves the establishing of suitable committees, and providing them with time and resources to act effectively.

In a secondary school there are commonly accepted groupings of staff on subject lines, and it would be expected that these, led by the departmental head, would be the committees for planning, implementing, and evaluating curricula. The role of the departmental head would be to lead the staff rather than direct them. School-based curricula have little merit if they are simply the creation of a handful of strong-minded departmental heads. A plenary meeting, or, in very large schools, a representative group, needs to consider overall curriculum policy, ensuring that the philosophy of each subject group is compatible with it, and making arrangements for the timetable and other co-ordinating procedures. The natural leader of this more broadly based group would be the principal.

In primary schools where there are usually no subject groupings of staff, special arrangements need to be made, either using the staff as a whole as the planning body, or creating subcommittees for special sections of the curriculum. Usually there are people on a staff with special interests, and it would be advantageous to recognise this fact and capitalise on it, even though in particular cases the person concerned might be quite junior in seniority. These staff members could be encouraged to take in-service courses in their specialty, keep up with new developments, act as contact members with advisory teachers and other consultants, be responsible for ordering books and other materials in their field, as well as acting as convenors for curriculum groups. A school would be unfortunate indeed if it did not have members of staff with a wide range of special interests. The familiar generalist role of the primary teachers has tended to obscure these special interests. An approach to curriculum development emphasising local features would soon bring them to light.

2.7 Relating School Organisation Appropriately to Teaching Methods

Teaching method is primarily a personal matter, but it needs the support of school organisation. This is particularly so if the methods used involve other teachers, or make demands on facilities outside the teacher's own domain.

The bearing of teaching methods on individual differences is discussed more fully in Chapter 7. Here only the implications of these methods for school organisation are considered.

There are three characteristics of any teaching method that are critical criteria in their effectiveness in catering for individual differences. These are:

1. The degree to which they encourage individual responsibility among students (which, in 2.5, is called the strengthening of self-discipline)
2. The extent to which learning tasks are presented as activities requiring participation by students
3. The effectiveness with which teachers co-operate with other teachers, and with other resource people, to widen the range of specialised contributions to the curriculum, and hence to capitalise on a wider range of student interests

These three objectives may be pursued in varied ways, according to the style of the teacher concerned and the various opportunities available in each teaching situation, but however pursued, it is likely that they have implications for the principal, other staff, and the life of the whole school.

At the most basic level the principal is involved in that he has to approve (or tolerate or prohibit) the conduct of a classroom where independent learning and an activity curriculum are practised. Typically it is noiser than the usual classroom, and there is more movement. The curriculum is more varied in the sense that it departs freely from the official syllabus, and also in the sense that a greater range of tasks is permitted within the class. Most probably also there is a greater spread in standards of achievement in basic or core subjects at the end of a year than might be expected with the more usual didactic methods where the limits of progress for children are more closely regulated. These matters have obvious relevance for the student's progression and for the work of the following year, as well as for the nature of the principal's report to parents.

At a higher level of involvement the principal would need to encourage these methods, and assist teachers to practise them, if his policies regarding the curriculum and the learning environment are based on a concern for the facts of individual differences, and for the positive encouragement of individuality. He could not achieve these policies through organisational measures alone, but unless his organisation is appropriate he is likely to detract from the effectiveness of the methods used, or discourage teachers from using such methods.

The extent of changes in organisation to achieve greater compatibility with teaching methods would depend on such factors as overall school decisions about objectives, curriculum and examination policies, staff co-operation, parental support, support by superiors, and, of course, the nature of already established patterns of organisation. The key to effective practice is the harmonious mobilisation of all the complex interactive influences in a school.

Methods that involve co-operation among staff are especially important in the attempt to cater for the varying interests of students. They embody the simple, but important fact that members of staff themselves vary greatly in their experience, expertise and general outlook, and can appeal in specialised ways to children's interests and understanding. Making the experience of a number of different teachers available to a group of children requires specific organisation, often involving substantial effort. The easiest form of organisation is to allot one teacher to each primary class, and one teacher of a particular subject to a secondary class, but apart from the changes that may be made from year to year, it does little to capitalise on the total resources of a staff for each student.

How various schemes of co-operation among teachers may be planned cannot be fully canvassed here. If the importance of the principle is accepted in schools it would be expected that varied expressions are likely to be conceived and experimented with.

These interpretations would reflect the ideas of individual schools with their particular resources and problems. A concept like *team teaching* is a general idea (the value of co-operation among staff in making the expertise of individual staff available to children) rather than a specific prescription for organisation. It can take many forms, involve any number of teachers, have varied objectives, and can vary widely in its degree of formality of structure. What is certain, however, is that team arrangements are unlikely to occur without the acceptance of a deliberate policy of support for them, and deliberate acts of planning to bring them about.

In the secondary school, teams of teachers are likely to be subject-based, with a panel of teachers contributing to different sections of a course, or dealing with a course on a massed lecture basis followed by smaller group tutorials. Visiting resource people and visiting student teachers, teacher aides, library staff and laboratory staff could well have a defined role in such a team concept. The likelihood that a responsive chord of interest would be struck in more students by such an approach is obviously increased. This kind of structure should be manageable fairly easily in a school that is departmentalised. A more radical concept is a multidisciplinary approach where a team of teachers from different departments combine to take a course. This enables the same concepts to be viewed from different perspectives—an extremely valuable experience, particularly for senior students, who when taught only on departmental lines are apt to miss the critical point that different subjects are abstract conceptual structures for analysing similar natural or social phenomena. A team of teachers composed, for example, of an historian, geographer, scientist, musician and physical educationist could subject important social concepts like *recreation, work, conservation* and *sex relationships* to scrutiny in a way that no single teacher could do. They might not agree on all matters, but this also would be salutary for students who all too often tend to regard knowledge as ready-made and complete, if only you can get the right book. If this procedure is impractical for a whole course (because factors such as external examinations are incompatible with it), it may be possible to attempt it on a limited supplementary basis. The value of the multidisciplinary approach is not only that it gives a more comprehensive perspective on knowledge, but it also is likely to appeal to different students in varied ways, and hence increase its impact.

Due to the traditional primary school organisation into grades or classes, rather than on a subject basis, co-operation among teachers is more difficult, and again requires planning if it is to occur. Modern schemes of open plan organisation are now fairly familiar, and commonly involve a degree of co-operation between two or more teachers. The idea that young children need the security of a single teacher is giving way to the view that a staff setting can be arranged in other ways than through the familiar one-teacher-one-class system, and that individual interests and talents are likely to be cultivated better by contact with a wider range of adults, both teachers and resource people from outside. Primary teachers, no less than secondary teachers, have special interests and talents, and these have been strengthened by the longer courses of training offered. The opportunity to express these in their daily work would benefit students, and also increase their own level of satisfaction in their work. A great deal would be done by informal arrangements among teachers within the present grade system, but planned organisational structures are needed if the principle of co-operation is to be given fullest expression.

An interesting example of a specialised approach to teaching, even with very young children, has been reported by Sandra Shephard in a New South Wales infants' school. It illustrates well how the attempt to meet a particular methodological objective requires school-wide organisation. Briefly, the scheme is as follows:

1. Three classes and three teachers form the basic unit.
2. Within the unit the curriculum is divided into three areas:
   (a) Communication and Expression (language skills, reading, writing, spelling, library skills);
   (b) Number, Space and Nature (number experiences, counting, computations, environmental geometry, mathematical games and models, problem solving, patterns in nature, elementary science, environment, health, and poetry—for lesson breaks and enrichment);
   (c) Cultural and Recreation Centre (arts and crafts, music, singing, creative dance and expression, physical education, social studies and drama);
3. During a day each class spends one session in each of the three centres, changing at normal recess and lunch breaks.
4. Each week the order of the class's use of the centres is rotated so that no one centre is favoured.

5. Over the year each teacher spends one term in each of the three centres. [This is not an essential feature of the scheme.]

Sandra Shephard's summary comment is this: 'We have found it works and has very few, if any, drawbacks, but has many positive advantages.'[20]

The experimental spirit of this design, aimed at using the special talents of teachers to increase the prospect of catering for the special talents and interests of children, points the way to the future. There is no single solution, no one best way. The essential elements are that the approaches made by different teachers are (or can be) unique to them, that in capitalising on these the varying needs of children are better provided for, and that, while some of the benefits of co-operative teaching may be gained informally, planning is needed to match resources and needs to best advantage.

2.8 Relating School Organisation Appropriately to Evaluation

The functioning of a school may be described in terms of three interrelated processes: (1) goal setting, (2) establishing procedures (organisation, curriculum, teaching, etc.) to give effect to agreed objectives, and (3) evaluation. The role of evaluation is to provide feedback regarding both objectives and procedures to ensure that the organisation functions efficiently. If the planned relationship of these three processes is disturbed, malfunctions are likely to occur in the system.

It is obvious that harmony is most easily preserved if the control of all three processes is internal to the system. When one or more is controlled from outside (particularly evaluation) the possibility of maladjustment among the processes is increased. Against this, it should be pointed out that a closed system, that is one in which all processes are internal, is more susceptible to stagnation.

Historically the evaluation of student's work, which is one of the commonest tests of efficiency applied to a school, has been substantially external, either through public examinations or school inspectors. Thus, examinations have had a strong influence on procedures in schools, virtually shaping curricula and significantly affecting teaching method and organisation, and, indirectly, objectives also.

They have been used to promote students through a school system, to determine (or guide) students' selection of schools and courses of study, to qualify them for entry to higher education and to employment, and to determine their eligibility for various kinds of scholarships and bursaries during their schooling and after it.

Thus evaluation, through school examinations, has tended to dominate the other processes, and distort the operation of the system. School objectives and procedures should relate to experiences realisable in school, and evaluation should relate specifically to these. It may, of course, quite legitimately include criteria appropriate to a phase of the student's progress beyond the point at which the assessment is made, but it should not be dominated by them. John Dewey established this very clearly more than half a century ago. He wrote as follows:

The mistake is not in attaching importance to preparation for future need, but in making it the mainspring of present effort. Because the need of preparation for a continually developing life is great, it is imperative that every energy should be bent to making the present experience as rich and significant as possible. Then as the present merges insensibly into the future, the future is taken care of.[21]

Thus the most significant challenge for a school is to create a life for each student which is as rich and significant as possible, and takes care of the future. Too close a preoccupation with immediate goals, without regard to future tasks, leads to a loss of relevance; too close a preoccupation with remote goals leads to a loss of zest for present tasks.

The distinctive aspect of evaluation that we are concerned with is that rising from the concern of an educational programme with individual differences, but this will be easier to analyse if the distinction is first made between examining *formatively* (that is diagnostically to identify students' difficulties so that alternative approaches or remedial teaching can be arranged), and examining *summatively* (that is terminally, to establish a student's standard of achievement). Each makes its own demands on organisation.

The relevance of formative evaluation to individual teaching is probably the most obvious, since diagnostic testing is aimed at understanding and assisting the individual case. A good deal of this testing can be done domestically within a classroom, but it is likely also that planning on a wider basis is needed to make full use of standardised tests, and even more so, to make use of the services of remedial teachers and other specialists. The scope and significance of formative assessment will be elaborated in Chapter 8.

Summative evaluation has the most obvious impact on schoolwide organisation since provision has to be made, at least in secondary schools, for schemes of assessment to meet external requirements. It is also more difficult to interpret within the framework of school objectives that stress the importance of individual differences, since the pressures on students tend to be towards the mastery of uniform subject matter and standards. This question also will be elaborated in Chapter 8, so that only a brief treatment, bearing particularly on school organisation, will be given.

Provision for individual differences can obviously be managed if evaluation is internal; on the other hand, the guarantee of standards appears to be more assured if evaluation is done externally. Recent moves in evaluation at the senior secondary level has grappled with the problem of trying to do justice to both these claims. Some of the compromises reached, which are being experimented with, are as follows:

1. The accrediting of schools to undertake the task of evaluation internally on the evidence of their capacity to do so
2. Evaluation being based on a composite of internal and external examinations
3. Internal examinations being moderated by subject reference tests, by consultation among teachers in different schools, or by aptitude tests

Although pressures on schools change from time to time according to such matters as changing employment conditions, restrictions on tertiary education, and social expectations of schools, there seems to be a fairly stable move towards increased responsibility on the part of schools for internal evaluation. This augurs well for their capacity to relate their programmes more realistically to their own students. It implies, however, that institutions and employers will be confronted with a more heterogeneous group in terms, at least in the scope, of their achievement, and possibly in terms of standards also, and will have to make provision accordingly.

One potential advantage of internal assessment is that it can be done cumulatively, rather than by a single final examination. The 'once-only' examination has been criticised for a long time on a formidable list of counts such as its unreliability, its undue pressure on students, its encouragement of coaching, and its inadequacy in catering for the varied accomplishments of students. Progressive evaluation, which allows a student to build up credits towards final assessment by assignments and by smaller tests, does have advantages, but it is not a panacea. In particular it does not necessarily reinforce a philosophy of individual teaching. If it means no more than the substitution of regular and frequent tests for infrequent, periodic ones, the standardised approach is actually intensified. Under these conditions progressive examining can reinforce the examination as the goal of teaching. It can also heighten the anxiety of students, and foster the undesirable attitude that a task is not worth doing unless it is given a mark, recorded, and credited to their account. This will be elaborated in Chapter 8.

The heart of the matter in evaluating the work of students is to make teaching and testing compatible. This is one of the major tasks for school organisation.

References

1. Broudy, H.S., 1972. *The Real World of the Public School*. Harcourt Brace Jovanovich: New York, p. 44.
2. Central Advisory Council for Education (England), 1967. *Children and their Primary Schools*. H.M.S.O.: London, p. 187.
3. Getzels, J.W., 1960. 'Theory and Practice in Educational Administration: An Old Question Revisited', in Campbell, R.F. and Lipham, J.M., *Administrative Theory: A Guide to Action*. Mid-West Administration Center: Chicago.
4. Biddle, B.J., 1970. 'Role Conflicts Perceived by Teachers in Four English Speaking Countries'. *Comparative Education Review* 14, 1.
5. Campbell, W.J. *et al.*, 1975. *Being a Teacher in Australian State Government Schools*. Australian Advisory Committee on Research and Development, Report no. 5.
6. *Ibid.*, p. 49.
7. Bush, R.N., 1958. 'The Teacher-Pupil Relationship in Australian Secondary Schools'. *Australian Journal of Education* 2, 1: 48.
8. Adams, R.S., 1970. 'Perceived Teaching Styles'. *Comparative Education Review* 14, 1: 56.
9. James, Brian, 1967. *The Advancement of Spencer Button*. Pacific Books: Sydney, p. 117.
10. Riesman, D., 1950. *The Lonely Crowd*. Yale University Press: New Haven.
11. Williamson, John N., 1974. 'The Inquiring School: Towards a Model of Organizational Self-Renewal', *Educational Forum* 38, 3: Kappa Delta, p. 358.
12. Pusey, M., 1976. *Dynamics of Bureaucracy*. John Wiley & Sons: Australia.
13. Morris, Ben, 1972. *Objectives and Perspectives in Education*. Routledge & Kegan Paul: London, p. 22.
14. Great Britain Board of Education, 1943. *Curriculum and Examinations in Secondary Schools*. H.M.S.O.: London (Norwood Report), p. 4.
15. Ridgway, L. and Lawton, I., 1969. *Family Grouping in the Primary School*. Ward Lock International: London, p. 10.
16. Piaget, J., 1971. *Science of Education and the Psychology of the Child*. Viking Press: New York, pp. 179–80.
17. Neagley, R.L. and Evans, N.D., 1967. *Handbook for Effective Curriculum Development*. Prentice Hall: Englewood Cliffs, N. J., p. 2.
18. Stenhouse, Lawrence, 1975. *An Introduction to Curriculum Research and Development*. Heinemann,: London, p. 40.
19. Whannell, R.A., 1976. 'Participative Decision Making in Queensland State High Schools'. *Administrators' Bulletin* 7, 7, University of Queensland.
20. Shephard, Sandra, 1976. 'Specialization in the Infants' School', *Primary Journal*. Dept of Education, N.S.W., 2, 5: 2–4.
21. Dewey, John, 1964. *Democracy and Education*. Macmillan Paperback: New York, p. 56.

6. Curriculum

Guidelines Relating to the Curriculum

3.1   *The curriculum, as it is experienced by individual students, is
a unique blend of the objective characteristics of the environment
(physical, biological, social and cultural), and the personal
characteristics of students which affect the quality of their
understanding and apppeciation of it. The school's role should
be to mediate between the objective environment and the characteristics of individual students in a way that promotes maximum
understanding and appreciation of it.*

3.2   *Because of the virtually limitless range of biophysical, social, and
cultural experiences open to children, either from direct experience or through interpretation and enrichment by the school
and other agencies, the diverse interests of students should be
catered for by making the curriculum flexible rather than
prescriptive in the range of themes and topics acceptable for
study. However, the methods and rules of inquiry must be
approached as an essential core of experience common to all.*

3.3   *The content of the curriculum may be arranged either formally
(in terms of subjects) or functionally (in terms of activities). While
both structures can be manipulated in various ways to improve
their appeal to the varied interests and aptitudes of students, the
functional mode is likely to be more effective as it is more flexible
in relating methods of inquiry to actual problems. Through the
functional approach both critical and practical knowledge are
built up, while pursuing tasks that are relevant to individual
children's interest and experience.*

3.4   *The child's contact with his environment is existential as well
as conceptual, that is it is assessed in terms of sensory and
affective responses to events, objects and people, as well as in
explanatory terms. Both are important components of the curriculum. Existential knowledge, being by definition unique and
personal, is related closely to differences among students, and
offers great scope for individual expression and satisfaction.*

205

3.1   The Curriculum As a Blend of Objective Characteristics of the Environment and the Personal Experience of Students

There is an inside and an outside view of the curriculum, and each needs to be considered in assessing the significance of the curriculum for the differences among students.

The outside view is objective and comprehensive, embracing all aspects of the environment that could conceivably be selected for study by particular individuals or groups. It includes physical and biological phenomena, social and cultural institutions, the processes and practices that they involve, and the public domain of knowledge by which they are studied. In this broad sense, the environment is the source of all curriculum and the sanction for it.

The inside view is existential, reflecting personal experience. It is the pupil's private view of the environment, revealing the knowledge, skills and values that he understands or accepts. It is an intimate microcosm of the world outside, a unique product of actual experience. The child reproduces elements of the objective environment, making what is outer, inner; he also reconstructs experience, transforming it in the process of assimilating it.

This process of transforming objective phenomena in the external environment into personal experience is regulated by the personal qualities of the child which direct his interests into particular channels or which give his activities and achievement a characteristic style. But it can also be mediated by the methods that scholars have developed for exploring the environment, and which teachers adapt for their own mode of intervention.

An attempt has been made to express these relationships in visual form in the diagram on page 207.

There are two main processes (1) *conceptual*, (2) *existential*. The loop lines indicate both.

The *conceptual process* may be explained in this way. Each child (centre circle) exists within his environment (the three segments of the outer ring). His personal characteristics (inner ring) affect the kind of transactions he has with his environment and the various needs he has for help in understanding his environment. He is assisted in interpreting his environment by the methods of inquiry and the concepts of the formal disciplines and by basic intellectual tools such as reading, writing, and computation (second ring). This ring represents the main area of intervention by the teacher. In this case the loops are intended to indicate that the child's experiences (whether physical, biological, social and cultural) are constantly being influenced (refined, enlarged, enriched, amended, consolidated, etc.) by his increasing contact with formal knowledge. This is elaborated in *3.2*.

*A Diagrammatic Representation of the Various Sources of Curriculum
and the Processes by Which the Curriculum Is Experienced by
Individual Children.*

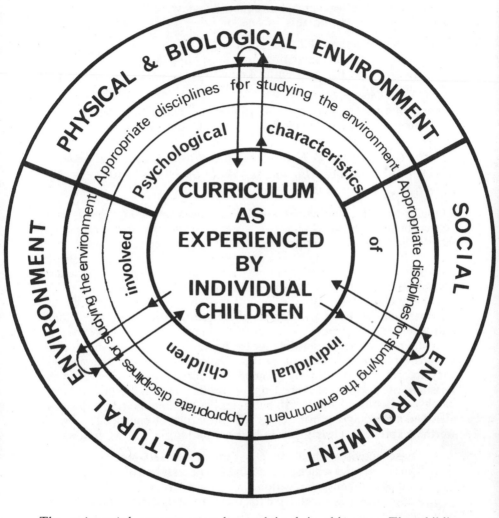

The *existential process* may be explained in this way. The child's
personal transactions with his environment are of a direct kind, their
main significance being not so much as to understand it, as to appreciate
it. In this case the loops may be considered to pass directly from the
individual child and his personal characteristics to the environment,
particularly in its cultural segment. This is elaborated in *3.4.*

Of the three elements in the diagram that influence the experience of children—their environment, the disciplines by which it is studied, and their own psychological characteristics—the environment offers most scope to the teacher to introduce diversity and richness into the curriculum. He may do this in one or other of the following ways:

1. By his selection of topics for study
2. By his mode of arranging and presenting knowledge
3. By his appeal to existential knowledge as well as to conceptual knowledge

Each of these options may be applied to the three major areas of environmental influence, biophysical, social, and cultural.

3.2 The Curriculum As Embodying Biophysical, Cultural and Social Elements, and Allowing for Wide Individual Choice in the Selection of Topics and Themes

Consider first the biophysical world as a source of knowledge. It must be accepted at the outset that it is virtually infinite in its scope and variety, and no single person can comprehend other than a very small part of it. Even scientists have expert knowledge in only limited fields, although their scientific training does assist them in assessing phenomena outside their special field in a disciplined way.

For the child at school, science is a veritable Pandora's box, offering unlimited choice. If we ask whether there are constraints on this choice, and whether accordingly some scientific knowledge has a prior claim over others (as those responsible for curriculum development might ask), the answers given (or implied by the selection of topics or themes) will vary according to the criteria adopted. Herbert Spencer's answer to the question of priority of knowledge straddles our three main areas, biophysical, cultural and social, but it applies within scientific knowledge also, and accordingly is instructive.[1] His hierarchy of knowledge 'of most worth', expressing clearly his utilitarian philosophy, is as follows:

1. Those activites which directly minister to self-preservation
2. Those activities which by securing the necessaries of life, indirectly minister to self-preservation
3. Those activities which have for their end the rearing and discipline of offspring
4. Those activities which are involved in the maintenance of proper social and political relations
5. Those miscellaneous activities which fill up the leisure part of life, devoted to the gratification of the tastes and feelings

Utility, as a criterion for selection of curriculum content, is important, and in one form or other has strongly influenced science curricula, particularly those that are planned as vocational courses or as a background to them. But it is an elusive criterion. It presupposes a relationship between the individual and his future life style which can scarcely be known at the time the judgement of usefulness has to be made. It also presupposes that the usefulness of particular knowledge is inherent and obvious, whereas, in fact, this may become apparent only after it has been studied. A distinction is often drawn between theoretical knowledge and practical knowledge, the latter being regarded as more useful. Unfortunately, children at school often have this rather contemptuous view of theory. In fact usefulness must always be based on some kind of theory, and it is an important task for the school to make this relationship clear.

In spite of these difficulties it is clear that the criterion of usefulness in selecting curriculum content is compatible with a concern for individual differences. The usefulness of studies no doubt has a social reference in that some societal need is being served by them, but it has a strong individual reference also. Knowledge is useful to a person when he can apply it in a way that increases his competence in work or leisure, and when it is a source of satisfaction to him. The elements of choice and personal involvement are thus recognised.

A more comprehensive criterion is that of relevance. This includes the concepts of usefulness and interest, but extends beyond them to include the processes whereby knowledge is built up. The methodology of knowledge is examined more fully in this chapter and in Chapter 7 in connection with teaching method. Here it is only touched on briefly to clarify the central question being considered—what topics or themes should be studied.

When emphasis is placed on scientific methods of inquiry and on the elucidation of leading scientific concepts that unite a whole array of apparently disconnected phenomena, the role of factual knowledge in a curriculum is changed. It may, of course, be still intrinsically interesting and useful, but it becomes also the raw material for scientific inquiry, and its relevance is judged also by the relationships and concepts that emerge from its study. These are useful, but in the wider sense of helping to build up knowledge, rather than being immediately useful in a practical sense.

In answer, then, to the question 'What topics or themes should be studied?', it would not be an exaggeration to say that it does not matter what topics are chosen, provided that they are pursued by students with interest and lead them to further study, provided they are studied in a way that gives scope for disciplined investigation, and provided that through their study, students enlarge their understanding and appreciation of the orderly pattern of relationships among phenomena.

This is certainly an appropriate proposition for primary school science, and with some reservation (the degree to which conceptual structure at a more advanced level is cumulative, and the degree to which vocational preparation is necessary), it is true for the secondary school also.

With the objective of science teaching shifted more towards an understanding of the methods of science and skill in their use, the way is opened for a greater appeal to individual interests and aptitudes among students. The focus of scientific study may with equal profit be on a study of marine life, or rocks, soils, plants, animals, birds, insects, the weather, the sky, air, water and a host of other themes, and among such a variety the chance of appealing to diverse interests is greatly increased.

Of special significance is the local environment because of its accessibility to first-hand observation and its familiarity. One of the most stimulating, and often surprising aspects of scientific study is how ordinary and familiar phenomena prove on closer examination to be quite extraordinary. Equally surprising and significant to students is the realisation that scientific instruments such as microscopes and telescopes, and chemical and other analytical techniques penetrate well beyond the boundaries of ordinary observation.

Remote environments can be studied through excursions, or vicariously through audio-visual aids of various kinds. A significant outcome of such study is that remote and local phenomena can often be linked through the pupil's growing insight into inclusive generalisations.

Thus the teacher, disposed to deal with scientific material that is relevant to his pupil's interests, either individually or in groups, need have no doubt as to its suitability simply because it differs from conventional textbook material. What is important is that he ensures that it is dealt with as an exercise in scientific inquiry.

Much that has been discussed in connection with the phenomenal environment is also true of the social environment, although there are some constraints that are different. It will be convenient to deal with the constraints first.

A child's social education is, to a degree, designed to reproduce a social type. The emphasis on socialisation as an objective and the form that it takes varies in different cultures, but in most there are codes of conventional manners and moral behaviour that are taught in home and school as norms. Individuality may, of course, still find expression in the detailed form of this behaviour, for example, in personal manners and in the quality of moral relationship, but there is common cultural basis for both which transcends individuality if social cohesion is to be maintained. Conventional behaviour and morality are not static, although they change slowly, and there is the problem in socialisation programmes of transmitting socio-cultural values while at the same time recognising the transitional influences involved. Failure to do this creates the so-called 'generation gap', although the gap may also be between other sections of the community.

Whereas in the case of scientific study the local environment is a familiar significant base for wider intellectual pursuits, in social studies it serves the purpose of socialisation, familiarising the child with formal and informal relationships and institutional life so that he may more effectively participate in them. Knowledge of one's own local (and national) geography, history, and sociology is an essential element in social competence, and not just a vehicle for more universal knowledge, important as this is. It is useful knowledge in the sense already discussed, and, as such, sets some limits to individual choice.

But there is, nevertheless, great scope for variety and choice in studying the social environment. As is the case in science, the methods of inquiry used by the social scientist have enormous value in their own right, and, once gained, free the individual to explore in a disciplined way all kinds of issues and novel situations. In no aspect of his environment does the individual face more persistent complex and urgent problems than in the social, ethical, political and economic sphere. Foreign affairs, historical events, local and national issues present a virtually unlimited area of choice for curriculum development aimed at strengthening the student's capacity for social inquiry and his will to attempt it in a disciplined way. The local social environment, no matter how apparently limited in significance, when studied through the methods of geography, history, sociology and other disciplines, is transformed into a scene of absorbing interest. Foreign cultures, both contemporary and historical, provide endless material for the extension of one's social experience, and can be studied through books, films and other materials. Learning the discipline of social inquiry frees each individual for his own exploration of the world of others.

An example of the scientific approach to curriculum development in social science with an emphasis on a method of study is *Man: A Course of Study* (M:ACOS) developed by Jerome Bruner.[2] This applies an anthropological framework of ideas in exploration of the ascent of man, combining the biological behaviour of fish, birds and baboons with simple human tribal life to give an insight into the development of civilised life. Such a course of study, if followed in detail in a school, would, no doubt, have its value, but it is rather prescriptive, and leaves little scope for independent work. However, as a suggestive framework for school-based courses that could exploit different, but equally good social material, it and similar courses are highly stimulating.

Perhaps the most significant expression of a disciplined approach to social questions is the interpretation that each person has to make of the myriad events that make up his day-to-day experience, and that come to his notice through newspaper, television and other media. The greater part of the news that he has to live with is a running commentary on his own society and related issues from other countries. He faces a barrage of wide-ranging economic, social and ethical questions, often presented in a way that seeks his allegiance to a particular viewpoint. He has to distinguish fact from opinion, and bias from reasoned conclusion in a welter of current affairs, often dressed up by 'media personalities' to increase their entertainment value. How well does the ordinary citizen cope with this? Probably not very well at all. His readiness to approach social issues with critical balance rather than with stereotyped thinking is weak or lacking, particularly in areas of life that touch his own material interests; his capacity to seek and sift evidence and to draw conclusions is defective, and his sensitiveness to humane feeling in social events removed from immediate self-interest is dull. The most urgent objective in teaching social science is to sensitise children to social issues and give them a mode and code of inquiry. This will not be achieved alone by stressing factual knowledge, but by choosing themes and topics that allow the student to explore social issues of all kinds. What topics are chosen can be left to the initiative of individual schools and teachers. In selecting them there is ample opportunity for catering for individual differences of experience and interests among students.

There are some risks in such an approach, since the habit of critical thinking on social issues is not always welcome to those who in various ways have a vested interest in maintaining the *status quo*. It also calls for a high degree of integrity on the part of teachers to be able to handle controversial topics impartially. But there is no effective substitute for it in a democratic society if the rights and obligations of each person in contributing towards social welfare are taken seriously.

We come then to the third area—the cultural environment. In a broad sense culture includes biophysical and social elements, but here it is used more narrowly to indicate artistic and creative activities such as the literary, visual and performing arts. In a special way these expressions of the creative spirit of a people help to give a culture its distinctive quality. They influence the development of children through home and other agencies, and it is important that generous provision be made for them in the environment that the school creates. To regard them as frills, of less importance than utilitarian studies, is to underrate their value in personal development and in the quality of social life. For some children with limited home backgrounds, the school is able to open up otherwise closed avenues to enjoyment and the development of standards of taste.

It is obvious—perhaps more so than in other aspects of the environment—that a wide choice of aesthetic activities is available, and that in this respect the flexibility of the curriculum is limited only by the teacher's own cultural resources—those that he can call on from other teachers and from outside the school, and those that students themselves initiate. Many students have already developed strong interests (musical, artistic, literary, dramatic, etc.) through private effort, and these should be allowed expression in the school. As has been pointed out earlier, the different cultural background of migrant children is an obvious source of enrichment to the life of a school.

In discussing scientific and social components of the curriculum it was pointed out that it is the choice of themes and topics that give flexibility of the curriculum to accommodate individual differences among students. The methods and rules of inquiry applying to each should be approached as a common possession. It is the same in the aesthetic field. The widest possible options for choice of aesthetic activities should exist, but within each the appropriate techniques of construction, performance or criticism should be applied. Greater freedom in the exercise of taste should not lead to lowered standards. On the contrary, it should be accepted that a chosen activity (whether it be playing a guitar, writing a story, constructing a model, painting a picture, throwing a pot, or countless others), should be pursued with concentrated effort and attention to technical detail, in due course helping to raise the general level of public taste. If the claim often made by mass media, that they are giving the public what they want, is true, it is a sad commentary on the degree of discipline with which the arts have been pursued at school.

Artistic activities are a blend of conceptual thought, technical skill and emotional response. The enjoyment of creative activity is primarily existential, requiring no justification beyond itself. This aspect of curriculum, so obviously relevant to the appeal to differences among students, is discussed in section *3.4*. Further consideration of aesthetic elements in the curriculum can be pursued there.

3.3 Formal and Functional Modes of Curriculum Structure

The generic modes of presentation of knowledge may be classified broadly as *formal* and *functional*. Within each category there can be variations.

Formal presentation treats knowledge as a self-contained set of propositions, generalisations, and relationships. It is necessarily abstract, being concerned primarily with concepts (ideas embracing a variety of phenomena and hypotheses) and theories (explanatory propositions or models expressing a set of relationships). It has a defined terminology and structure that guide the sequence in which ideas are dealt with. Not the least of its formal characteristics for teachers is that it is set out in a textbook, a programmed text, or an audio-visual medium for teachers and pupils to follow. Traditional school subjects, particularly those in the secondary school, provide plenty of familiar examples.

Functional presentation, by contrast, takes as its focus of interest some object or event (or related group of them) in a naturally occurring or contrived setting. There is greater emphasis in such a presentation on events of intrinsic interest and on the process of knowledge—the methods of inquiry by which phenomena are investigated. Examples are the study of the sea-shore at low tide, the systematic examination of a defoliated plant, or the migratory habits of local birds.

With these definitions in mind we can consider the suitability of the different types of curriculum in adapting to the differences among pupils. Both formal and functional approaches may be varied to increase their appeal to different children, or to help understanding. Variations in the formal approach will be dealt with first:

Variations in the Formal Approach

1. *Variety of applications.* The significance and usefulness of theoretical knowledge for most pupils become more apparent as the range of its applications are understood and appreciated. In this way the level of abstraction is reduced. Some pupils can successfully manage sustained abstraction; others need frequent recourse to illustration of concrete objects and operations within their experience. Audio-visual aids are particularly useful in this regard. The same idea can thus be understood by different children by the varied use of illustration. Particular interests that children may have, and which are recognised by alert teachers, can be appealed to and used for illustrative purposes. Application thus enhances relevance, and adapts theory to observation and practice.

2. *Graduated steps of analysis.* A complex idea or set of relationships may be presented whole or divided into smaller steps. A pupil who may not understand a concept or relationship at first may be helped to do so by a more gradual presentation. This procedure is often diagnostic as well as explanatory, in that it pinpoints specific difficulties. Provided class organisation and

teaching methods are sufficiently flexible, differences in comprehension among pupils may be provided for in this way. Schemes of programmed instruction are usually constructed on this basis of progression by small steps. Since the steps are so small that virtually anyone can follow them correctly, this type of curriculum becomes a self-teaching device which a pupil can proceed with at his own pace. Many kinds of self-teaching equipment are now available, and are of great assistance to teachers who have trained their pupils to be self-reliant in such tasks. For some children, quick to see relationships, the lilliputian steps of the programmed text are often unnecessary, and may be quite tedious.

3. *Selection of topics and themes.* Another common way already discussed in which a formal curriculum can be varied to suit particular pupils, is by the inclusion of particular themes or topics and the omission of others. The criteria used for this selection can be the level of difficulty of the topics, their importance for an understanding of the subject, their relevance to the pupils, or the availability of resources. An underlying assumption is that valid judgements based on criteria of this kind can be made for a whole class of pupils. This may well be a dubious assumption, disregarding the differences within the class.

Variations in the Functional Approach

The functional approach to the development of knowledge is by its very nature variable in the hands of different teachers, in that topics for study are selected on the criterion of their significance for the pupils. The projects may be undertaken by the class as a whole (perhaps with some division of tasks among different pupils, by groups with the class, or by individual pupils). Class organisation and the teacher's methods and evaluation need to be compatible with such an informal curriculum for it to be effective.

Units of work preplanned by the teacher fall midway between formal and functional curricula. Their structured character aligns them with formal curricula; their focus on practical topics and problems suggests a functional approach.

Formal and Functional Curricula Compared

The two approaches have basically the same objective, namely to increase the pupil's understanding of his environment. The formal curriculum attempts to do this by presenting knowledge in the form of systematic disciplines (chemistry, physics, biology, geology, etc.) and applying this to the environment. The functional approach takes a particular aspect of the environment, and applies appropriate methods of inquiry to it and relates it to relevant scientific concepts and principles. The teacher obviously needs to have a good command of the various concepts and generalisations involved to be able to guide the pupil in his investigation. Each task successfully undertaken is a bridge for the pupil between the 'real' world and the 'theoretical' world.

Obviously in both cases an understanding of the various disciplines is an essential gateway to comprehension of the environment, and it might appear at first glance that the most systematic and economical way of achieving this is to teach the disciplines directly, and show by application how, in fact, they do illuminate the phenomenal world. Schools have had considerable experience with this approach to curriculum development—particularly at secondary school. Primary schools traditionally have devoted most of their effort to teaching the basic tools of learning, but to the extent that they have taught substantive subjects they have tended to follow the lead of the secondary school in adopting a discipline-centred approach.

In spite of its apparent short cut to success, the formal approach, at both primary and secondary school, has not been very successful, at least for the majority of pupils. Various explanations of this can be offered. Teachers, who have a mature understanding of a discipline themselves, developed through study at secondary and tertiary level, may underestimate the pupil's need for concrete illustrations, and tend to treat the subject primarily as a self-contained logical system (which, in a sense, it is). This overstrains most pupils' capacity for a theoretical type of thinking. It also taxes their interest in schoolwork in that the subject appears to be like an endless preparation for a journey which is never taken, as does excessive preoccupation with reading, spelling, writing and computation as skills in the primary school, without the substantive study that they make possible.

Other measures that might be taken by careful teachers, such as a more detailed analysis of complex concepts for pupils who are having difficulty, or the omission of certain difficult sections of a course, assist in making a formal curriculum more flexible, but when all such possible steps have been taken it is still true that the traditional discipline-centred curriculum suffers from two inherent defects which limit its appeal to many pupils. One is its theoretical form, requiring sustained abstract thinking which many pupils find difficult; the other is the reduction, or even elimination, of the satisfaction and achievement that were originally intrinsic elements in the processes of inquiry and discovery by which these organised bodies of knowledge were progressively built up by scholars. The removal, or mitigation of these defects, is a direct objective of the functional type of curriculum.

As has been indicated, it attempts to do this by focusing on objects, events, problems and tasks that are relevant to children's interests, and by exploring them in disciplined way. Conceived in this way a curriculum is not a set of prescriptions, but a pursuit of knowledge built up progressively by individual students. It is a sequence of activities in which the students gain skill in using appropriate methods of inquiry and proof, while at the same time increasing their insight into the structure of disciplines as this is understood by scholars. It is to be hoped, also, that their commitment to the intellectual values that guide inquiry increases. Learning in this way is akin to the research work of the scholar. It is active, responsible and satisfying.

This emphasis on curriculum in terms of function may be summarised in this way:

1. The students learn the characteristic methods of inquiry that have been developed to explore the material and social environment: careful observation, various forms of measurement, hypothetic inference, experiment, and proof. Some of these methods involve skills such as calculation, using equipment, finding information, as well, of course, as effective verbal expression, and these, too, have to be practised and learnt.

2. They learn to appreciate the rules that govern such activity (the morality of inquiry): respect for evidence, objectivity, and suspended judgement. From these they increasingly should be able to distinguish fact from opinion, and to conclude what the facts conclude, even though the result is unexpected, or even contrary to their own belief. With growing understanding of the environment it is to be hoped also that they would become more sensitive to the wonders of nature, and more humble in their attitude to it, and more aware of the problems of civilised society.

3. As selected areas of the environment are explored by the methods referred to in (1), the students' insight into organised disciplines becomes clearer, more ordered, and more comprehensive. Their knowledge becomes more conceptual and generalised as the regularities of nature are better understood. Thus the theoretical structure of the disciplines emerges, progressively more articulated as the pursuit of knowledge becomes more sophisticated, and also more powerful as a tool for further inquiry. It is this kind of knowledge that the scholar has in his special field. It is made up of concepts, systems of relationships (models or theories), laws and evaluation schemes. Armed with such knowledge he can predict and evaluate, and extend the boundaries of knowledge.

Few reach this level of achievement, but progress towards it is the gateway to understanding of the environment for all.

In view of the importance of this theoretical form of knowledge it may be unconvincing to many to deny it pride of place as the substance of curriculum. But no matter how developed a discipline may be, it still remains instrumental, and is justified by the understanding and control that it gives over the social and phenomenal world. It derives from this world and must keep returning to it if it is to avoid the charge of sterility. It is precisely because this is forgotten by some teachers that their teaching is rejected by students. It is undeniable that there is a sense in which the concept *knowledge for its own sake* is significant, and this will be discussed in connection with existentialism, but primarily a structured discipline is a tool for exploring and controlling the environment, and for inventing new technologies.

The perspective on curriculum that emerges from this approach is one of *contrived interaction* between processes of inquiry on the one hand (embracing scientific methods, intellectual code, and theoretical formulations), and substantive phenomena on the other. Both inquiry processes and factual knowledge gain from this reciprocal relationship. Investigation of new problems leads both to a clearer understanding of them and to gains in grasp of methodology and theory.

The detailed nature of this interaction is very much a function of the maturity, experience, motivation and aptitude of the pupil engaging in it, and is hence moderated by individual differences. Clearly, younger pupils will be more concerned with factual knowledge and older ones with theory, and within age ranges there will be wide variation derived from other influences discussed in previous chapters, but at all levels, both factual knowledge and theory should be present. No doubt this is what Bruner had in mind when he proposed the bold hypothesis that any subject can be taught in some intellectually honest form to any child at any stage of development.[3]

An activity curriculum such as has been described can hardly be discussed apart from the methods used by the teacher in teaching it. Product and process become fused. Clearly a major consideration for teaching method is the procedure used in continuously relating fact to theory in a balanced way. A closer examination of this is made in Chapter 7 dealing with guidelines in teaching method.

3.4 Existential Knowledge As an Important Element in the Curriculum Catering for Individual Differences

It is usual to identify schoolwork with conceptual knowledge, that is with inquiry, insight, explanation, inference and other rational processes, together with the skills that are the means to them (reading, writing, computation, listening, etc.) Not infrequently, particularly in the primary school, the means triumph over the ends, and training in techniques predominates, but the rationale for these curriculum objectives directed towards understanding the environment is clear, even though at times it may be underemphasised or lost sight of.

But there is also a different kind of knowledge and a different way of reacting to the environment. It is not easy to describe this alternative form of knowledge, since the ordinary vocabulary pertaining to knowledge usually assumes a scientific form. Terms such as *intuitive, direct, sensory*, and *existential* are used, and these overlap readily with affective terms such as *appreciation, attitude, satisfaction, emotion*, etc. The emphasis is on reacting to some object or living creature *for itself*, and not necessarily seeking to explain or analyse it. This latter process requires that the object or creature be put into a particular context and related to other objects or creatures. But we can react to warmth without knowing, or seeking to know, the physics of temperature. Indeed, often in this case it is the existential response that is most significant. Similarly, we can appreciate a flower without understanding it as a botanist would, and we can appreciate and value a person without using biological or psychological analytical methods. Thus each object or creature can be viewed both scientifically and existentially. Both perspectives are important, and a comprehensive school programme should take account of both.

The existential perspective leads readily to various forms of art— the visual arts, bodily movement, crafts, music, drama, and literature. Each of these is likely to have a deep involvement in sensory and affective experience for its own sake. An example of this experiential and personal element is taken from the poem 'Granchester', by the English poet, Rupert Brooke. It was written in 1912 in a Berlin cafe, and expresses his nostalgia for home in intimate visual images:

> Just now the lilac is in bloom
> All before my little room,
> And in my flower beds, I think,
> Smile the carnation and the pink,
> . . . .
> . . . .
> Stands the church clock at 10 to 3?
> And is there honey still for tea?

Having distinguished the existential from the conceptual it is important to stress that both may form part of the same experience, and, in particular, that art need not be exclusively existential. In fact many art forms are abstract and symbolic, and predominantly conceptual; others make use of scientific knowledge of the properties of the materials they use, and perhaps also of the subject of the work. A simple example of the union of the scientific and the artistic is when a child learns the properties of the timber, clay, metal or other material he is working with. His knowledge of these properties, his skill in manipulating them, and satisfaction from the utility or aesthetic quality of the created product, all blend into a unified experience.

Acceptance of existential experiences in the curriculum, undertaken for pure enjoyment, greatly enriches it, and enlarges its offerings to different pupils. It also increases the appeal of school to children, providing a balancing function to intellectual tasks.

The biophysical world provides unlimited scope for exploiting sensory and affective experiences, whether in more formally organised subjects such as physical education, music, art, manual arts, dramatic art and literature, or in functional activities. These are not frills or soft options. They cater for human needs, at least as compelling as the need for rationality, and for many children they are at least as significant a form of self-expression as are the more intellectual forms. They also help to make school an enjoyable place.

References

1. Spencer, H., 1929. *Education.* Thinkers' Library: London, Ch. 1.
2. See discussion by McClure, R.M., 1971. *Seventieth Year-book* of the National Society for the Study of Education, pt 1, University of Chicago.
3. Bruner, J.S., 1961. *The Process of Education.* Harvard University Press: Cambridge, Mass. p. 33.

7. *Teaching*

Guidelines Relating to Individualising Teaching

4.1   Teachers should have a sincere and sensitive regard for the personal characteristics of their students, particularly in ways that increase the student's feelings of self-worth. This attitude of acceptance of students is likely to increase the effectiveness of teaching by creating a favourable climate for learning.

4.2   Since students differ markedly in their motivation for learning, teaching is likely to be more effective if it can be related to each student's needs and values. The development in maturity of children's present motives—towards those based on educational values (intellectual, aesthetic, social and moral) and on achievement in educational tasks as intrinsically satisfying—is best approached directly through appropriate curricula, using methods of teaching that appeal to children, and by creating a pleasant and supportive school environment, rather than indirectly by schemes of rewards and punishments.

4.3   Teaching methods should be directed towards encouraging active student participation in school tasks. They should emphasise various forms of expression by students (inquiry, discovery, writing, speaking, acting, composing, constructing, etc.) rather than relying too much on impression, which can easily lead to relatively passive responses by students, or to servile learning which is reproductive rather than productive. They should also make use of student differences in cognitive style, that is in their preferred modes of learning. They should stimulate creativity, allowing for divergent thinking and action by students. Finally, they should exploit the curriculum in a way that differentiates the various elements of school tasks to cater appropriately for the various interests and aptitudes of students.

221

Introduction

The guidelines discussed in this section deal with teacher behaviour in relation to student differences. The term *teacher behaviour* is chosen rather than *teaching method* to indicate the variety and breadth of contacts that can occur between teachers and students. It includes what would ordinarily be called *teaching method*, but suggests also a wider range of encounters between teachers and students which have a significant bearing on the student's attitude towards school, for good or ill. In fact, in the statement of guidelines, the expression of the teacher's interest in students is placed first, highlighting this as a factor in success.

Teaching methods are generally discussed in terms that apply to students in general, or at least in groups, and are based on characteristics of human learning that have been established also as general. This is to be expected in a movement designed to establish a scientific basis for pedagogy. The educationist expectedly turns for guidance to the common scientific model which seeks to establish predictable outcomes for a specified population from determinate inputs and processes. It is also to be expected, when viewed sociologically, that the task of creating an effective methodology for teaching should be approached within the context of popular, mass education. The scientific movement in pedagogy and the spread of popular education are linked in spirit, as well as in time. A good example of this is Herbartian pedagogy which dominated the early years of the nineteenth century popular education movement in Europe, and which strongly influenced America.

This emphasis of methodology on uniform processes, not surprisingly, has reinforced class teaching as a prototype of teaching. It is still true today, after at least a generation in which the importance of individualised teaching has been stressed in educational literature, that the image of the good teacher is that of the good class teacher—one who can keep a whole class working together, like a conductor with his orchestra, or with his choir singing in unison.

It is clear from the material presented in Chapters 1, 2 and 3 that psychology provides a greater understanding of children than has been effectively put to use in education. In part at least, this is because much that psychology is concerned with in the behaviour of children does not fit easily into the dominant mode of mass instruction. This is particularly true in relation to personality and mental health, but it is true also of many aspects of cognition and learning. In psychology, investigation by means of case studies has long been necessary as a supplement to surveys and experiments with mass populations, and in psychological practice a clinical approach is common. The counterpart to this in education has been seen not so much in teaching as in educational guidance. The guidance movement, of course, has been salutary, both for its special contribution to the children it deals with, and for its influence on teaching. This influence, however, with its orientation towards concern for the individual student, has not been immediate or strong; in fact guidance and teaching have had an uneasy relationship because of their different approaches towards the individual; but it is having a desirable effect. When guidance and teaching are more completely suffused with the same spirit of concern for the individual child, teaching method is likely to be able to make greater use of available psychological knowledge.

It also needs to be brought out in an introduction to teaching that the research and scholarly methods used by scholars in establishing and extending bodies of knowledge are relevant to the methods that the teacher should use in teaching these subjects. Bodies of knowledge may be classified in various ways as pure, applied, multidisciplinary, etc., but the boundaries between them are not always definite. Accordingly the methods used in the various disciplines overlap to some extent. Scientific method is used not only in the traditional sciences, but in many other fields in which observation, experiment, hypothetic inference, and similar aspects of scientific method apply. Other methods are used in the social sciences, in language study, and in the humanities. When individual learning is emphasised, the student is likely to make more use of these methods of inquiry, as he is put in a position somewhat similar to that of the research scholar himself. The teacher also is more likely to relate his methodology to them as well as to the methods suggested by the psychology of learning. This important link between teaching method and the methods of knowledge is a reminder of the close association between teaching method and the curriculum which has been referred to in previous sections.

It should be made clear that the guidelines in this section do not deal with special methods that are used with handicapped or subnormal children, and others that deviate widely from the normal. In practice, what needs to be determined is whether segregated teaching is necessary. Teachers' judgements as to what constitutes 'special' are influenced by their own teaching methods, and particularly their tolerance of differences within their classrooms. An inflexible approach to teaching the class as a whole is likely to lead to labelling many children as *special* who could, under other circumstances, be taught without segregation.

The guidelines that follow relate to three aspects of teacher behaviour which are regarded as particularly important in dealing with individual differences—(1) the personal relationship between teacher and student that establishes and sustains a favourable setting for learning, (2) the motivation of learning, and (3) the encouragement of various forms of active student participation in their own learning.

4.1 The Importance of Personal Relationships between Teachers and Students

Ben Morris's notion of education as 'an adventure in mutuality' has already been mentioned.[1] This idea of a reciprocal relationship between teacher and student does not fit readily into every teacher's view of authority and discipline in teaching, yet it is an essential basis for it, if the differential treatment of students is to be taken seriously.

In an earlier section the concept of discipline was presented as the effort needed to meet the requirements of a task. The role of the teacher in this exercise of discipline may be coercive, either because it is considered to be the only practicable solution, or because coercion is elevated into an educational principle ('self-discipline is strengthened by the exercise of imposed discipline'). But coercion does little to ensure the continuing development of self-discipline; indeed it may be counter-productive, and often is. John Holt stresses this point—'. . . the child who learns something to please or appease someone else forgets it when the need for pleasing or the danger of not appeasing is past.'[2]

Pusey,[3] as pointed out earlier, makes an even more serious charge against the use of formal authority in teaching than merely its ineffectiveness in the long run. His claim, in effect, is that it is anti-educational, producing reactions of aggression, ingratiation, or withdrawal among students. The withdrawal reaction, which he asserts is the most common, raises a barrier between teacher and student and frustrates any attempt on the part of the teacher to encourage a creative response from the student. The result is a disabling learning pattern in which formality and routine on the part of both teacher and student are progressively reinforced.

The teacher's role, rather, should be constructive, stimulating and supportive; he should assist students in the choice of tasks by suggestion and criticism, give the most appropriate sort of help to them in carrying them out, give encouragement and recognition, and foster self-confidence. This view of teaching may sound idealistic and impractical. No doubt it is, in the sense that not all teachers find it easy to approach their work in this spirit, or even have been encouraged to do so, that not all students have learned how to work in the responsible, independent way implied, and that not all schools are satisfactory as a setting for such personalised teaching, but it is a desirable objective, even though unattained, or even unattainable.

Carl Rogers writes of teaching as an 'over-rated function'.[4] By 'teaching' he means formal instruction. The important aim for education in his view is the facilitation of learning, 'the way in which we might develop the learning man'. This aim is likely to be achieved, he believes, not primarily through teaching skills, but through 'certain attitudinal qualities which exist in the personal relationship between the facilitator and the learner'.[5] It is these qualities, *genuineness, acceptance*, and *empathic understanding*, which create a climate of freedom to learn.

By *genuineness* he means that the teacher comes into direct personal encounter with the learner, being himself, rather than playing an assumed role. According to Ben Morris[6] whose thinking on this is very much in tune with Rogers's, children know intuitively what we feel about them—in discerning the real feelings of others they are much more perceptive than most adults—and they react accordingly. The implications of these ideas for the teacher are serious indeed. If a teacher must be himself in his relations with students, and if his attitudes towards students are transparent, the inescapable imperative is that he be a person worth knowing, and one whose contact with students is likely to be beneficial—a heavy responsibility for those who select and train teachers!

The second quality, *acceptance*, is an elusive one. Martin Buber uses the same term, and his rather spiritual meaning for it has already been presented.[7] Rogers explains it in a variety of forms: 'prizing the learner, prizing his feelings, his opinion, his person', 'a basic trust—a belief that this other person is somehow fundamentally trustworthy'.[8] This confident and optimistic view of children is certainly not shared by all teachers (some of whom incline more to a doctrine of original sin), and for those who do share it, it is likely to be a product of growth through reflection and experience. Many teachers (probably most), believe that students need to be manipulated for their own good, and come to a different view (if they do so) by taking risks. For example, some teachers might allow a student to give disproportionate time to a particular subject or topic in which he is engrossed, and accept the risk that other studies may suffer. They have to balance the return from capitalising on an expressed positive interest and the hope that the balance can be redressed later on with the overall benefit of rationing the student's time through a prepared timetable. The adventurous teacher will opt for the former, and in time come to trust his judgement that these risks are worth taking because, at least, something of great value has not been lost, and, at best, because there are other evidences of improvement in the student's attitude towards school and in the quality of his learning. Empirical evidence for the value of such a subtle quality as trust is, by its very nature, hard to get, although there are the personal testimonies of a number of creative educators in various parts of the world. For the most part, its justification must be considered an act of faith.

The third quality, *empathic understanding*, is the capacity to understand another's behaviour with some of the direct awareness that the person himself has. Experientially this phenomenon is real enough, and not uncommon, although it is expressed more often in literary and dramatic writings than in the literature of psychology, and is hard to express in scientific terms. Teachers who have a liking for young people are perhaps better able to see things from the student's perspective, but this is by no means always the case. Liking (or love) for another is often associated with obtuseness regarding the real feelings of the person liked. Moreover, liking in a classroom can easily be perceived as favouritism, and this is likely to be a disruptive element in student-teacher relationships. A more neutral approach (warm, but not aloof or judicial) is likely to diffuse constructive attitudes throughout a group, with a better prospect of enhancing the self-image of all.

The word *acceptance*, used in previous paragraphs, is more inclusive than *liking*, and probably is a better general word to describe the relationship that might result in empathic understanding. This kind of understanding should not be identified with rational understanding. A teacher may attempt to diagnose a student's behaviour with a view to making a judgement and prescribing some form of treatment, without having a truly personal relationship with the student. On the other hand a teacher who has such a relationship may wish to use rational diagnostic methods. His attitude towards the information so gained is, however, less likely to be judgemental. This point has important implications for the assessment of students—a topic to be dealt with later.

Empathic understanding is, of course, likely to develop and be expressed more in teacher-to-student encounters than in a class situation. Class teaching does not prevent the occurrence of empathy with individual children; it just makes it harder. With many teachers the habitual handling of the class as a whole leads to diminished regard for the importance of getting to know the perspective of those being taught. It is not that teachers as a group are unduly egocentric, but that their usual pedagogical style leads them (unwittingly) to embrace an excessive preoccupation with their own thought processes (relating to subjects). This produces a form of behaviour that is akin to egocentricity when it is expressed in terms of relationships with students.

Whether students actually learn more when this empathic understanding exists is hard to prove. But it is not unreasonable to expect that their attitude to learning is likely to be more wholesome, constructive and enduring because of it. If this is so, it is an achievement of crucial importance, if success in education is to be judged by the momentum it can create in people to continue their own development in a creative and critical spirit.

The discussion so far has rested on psychological evidence—both that presented in earlier chapters and on the views of Morris and Rogers. It would be appropriate to consider also the evidence of a leading educational administrator, Sir Alec Clegg. Clegg's name in education in England is something of a household word. He has not only led a major movement in his own education authority, but, by articulating and publicising its problems and its successes, he has had an influence well beyond it. The balance that he has been able to keep between idealism and practicality is a major source of his authority. He believes that the teaching of facts and skills has been over-emphasised, and that existential goals such as the enjoyment of fine writing, the vision of good and evil in the world, and the beauty of craftsmanship, are just as important as the skills of writing, the knowledge of history, and the artistic skills that underlie them.

Clegg has reported examples from schools in Yorkshire of striking achievements in creative expression by children, many of whom come from impoverished backgrounds.[9] He has also attempted to analyse the qualities of the varied teachers who were able to stimulate such work. It is of particular interest to the case presented here that half of the fourteen qualities he lists directly relate to the personal relationship between the teacher and his students. These are listed as follows:

1. They are compassionate people who believe that there is good in every child, however repellent he may seem.
2. They may be quite inexpert in the use of an expressive medium such as writing or painting or modelling, but they are sensitive to what that medium can do for children.
3. They know how to question and criticise in ways that will encourage rather than repress.
4. They can share the multifarious experiences of children in ways which establish a bond of trust between themselves and those whom they teach.
5. They know how to engineer success for the child who stands in need of it, and how to protect a child against perpetual failure.
6. They know when to step in and help, and when to hold back and let the child find out.
7. They are constantly refreshed by the freshness which they can induce in their pupils.

Clegg believes that the teaching qualities that draw out the best expressive work of the child induce a zest and eagerness that cannot fail to have an effect on the child's general intellectual growth, but that this rarely happens in reverse.

This section may be appropriately concluded on this same practical note by quoting the comments of a colleague—a very successful teacher, unusually sensitive to the need to recognise the individuality of each student. The objectives he sets for himself to keep his teaching at a personal level are listed as follows:

1. To try to talk to each student each day, in class or out of it, about something of importance to him.
2. To try to listen to each student so that he has the opportunity to put forward his viewpoints, interests, successes, failures.
3. To try to give each student the opportunity to do something each day that he is proud of and that is worthwhile to him and to others.
4. To try to give each student the chance to do something better than he did it the day before, particularly in an area that seems important for his success in school.

It has been pointed out in Chapter 1 that the child's self-concept is one of his most significant personality traits, and that how he views himself and his role in his immediate social setting will determine, in large measure, his strivings and achievements. It is because of this that the quality of personal relationships in school is so important.

4.2 The Need to Motivate Students' Learning by Taking Account of Their Personal Values and Interests

The activity of the teacher is specified in the first place by the character of his partner.[10]

This dictum of Oakeshott's applies with obvious relevance when the character in question is the student's motivation for learning, and it is clear that the appropriateness of the teacher's activity will depend, among other things, on his knowledge of this motivation.

To be able to deal with each student in a way that takes account of his personal values and interests (developed for the most part outside the school), and that relates them to school tasks, is asking a great deal, and in practice it may only be partially successful. Yet it is the best guide for a teacher to follow.

An alternative is to invent systems of rewards and punishments. At best these are likely to be effective in only a limited way, and to lose their force when the student moves out of the school's influence; at worst they are actually harmful, either acting as a disincentive, or substituting trivial for serious objectives. John Holt has written with feeling about this—

> We destroy the disinterested (I do *not* mean *un*interested) love of learning in children, which is so strong when they are small, by encouraging and compelling them to work for petty and contemptible rewards—gold stars, or papers marked 100 and tacked to the wall . . .'[11]

Holt's judgement may seem unduly harsh, particularly to those who see at least a defensible short-term benefit in praise and censure in dealing with children. Also, his implication that it is only the experience of school, rather than that of outside influences that destroys the child's disinterested love of learning, requires some modification in the light of the complex aetiology of motivation outlined in Chapter 1. But his message is clear and important: learning should be encouraged for its intrinsic interest and value to the individual.

To describe the motivation of learning as a process of interpreting, guiding and mobilising a child's drives and interests may give the impression that it is exclusively a matter of tapping and harnessing an existing force, rather than trying to establish a new one. It is, of course, both. A child's existing pattern of drives is a product of development, and its growth and modification will also be a product of development.

Education influences this process in two ways: by opening up new interests for the student, and by fostering rational processes of thought that encourage him to subject existing values to critical assessment. Thus, to new skills and knowledge that the student acquires, are added new or modified interests, values, attitudes and expectations. For some students, particularly at senior secondary level, the changes in value systems learnt earlier in home and social group may be strong and enduring enough to change the course of their life.

A careful analysis of the complex motivational elements of personality was made in Chapter 1. These included the concepts of *need* (particularly the need for achievement and the need for affiliation), *values* and *attitudes, aspirations* and *expectations*, and the integrated concept of *self*. Chapter 2 dealt with various manifestations of the self in maladjusted children. Individual differences in these sources of motivation, and their implications for teachers were also discussed. These can be accepted by the reader as being part of these guidelines, and there is no need to retrace the same ground in this section.

What is attempted here is to supplement the points already made, particularly with respect to achievement and affiliation needs, and to relate the earlier discussion of values to the educational values (intellectual, aesthetic, social and moral) to which the school is inescapably committed in attempting to interpret and transmit culture.

Achievement and Affiliation Needs

Achievement motivation has been described as a striving to excel, either because of a pride in accomplishment, or a desire to avoid failure which might bring shame and embarrassment. The affiliation need is a concern for seeking friendly relationships and for being approved of by people who are considered to be important to the person.

It could be assumed that the need to achieve to avoid failure is really a version of the affiliation need. In such cases the basis of striving is to gain the approval or avoid the censure of people whom one regards as important. Thus, the student may work hard to please his parents, or to meet their expectations of him, because he loves or fears them. A dramatic example of this in literature is to be found in A.J. Cronin's novel *Hatter's Castle*. Nessie is spurred on to do well in her vital scholarship examination to please her father, James Brodie. The father's concern about her success in school is inspired more by his obsessive competitiveness with the son of a business rival than by unselfish love for his daughter. As the pressure on her to do well mounts, her fear of failure also grows, reaching neurotic proportions. The climax comes immediately after her failure to win the coveted scholarship becomes known. She has hanged herself in her room.

Fear of failure does not reach such grim proportions for most of us, but it is probably an element in most people's striving for achievement. There are a few who have won invulnerability by immersion in tasks which are intrinsically satisfying, and who, accordingly, are quite independent of social approval. There are a few who achieve it by dropping out of competitive society, gaining peace of mind by creating their own mode of life, whether alone, or in a group with like-minded people. For most, however, recognition in some form, from some people (peers, elders, authority figures, etc.), and to some degree, plays a part in achievement motivation.

Since it is apparent from the comments above that achievement motivation is usually a complex product, involving both intrinsic interest and recognition from others, keeping these elements in balance is an important task for the teacher in his handling of motivation. Relating schoolwork to the student's pattern of striving for achievement is an obvious formula for success for the teacher; but it is equally obvious that school tasks are not the only ones that interest children, and that not all school tasks are equally appealing. Considering the range of possible interests and values that schools deal with in their various subjects and activities, it is to be expected that only some of these will appeal to individual students, and that for many children the extrinsic motives of approval and disapproval are needed as a spur to effort, at least at some stage of their development. It is this element that needs to be kept carefully in balance if a wholesome form of striving is to be encouraged.

Spindler was quoted in Chapter 1 as claiming that the value system of youth is 'emergent' rather than 'traditional', and that these emergent values stress sociability and conformity rather than the work-success ethic and a striving for independence and originality. Riesman's similar reference to 'other-directed' behaviour has already been commented on. These suggestions are alarming, not because of the departure from traditional values, but because of the serious threat that these 'emergent' values represent to character development—particularly where this is dependent on adventurousness in thought and action. The influence of the 'others' weakens children's confidence in their own skill and judgement, and sets up statistical norms (popular opinion) as the major imperatives to action. Some of the most bizarre examples of 'other-direction' are the various manifestations of teenage hysteria in the entertainment field. These may be relatively harmless (and good for business), but when the same mentality invades serious intellectual endeavour and aesthetic standards, the risks are great indeed. Riesman's account of the development of 'other-direction' suggests an element of inevitability, as it moves like a Greek drama towards a tragic climax— '. . . men are created different; they lose their social freedom and their individual autonomy in seeking to become like each other'.[12]

The social influences that shape this development are complex and interrelated: affluence, urbanisation, the decline in family size, the weakening of family influence, the pervasiveness of radio and television, the breakdown in privacy, and the economic shift from the predominance of primary and secondary industry to that of tertiary activity (service industries, entertainment, etc.) in which persuasion and other marketable expressions of personality replace material achievement.

It is distasteful to an educationist to be asked to accept the idea of inevitable outcomes of children's development from social forces outside his control. In a sense, the whole educational enterprise is an attempt to swim against the stream, to help strengthen each child's capacity for autonomy in the face of influences (both from outside and within) that tend to constrain it. Thus, the teacher's approach to the child's motivation should emphasise more the achievement motive, and restrain appeals to praise and blame. This statement may suggest that the relationship between teacher and student should be cold and formal. Enough has been said in the previous section to indicate that this is by no means what is implied. All learning should be conducted in an environment that is supportive. The student should be able to take it for granted that he is accepted as a person, that his effort is appreciated, and that the lack of it is a matter of concern to the teacher. This social climate is a *sine qua non* of an educational situation. But this can be established without sentimentality. Some teachers, particularly of young children, give the impression that even the simplest of correct responses by a child merits praise. Responses such as 'Good girl', 'You're a clever boy', or 'I'm very pleased with you' are used almost meaninglessly, but strengthen the child's expectation that everything done should be recognised and rewarded. The sparing use of praise, in itself, does not create a more favourable climate for strengthening achievement as a motive, but it paves the way for it. Very young children, being more egocentrically inclined, have a greater dependence on the teacher's approval than older children, and it is important that the judicious rationing of merely sentimental praise be begun early so that the dependence pattern is weakened.

By the time the child is in the primary school the intrinsic challenge and interest of school tasks should be strengthening, and the use of praise and blame become subsidiary. The main measures that the teacher can use to promote intrinsic interest are the curriculum itself and the use of constructive criticism which involves analysis of the task in hand and assessment of the steps taken to carry it out. This meaning of criticism is quite different from reproof; it is, rather, the evaluative aspect of achievement. By secondary school, constructive criticism, as an instrument of clarification and assessment, should be the major reaction of the teacher to children's work, and of course it assumes even greater importance at the tertiary level.

To view achievement in this way, with constraint on the use of social approval, and emphasis on the quality of effort and performance, is idealistic, and assumes a higher level of maturity of development in students than is commonly found, but the idealistic nature of all the guidelines is recognised, and has been pointed out earlier. How well the value system of the student equips him to pursue an increasingly autonomous course of action in school depends on the degree to which he has come to accept educational values. This point is taken up in the next section.

Educational Values and Student Motivation

The pursuit of knowledge, skill and taste has an essential moral quality, as well as requiring the acquisition of techniques. This is the code or value system underlying educational endeavour. It is his dedication to this code that is the most characteristic feature of the genuine scholar. Others *use* knowledge (for example in industry), but they do not necessarily accept the code or discipline by which that knowledge was established in the first place. In cases where knowledge is exploited for personal or sectional gain, the moral standards that guided the original research may be ignored, or displaced by considerations of power or expediency. The controversy about atomic power is an example of this.

The morality of scientific thought lies in the acceptance of scientific method. One can have some scientific knowledge without accepting its rules of inquiry, but the clear aim of scientific education includes the acceptance of these rules, as well as appropriate techniques of inquiry, factual knowledge and the conceptual structures of the various sciences. Similarly the teaching of the social sciences, the humanities and arts involve the acquisition of appropriate discipline—the standards of procedure. Social sciences, particularly, which touch the lives of students perhaps more directly than other subjects, call for careful adherence to objective standards, and sincerity of judgement where objectivity is in doubt. Expediency, self-seeking, cynical distortion of the facts, prejudice and ignorance surround the students in public life and in business. If those who teach the social sciences fail to teach the discipline by which conclusions are reached, the major value of these subjects will have been lost.

The difficulty of overcoming prejudice with children is amusingly illustrated in the following anecdote from an English slum school. The cautionary tale is now twenty years old, but the theme of racial intolerance is at least as much alive now as it was then.

MASTER SNIPE ON RACE RELATIONS
'Forriners is stoopid bastuds'.

That was, so to speak, the key sentence in Snipe's composition, and it did not dismay us. Rather the contrary. It was the kind of sentiment one would expect of Snipe, and it was forthright, honest, and no more malicious than any other of his opinions. Snipe is capable of making libellous accusations against his own mother; has, in fact, made them from time to time.

The point about his verdict on foreigners is that it was not peculiar to him, but a laconic summary of the reaction of the whole class. That is why we were so pleased with it. It was unequivocal, it was typical, and it was unfavourable. It was the ideal starting point for our project on race relations. We could reasonably hope that after a term's brain-washing Snipe's views would be equally unequivocal, equally typical, but quite different.

Our project had no official sanction or backing. It was a purely private affair, its aim being to combat, in some small degree, the endemic xenophobia of our pupils. We hoped to induce in them a slightly more tolerant attitude towards races other than their own; the human race for instance. Subtopia may be able to afford generous ideals and large visions of mankind united, but down by the docks all creation is divided into Them and Us. There is no question of colour in this. Brown and black and yellow skins are included among those who belong, though the dockside community has its own family tensions. Foreigners are those who do not belong, whether from over the sea or, it sometimes seems, from the other side of town. Foreigners in the usual sense are, of course, well known to our boys, who see them every day of their lives: little brown deckhands, Chinese cooks, shambling Americans, big Scandinavians, and a host of others. Our boys know, too, how to deal with them. You sell them inferior clothing or drink at superior prices, and keep as much of the change as their unfamiliarity with our currency will safely allow. Hence, perhaps, Snipe's description.

Nor did our project follow the usual careful, scientific pattern. We decided, for lack of both time and inclination, to dispense with those formidable before and after questionnaires beloved of international organisations and institutes of education; questionnaires which test what is known as 'attitudes', and usually succeed in proving that children who have studied a subject for a term or two know slightly more about it than children who haven't. Irresponsibly and un-professionally we took this for granted. Besides, we couldn't put the usual questions to our boys: 'Would you be prepared to marry a Negro?' for instance. After all, quite a number of their parents already had, and it was frequently the Negro who had second thoughts about the wisdom of the alliance.

So we merely invited our guinea-pigs, at the beginning of term, to write a composition on 'Foreigners' and then got on with the treatment. 'Project' is no doubt too pompous a word for what we did. There is no series of special topics, no concerted study of any one nation or group of nations. We simply angled our lessons on all possible subjects to make the boys aware that other nations and other people existed and had contributed something of importance to the scheme of things. The idea was to widen their horizons, or rather to urge them to climb over the horizon and register the fact that there was something on the other side. We sought to maroon them on scattered bits of the circumference of knowledge and let them grope their own way back to the gritty streets and oily waters of home. In passing, it should be noted that it is of little use anyway to start at the centre with our boys, and work outwards. Every new teachers determines to begin with what boys already know, and build his edifice of education, brick by progressive brick, on that. And every teacher abandons the idea for the same reason—the impossibility of ever reaching the starting point.

During that term, I think, some good work was done, without the boys becoming too aware of the fact. A rudimentary acquaintance was struck with Greece and Rome, and the fact established that Hadrian's Wall had not been built by Marlon Brando. The revelation was made, little by little, in order not to shock the boys too much, that foreigners had in their time contributed some items of value to the world's treasury of art and music and literature and science and useful inventions. Most of this they had to take on trust from the teachers, and it probably did not worry them overmuch anyway. But foreign intrusion into the world of sport was a fact of which they were already humiliatingly aware. They had read about and seen films of Hungarian footballers and Russian athletes and American boxers. When these things were mentioned, Snipe, who was going through an anti-sportive phase since being dropped from the school team, gave a great sneering sniff and pretended to read a library book. The others mostly rationalized. 'Well, sir, we taught the Hungry'uns all they know. Them Russians, sir—you know what they are . . .' The Americans, more familiar from films, they hardly regarded as foreigners at all. Americans were Us with more pocket money, gayer clothes, even more detestable cops. They could be tolerated for providing a solacing celluloid dream world, an understandable materialistic paradise, just attainable in imagination at least.

Medicine caused us some trouble. We brought in the Greeks again, and Pasteur, and even Freud, and several other exotic benefactors of mankind, but found considerable resistance to the view that foreigners had contributed anything of note to this sphere of human knowledge. The reason, we discovered, was Billy Green, who had converted all his friends to his own unshakable belief that all medical advance stemmed exclusively from his dad, a cheerful and beery character who, every Saturday for 20 years, had purveyed at the back of the city market a universal remedy known as 'Green's Gravel Pills'.

Still, setbacks of some kind were to be expected. On the whole, they were remarkably few. We managed, by and large, to do foreigners proud. Even history lessons extolled the achievements of foreigners, instead of presenting the inhabitants of other lands as mere adjuncts to the story of the island race, the hapless recipients of English missiles. By the end of the term we were all reasonably satisfied that our boys were no longer confined in the shackles of ignorant nationalism, and that their patriotism would be all the

sounder for being better informed. They had at least an inkling of
the glory that was Greece and the grandeur that was Rome, the
civilization of France, the genius of Germany and Russia, the cultures
ancient and modern, of China and India; as well as an appreciation
of the debt we owe to these countries and others, and of the
importance of approaching maturity in the younger nations of the
modern world.

We set, with confidence, the end-of-term composition on 'Foreigners'. Again we were not disappointed. And again it was Snipe
who summed up, in one pregnant sentence, the change of attitude
that had taken place. He wrote:

'Forriners is kunnin bastuds'.[13]

The challenge to schools, then, in regard to the motivation of their
students is abundantly clear, if difficult—to seek their commitment to
the intellectual, aesthetic, and social values that underlie the main areas
of knowledge. Its chance of success, as with other facets of the school's
work, is likely to depend not only on how effectively this goal is pursued
in school, but also on the educative influences playing upon students
out of school and in their subsequent life, and on the maturing of their
own reflections on their value system.

In placing such high importance on these educational values, it should
be stressed that they are not basically remote from ordinary experience,
as is often suggested by the separation conceptually of academic and
practical affairs, and by the fact that in actual practice the culture of
the school often becomes divorced from the out-of-school life of many,
if not most, of its students. The young child's unprompted, and often
unguided, attempts to understand his environment, although limited
somewhat by animistic thinking, are not basically different in motivation
or method from that of the older student's more sophisticated formal
inquiry. Objectivity and regard for factual evidence are present, even
though not explicitly formulated. So are accuracy of observation and
rejection of fantasy (even though this occurs only gradually in some
cases). In social inquiry, in various manipulative skills, bodily movement, construction, and artistic expression there is a similar impulse
towards accuracy, as in a cultivated adult, even though the canons of
taste and expression are rudimentary. In short, the value system of
educational endeavour is not something apart—a goal attainable by only
a few. That it is often believed to be so is due to the competition of
stronger claims on the allegiance of children as they grow up, or to
failure on the part of the school to relate its work to life outside it
in a way that makes clear the relevance, importance, and usefulness
of educational values.

Competition from alternative values is probably the most serious impediment to the development of educational values. Educational values, as has been stressed, are distinguished by the desire to understand, to achieve high standards of performance, and to think and act creatively. Material values, on the other hand, are concerned with the acquisition of possessions, with the increase in prestige or power, or the gratification of personal pleasures. If these compete with scholastic values, as they commonly do, it is the material values that are likely to prevail. This pessimistic judgement about the success of education may be offset to some extent by the observation that progress in the spread of educational values through popular education and their expression in adult society is bound to be slow. It could be added that it is already not without its successes. The strengthening of altruistic movements such as a heightened concern for the environment is an obvious example.

It is motivation in this sense, of strengthening each individual's capacity to value and apply civilised standards, and not merely to capitalise on its knowledge and techniques, that the school must be concerned with. Any other interpretation is either ephemeral or trivial.

4.3 Teaching As the Encouragement of Active Student Participation in School Tasks

A good deal has already been stated or implied in previous sections about the style of teaching that is appropriate to cope with individual differences. Teaching is a complex activity, and it is to be expected that in discussing its organisational aspects, the curriculum, discipline, and other topics, reference would be made to the teacher's methods. We now take up the discussion of these in more detail.

A teacher's methods are very much a product of personal development through experience. He is likely to be influenced by his own early experiences as a student, by his training, and his early years of teaching when he is experimenting with approaches that seem to suit him, and seem to work. He is influenced also by ideas from books, and from other teachers, either because they confirm his own comfortable habits, or because they unsettle and challenge him. But the main influences in his development of a philosophy of teaching style are his personal and professional values, and particularly his attitude to children and to knowledge.

If his attitude towards children is one of acceptance of differences, and a readiness to treat each as unique, all the personal relationships that make individual teaching a reality are present. He will enjoy talking to students in and out of school, and be genuinely interested in their affairs. He will be courteous to all children, and compassionate to those in trouble. He will avoid sarcasm, and be disinclined to compare children, preferring to deal with each in his own way. He will be disposed to deal with learning at a personal level, rather than by mass teaching; he will accept that children will achieve success in different ways, and will avoid imposing his own priorities on them.

If he sees knowledge as an ongoing process on inquiry, rather than dogmatically as a fixed set of prescriptions, he is likely to develop a teaching style that emphasises individual learning. He will see knowledge as activity of thought, and not as something that can be passed on to another like an object; he will appreciate the vastness of what can be explored in the environment, and hence the wide choice of curriculum material open to children. He will emphasise the methods of knowledge as a gateway to factual knowledge rather than as ends in themselves. Accordingly he will be concerned that children learn to read, but equally concerned about the use to which the skill is put; he will be concerned that children learn the method of scientific inquiry, but not restrict their use of it to an abstract body of ideas called chemistry or physics. He will make no pretentions towards omniscience, and will have no status problems in admitting his own ignorance or uncertainty, and exploring questions along with his students. In short, he will see knowledge as an active inquiry into a bewilderingly complex environment. By the very nature of this task it is necessarily individual, although there are guidelines and help available from others.

The methods used by teachers who are oriented towards individualised teaching are difficult to express in standardised form, but they do possess a common spirit, and make use of broadly similar strategies, even though the detail may be personal. The strategies are listed below, and are discussed in succeeding sections:

1. Stimulating expression
2. Making use of differences in cognitive style
3. Stimulating creativity

Stimulating Expression

Systems-type models of teaching that emphasise 'input' by teachers and subsequent 'output' by students rely heavily on *impression* as the major learning response of students. Learning through impression is, of course, important, but it can be criticised as tending towards passivity on the part of students. This need not be so, as attending, listening, watching, imitating, and other modes of behaviour associated with impression are forms of activity, and require concentration and effort. Lowered concentration and wandering attention are, however, common enough, and affect learning adversely.

An associated phenomenon is servile learning, resulting either in an uncritical acceptance of the ideas of other people, or a confusion between one's ability to follow a teacher's exposition and the capacity to reproduce or reconstruct it afterwards. Teachers who spend considerable time in planning suitable lessons, and effort in presenting them, often receive a very low return in student response for their investment.

The systems model is commonly used as a class method, and, as such, often fails to secure each student's involvement and acceptance of responsibility. In the hands of a dull or dogmatic teacher, or one who is so insecure in his own knowledge that he cannot afford to risk straying from his prepared material, student involvement can be at a very low level indeed. Charles Dickens has pilloried this type of teaching in many of his novels. This picture from *Hard Times* of a 'sit-stillery' type of classroom with tiered seating is a good example—

> The inclined plane of little vessels arranged in order, ready to have imperial gallons of facts poured into them until they were full to the brim.[14]

Appealing to *expression* virtually reverses the systems model. It emphasises output from the beginning. Input follows output, not leads it, as the student's need for assistance is progressively revealed. Expression also enhances the student's acceptance of the task, and his sense of discipline and responsibility in discharging it. The skill of the teacher in this kind of situation lies in creating the conditions which lead to the activities (the merging of curriculum and method), in ensuring that available resources are put to good use, in giving assistance to each student as it is needed, and in encouraging him to a point where a helpful assessment of achievement is possible.

The appeal to expression as a criterion of method does not lead directly to clear-cut methods of teaching. It is, rather, a broad guideline which can be interpreted in many different ways by teachers, according to their preferences, the maturity of the children and their experience in independent work, the subject involved, and the facilities available.

One fairly systematic form of it is project work, in which a problem is identified, a strategy of inquiry is worked out, tasks are allocated to members of the project team, and a written report or other statement of results is planned. This is an inquiry, discovery, or research strategy. Students tackle a realistic problem, with appropriate methods, and pursue it in an independent and responsible way. Projects are particularly suitable for scientific-type studies, for example, studies of the physical or biological environment, or for historical, geographical or sociological studies of the social environment. They provide for the student a disciplined form of learning, akin to that of the research worker who is trying to break new ground, and who is personally involved with the task in hand.

In this connection it is relevant to stress again the connection between pedagogical method and the methods used in the various disciplines to create new knowledge—a point made earlier in discussing the curriculum. Activities involving inquiry can exercise the student in the research methods appropriate to a particular form of knowledge, as well as lead him to the discovery of new facts. This skill in inquiry (whether applied to scientific or social phenomena) is a valuable possession, undoubtedly more lasting and useful than specific factual knowledge. Facts may be forgotten, or subsumed under more inclusive ideas gained later. But the methodology of inquiry gives a student an insight into the grammar of knowledge—its structural rules, as well as its factual elements.

Thus the teacher can capitalise on the methods of the scholar (first-hand observation, the use of original sources, repeated measurement, experimentation, analyses of data, inference, verification, and the like), interpreting them in ways within the grasp of the children concerned, and in connection with problems within their experience. He can likewise encourage children to observe the scholar's rules (objectivity, caution, thoroughness, etc.). Thus a powerful method of learning can be transformed into a powerful form of teaching—a striking example of the expression model.

Forms of expression in language are also worthy of special mention. The close association of thought and language has been discussed in Chapter 3, and it is clear that the freeing of children's intelligence can be stimulated by helping them to gain a better command of verbal expression. This is, of course, achieved in part by inputs from reading and listening, but it requires, most of all, active expression in writing and speaking. The responsibility for explicit formulation of ideas in written and spoken language both reinforces the thought process involved and reveals the need for greater clarity where this is lacking. It is both an exercise in logical thought and a test of it.

There is at present much criticism of children's competence in basic scholastic skills. The following statement by Leonie Kramer expresses this very positively:

> There is a noticeable falling off in students' capacity to argue logically and coherently. Many students have little understanding of what a logical argument is . . . Secondly there are the much publicised grammatical failings of students. This whole area of technical

deficiency is of course, important, but it is always related to deeper failings in understanding, clear thinking, and accurate reading . . . Thirdly, many students have a very limited and impoverished vocabulary. They lack the range of words which makes for discrimination in thinking and comprehending. They bring to their writing and speaking a great deal of colloquial jargon which is a debased form of expression and does not permit them to clarify their ideas.[15]

It is not proposed to enter this debate on educational standards here; but it is undeniable that effectiveness in the communication of thought, particularly thought that is conceptually sophisticated, depends on the control of the vocabulary and structure of the language used. Children do have different forms of language for different occasions, and there is no harm in this if they are able to distinguish the needs of the different occasions. They do differ also in their language style (through home and neighbourhood influences), and in their capacity to develop the alternative style of the formal structure of disciplined inquiry and exposition of complex ideas, and need to be helped individually to do so. This development will not easily come from mere exhortation on the part of teachers, nor from similar models of it in the student's reading (where it is relatively easy for the student to impose his own language patterns on the materials through a translation process in inner speech). It has a better chance if it is expressed in written or spoken form, thus providing a public setting for what is essentially a public form of expression.

Students' opportunities for sustained speaking (as distinct from answering questions) are decidedly limited, and it is a promising change in modern practice to allow more opportunity for them to speak to others by the increased participation of adults other than the teacher (teacher aides, resource teachers, remedial teachers, parents, etc.) in the school's work. Opportunities for written expression are easier to make, but care needs to be taken not to divorce this from the rest of the school work. 'Compositions', done as separate exercises, can easily become artificial in substance and stilted in form. The best compositions are those that deal with the great variety of ideas that come up in the pursuit of school tasks, whether these be literary, scientific or practical. To express clearly in speech or writing how to make a cake (or better still, how the student actually made a cake), to write an informative letter to a friend or firm, or to report lucidly on the findings of an environmental survey, is to use composition in the most useful and instructive way. Straining after effect usually spoils children's writing or speech. Style comes best by striving for simplicity and lucidity.

Language, of course, is not the only vehicle of expression, important as it is. Children use other forms, some symbolic, some concrete. Examples are bodily movement, the use of colour and sound, constructive activities, and mathematical relationships of quantity and space. Indeed for many children some of these are a preferred kind of 'language'—particularly as a mode of creative expression. We return to this in a later section.

Making Use of Differences in Cognitive Style

In Chapter 3 the notion of cognitive style was raised. This is the preferred mode of learning and acting that children show in handling school tasks. The variations are extensive and significant, as can be seen from the following summary:

1. *Sensory orientation.* The student's preference for aural, visual, tactile, kinaesthetic, and other sensory modes.
2. *Responsive mode.* His characteristic response pattern, for example, his preference for solitary or social activities, or for reflective criticism or acceptance of ideas presented to him.
3. *Thinking pattern.* His preference for deliberative, methodical, reflective, or intuitive pattern.
4. *Field dependence/independence.* His ability to consider an object or relationship as being only within the context presented, or to relate it to other contexts.
5. *Mode of categorisation.* His preference for classification on the basis of objective features, such as size and shape, common elements, of common relationships.
6. *Bruner's modes of thought structure.* His preference for *enactive, iconic,* or *symbolic* forms of thought.

This list, although formidable, is almost certainly only a crude approximation to the much greater range of differences in style that do exist, particularly when subtle nuances of personality are taken into account.

In teaching children the teacher is faced with this wide variation in their preferred modes of thinking, learning and acting, as well as with the range of their interests, motives, values and aptitudes. The problem is further compounded by the fact that he, too, has his preferred modes of thought and probably gives unwitting stress to them in his teaching, thus appealing more to some students than to others. This suggests that teachers should become more aware of the unconscious bias in their own presentation of work. It is commonly believed that teachers incline towards a form of thought that is *symbolic* rather than *enactive* (to use Bruner's terms), and that their intellectual background predisposes them to use a verbal, rather than a visual or concrete mode.

While the fact of variation in cognitive style among students and teachers obviously complicates teaching method, it also has the advantage that strengths of style can be capitalised on. The pedagogical problem is well posed by Riessman—

In everybody's style, there are certain strengths, and each of us has his own Achilles heel. The issue in developing a powerful change in a person is related to how one gets to the Achilles heel and how one utilizes the strengths. This is the central problem of the strategy of style.[16]

The attempt to relate teaching methods to student characteristics has been pursued most vigorously in America where the dream of creating a scientific pedagogy persists most strongly. Among others, it has given rise to a vigorous movement labelled *attribute* (or *aptitude*)-*treatment intervention* (ATI for short), the attempt to match individual differences in learning styles (attributes) with appropriate teaching styles (treatments). The movement has stimulated much research, but success has been elusive. According to Cronbach and Snow, progress towards the goal of identifying and understanding ATI has been slight, but they add—

One reaction to this regrettable state of affairs would be to abandon ATI research on the grounds that such effects are non-existent. We urge against this defeatist course. It is inconceivable to us that humans, differing in as many ways as we do, do not differ with respect to the educational treatment that fits each one best. To abandon the ATI model is to assume that there is only one path towards educational development, and that individual differences have no implications save the fatalistic one, telling the educator that some pupils will advance more rapidly than others, no matter what he does.[17]

It may appear to be presumptuous in this brief discussion, in view of the considerable thought given to the ATI model, to suggest why it has been so unproductive, and to question whether its abandonment need lead a teacher to accept the fatalistic conclusion that his intervention is of little or no account in influencing the progress of students.

It appears that the terms being matched in the ATI model (teacher intervention on the one side and student differences on the other) are conceived much more formally in research than would occur in actual teaching situations. Instruction is conceived in system terms that can be generalised, standardised, and programmed (either in a person or a machine). Differences in students are expressed in categories, when they should be expressed in dimensions, providing for an infinite variety of gradings. By a process of hardening of the categories (often aided by the statistical methods imposed on the data during research), the categories become styles, and the actual behaviour of children recedes into the background. This behaviour is almost certainly more flexible than the categories suggest; it allows overlap, interaction and substitution in the handling of different kinds of experience, and indeed of similar experience at different times.

The expectation that for different learning styles there is a mirror image of instructional style in educational technology is unrealistic, and seems bound to fail. The formal means-end models of instruction makes sense in didactic teaching situations (narration, exposition, demonstration, and the like) where the overriding purpose of the teacher is to achieve an explicit objective; but they are inappropriate in more informal situations that allow students individual interpretation, variation in pace, and other features of self-expression. In these situations the great need is for flexible, not predictable, behaviour on the part of the teacher. His responses need to deal sensitively with the varied and changing needs of the students.

There is certainly no need for a teacher to take a fatalistic view of this facilitating role. On the contrary, the personal help that is given in each transaction with students is valuable, and its effects in particular cases may be incalculable. But by the very nature of the situation, the encounter is a personal one, and cannot be generalised into a method.

What, then, is the significance of cognitive styles for the teacher who wishes to direct his teaching as much as possible towards meeting individual needs? A number of answers can be given, and each is important.

First, the opportunity for a student to use a preferred style of learning is increased if the curriculum is conceived in broad and flexible terms. The greater scope for the exercise of different cognitive styles is obvious if tasks include such varied opportunities as reasoning, analytical writing, creative writing, factual memorising, mathematical analysis and computing, constructing with a wide range of materials, musical performance, dramatic expression, painting, bodily movement, etc. To cater for differences in style by multiplying the opportunities for choice is obviously much less systematic than by diagnosing the cognitive styles of children and devising for them (if one can) an appropriate form of lesson planning; but it is probably more realistic, and more likely to succeed—at least for some.

Second (a variation on the first), if an integrated approach to curriculum is used, there are many opportunities for the same task or topic to be treated in different ways by different students according to this preferred style. For example, an episode in Australian history might be expressed visually by the artistic minded, in constructive activities such as the reproduction of historical buildings or dioramas, in narrative by those preferring written expression, in role playing, musical composition, and so on. Each deals with the same reality, and each in his own way.

Third, while the teacher may find it difficult to *plan* for the differences which children do, in fact, exhibit in their approach to a task, he can be *alert* in anticipation of them, and deal with them constructively— acknowledging them by pointing out to the student how other children are handling a task, by suggesting alternative or additional ways of acting to increase the child's range of responses. A child who expresses a set of quantitative relationships graphically might be encouraged to express the same ideas in prose; one with preferred verbal facility might be encouraged to express ideas visually in pictures or kinaesthetically in dramatic expression. Acknowledging the fact of preferred cognitive styles in itself does not imply either the desirability of reinforcing them or of encouraging other styles. Much depends on the child's background of opportunity for expression. The preferred cognitive style of a disadvantaged child for example, may have developed mainly by default because those who had the opportunity to stimulate him to experiment with alternative forms of expression failed to do so. In such cases new experiences and opportunities at school could enlarge his capacity to respond. Other children might have had the opportunity to base their preferred style on adequate experience.

In summary it could be said that the critical factors in capitalising on variations in cognitive style are these:

1. An understanding on the part of the teacher of the kind of variation in style that can occur, and a sensitiveness to its occurrence in particular cases
2. The provision of a rich curriculum that offers scope for the exercise of different learning styles
3. The teacher's sense of timing, which enables him to suggest alternative learning styles in cases where this would assist the student.

There is no doubt that whatever success the teacher may have in appealing to the preferred cognitive styles of students he is likely to improve the effectiveness of students' learning, and also their sense of satisfaction in this achievement.

Stimulating Creativity

As has been pointed out in Chapter 3, thought and consequent action may be convergent or divergent. Convergent thought leads towards an expected or required conclusion, guided by an authority such as a teacher, or by the logic of the relationships involved. It leads to known and standard outcomes, provided the correct processes of thought are followed.

By contrast, divergent thinking departs from the known and the expected, being creative rather than reproductive. For example, Lewis Carroll is using thought divergently when he makes Humpty Dumpty say 'When I use a word, it means what I choose it to mean, neither more nor less'.[18] A great deal of the charm of *Alice in Wonderland* and *Through the Looking Glass* is achieved by a similar use of the unexpected. Many other writers rely on the use of divergent thinking for their effects. Another example is this conversation piece from Wilde's play *The Importance of Being Earnest*

> Jack Worthing says to Lady Bracknell: 'I have lost both my parents'. Lady Bracknell answers: 'Both? . . . that seems like carelessness'.[19]

Many forms of humour depend on divergent thinking, as do many artistic effects. It should not be assumed, however, that divergent thinking is restricted to these forms of expression. Scientific and mathematical thinking may also be divergent, although in schools they are usually presented as a set of structured propositions involving mainly convergent thinking. That these propositions have evolved from highly inventive and speculative thought is often forgotten by teachers, and usually not realised by children.

It should be stressed also that divergent thinking is not the same as negativistic thinking, although creative people often do find themselves in opposition to established views. Negativism is usually more akin to dogmatism than creativity, expressing rigidity of thought rather than openness and originality.

Both convergent and divergent thinking should have an accepted place in schoolwork the first in the dissemination of factual knowledge and the practice of logical argument, the second in the encouragement of special interests and originality. Convergent thinking, however, has been dominant, particularly in the secondary school where the curriculum has been conceived as an authoritative fund of knowledge and body of skills to which children should be introduced in the most direct and positive way possible. Creative activities, on the other hand, have frequently been regarded as marginal to the central tasks of the school, and associated mainly with aesthetic subjects and extracurricular activities that are not part of the core of essential studies.

Yet creative expression is obviously the best guarantee that there is of the child's activity of thought. In Thiele's words,[20] creativity in English involves '*making* rather than *having things made, giving out* rather than *taking in*, *contributing* rather than *receiving* and *accepting, activity* rather than *passivity.'* What activities excite the students' creative expression, and the standards achieved in them are, of course, also important, but the learning mode is clearly significant. Adventure has a many-sided appeal to youth, and it ought not be too difficult to capitalise on this in school work. Certainly, a school programme in which creativity had no place would be impoverished indeed.

But can creativity be taught? Guilford's ideas described in Chapter 3 may give a lead in answering this question. He distinguishes between two forms of divergent thinking—*production* (yielding quite new ideas), and *transformation* (yielding new versions or adaptations of existing ideas). It is the second of these which more obviously suggests a methodology, since it is easier to conceive ways of encouraging students to interpret their experience in novel ways than it is to seek ideas which lie outside experience. One can exhort students to be 'creative', but this hardly amounts to a methodology, and in any case it is unlikely to yield anything of value. This is not to say that divergent production will not occur with children (and the point will be taken up later); but it does mean that novel reconstructions of children's own experience are more amenable to intervention and assistance by a teacher than are uniquely new ideas. A teacher can contrive situations and encourage creative responses more readily as an extension of events and experiences that have an element of familiarity both to him and to his students than when working from an unknown base.

The point can be illustrated by examining the type of items used in creativity tests in the research literature.[21] In word association tests the subject is asked to give as many definitions as possible of familiar stimulus words such as 'bolt' and 'brick'. In tests of the uses of things the subject is asked to indicate as many possible uses of an object such as a paper-clip. In tests involving fables, subjects are asked to compose alternative endings, and so on. The starting point is well within the experience of all concerned; the creativity of the individual is measured by his capacity to go beyond this. This approach used in testing underlies most of the suggested methods for encouraging creativity in school work.

T.C. Blythe, for example, states that some of the most successful topics in his experiences with children's creative writing were these everyday ones: 'washing machine', 'spin-drier', 'exams', 'Anzac', 'autumn', 'thoughts after looking at a picture', 'it annoys me', 'the job I dislike most', 'in the garbage bin', 'thunderstorm', 'going home in the rain', 'wet day', 'bathing the baby', 'riding a bike in the wind', 'school's out', 'lunch', and 'watching the sprinkler'. His ground rules for encouraging creative writing are 'choosing topics with more than usual thought and imagination; awakening in every child a lively consciousness of himself and his environment; freeing him from his dependence on 'school English' and on his conditioned desire to write what he thinks his teacher will like; giving him a conviction that creative writing affords him a rare opportunity to make something which is really his, which nobody else could have made, and for which he is completely responsible'.[22]

Margaret Langdon's method of 'intensive writing', is also based on children's experience which is suffused with more than ordinary feeling.[23] Similarly the remarkable record of children's writing presented by Clegg in *The Excitement of Writing* indicates clearly that creative writing in these Yorkshire schools in the sixties was 'neither a luxury allowed by indulgent teachers, nor a form of psychotherapy, but a mode of expression that children readily practise'.[24]

The strategies employed to achieve this were quite simple: frequent opportunity for writing, encouragement by the teacher rather than criticism of minor points of formal accuracy, stress on sincerity of expression rather than on striving after effect, emphasis on wide reading to assist with vocabulary, spelling and punctuation, and correction and criticism by fellow pupils rather than by the teacher. Formal exercises in composition and drill were emphatically rejected. The themes chosen were everyday ones; it was the sincerity of treatment that produced prose that was clear and effective, and that had, in many instances, a sense of style.

There could be no better rebuttal than these compositions of the criticism often made today that allowing children to write creatively leads to work that is unreal in substance and slipshod in form. If we want students to learn to use language effectively for a variety of purposes we are more likely to achieve this by encouraging them to express their own ideas, rather than to reproduce those of others. Certainly the formal requirements of language must be learnt, and for this purpose the writings of others should be studied with care, but formal correctness is of little value to a person who has nothing of significance to say. Stimulating creativity need not be approached as an excursion into fantasy (although this can happen with children), but rather as an attempt to encourage students to identify matters of genuine concern to them, and to make a personal statement about them. The level of originality achieved, when judged on external standards, will obviously vary. It is obvious, too, that few schoolchildren will create new ideas of any great consequence to others. But in seeking to be creative there is at least a chance that students will gain in respect for sincerity of expression, if not in achieving originality. In a society in which banality and insincerity in the media and elsewhere are so common, this would be a significant achievement.

The foregoing discussion of creativity has been restricted to written expression, but it could just as appropriately have been directed towards dramatic art, painting, pottery, woodwork, music, or even the more traditional school subjects such as mathematics and science. Each has its special character, and, in matters of detail, its own methodology, but the general approach outlined is relevant.

It is appropriate also, at this point, to return to the idea of *divergent production*, lest it be thought that inventiveness in schools is conceived only in terms of adaptation or extension of ordinary experience. No doubt children do generate some genuinely new ideas, movements, shapes, sounds, colour combinations, rhythms, etc., without the stimulus of actual experience. These are precious products, and any school must be accounted successful in helping to produce them. It is not at all obvious, however, how such spontaneity can be cultivated or managed.

Probably the most promising approach is to regard creativity as being inherent in all schoolwork, and not as a quality that is restricted to particular subjects or particular lessons. If teachers can create an open climate hospitable to its expression, within a rich and varied curriculum, by stimulating and challenging students to be alert to alternatives to conventional wisdom, whether it be in aesthetic expression or in problem solving, the chances of genuine invention occurring are greatly increased. There is need, also, for teachers to take children's alternative ideas seriously. Clearly, some students are potentially more creative than their teachers, but it is not easy for teachers to accept this.

The fact that there are children who show relatively early a marked flair for a particular activity raises the question whether special provision should be made for them. Although the complex questions of teaching exceptional children have not been dealt with in this book, a brief reference to those creative children generally described as 'gifted' is merited.

The Schools Commission includes the education of these children in its list of priorities for special encouragement under its innovation programme. The point is expressed thus:

. . . provide special educational opportunities to students who have demonstrated their ability or interest in a particular field of study, including scientific, literary, artistic or musical studies.[25]

The Commission's philosophy is that individual differences should be catered for in a way that allows children to remain members of normal school communities. In line with this policy they suggest the following special provisions for gifted children:

1. Where the students' special interest lies within the normal curriculum, there should be greater flexibility in school organisation to allow them opportunity to study at higher levels.

2. Where the special interest lies outside the normal curriculum, the use of resources outside the school should be sought. A radical modification in the individual student's timetable within his normal school would be needed to accommodate such arrangements.

Outside resources envisaged by the Commission include tertiary or other educational institutions, for example, ballet schools; resource people in the community who might be brought into the school; and the creation of special interest centres with highly qualified staff to supplement the work of schools.

The Commission reflects fairly faithfully the egalitarian philosophy that has permeated Australian educational policy generally. By contrast, in many overseas countries provision for gifted children in special schools is accepted practice. However it is done, clearly there is a need in Australia for greater attention to the gifted child. Start, in commenting on a Melbourne survey of the provision made in Australia for teaching gifted children, sums up its findings with this forthright statement—

Patently there is more concern for the under-achievement of the slow child than for the potential waste in the under-achievement of the bright child.[26]

References

1. Morris, *op. cit.*, in ref. no. 13, ch. 5.
2. Holt, J., 1969. *How Children Fail*. Pelican: London, p. 171.
3. Pusey, *op. cit.*, in ref. no. 12, ch. 5.
4. Rogers, Carl, 1969, *Freedom to Learn*, Merrill Publishing Co.: Columbus, p. 103.
5. *Ibid.*, p. 105.
6. Morris, *op. cit.*
7. Buber, *op. cit.*, in ref. no. 17, Introduction.
8. Rogers, *op. cit,*, p. 106.
9. Clegg, A.B., 1976. 'Loaves and Hyacinths'. *New Horizons in Education*, W.E.F., no. 55.
10. Oakeshott, M., 1967. 'Learning and Teaching', in Peters, R.S., *The Concept of Education*, Humanities Press: New York, p. 157.
11. Holt, *op. cit.*, p. 165.
12. Riesman, *op. cit.*, in ref. no. 9, ch. 5, p. 373.
13. *Times Educational Supplement*, 5/4/1957. The author appears only as C.H.
14. Dickens, C. 1854. *Hard Times*, ch. 1.
15. Kramer, L., 1977. *Newsletter*, 16, 1. Australian College of Education, Queensland Chapter: Brisbane.
16. Riessman, Frank, 1964. *Teachers College Record* 65: 484–89.

17. Cronbach, L.J. and Snow, A.E., 1969. 'Individual Differences in Learning Ability As a Function of Instructional Variables'. U.S.O.E. *Final Report,* O.E.C., 4–6–061269–1217: p. 193.
18. Carroll, Lewis 1871. 'Through the Looking Glass', *The Complete Works of Lewis Carroll,* Nonesuch Press: London, p. 214.
19. Wilde, Oscar, 1899. *The Importance of Being Earnest,* 1969 edn Methuen & Co.: London, Act 1, p. 45.
20. Thiele, C., 1976, 'Creative English in the Primary School', in Tronc, K. and Cullen, P., *Quality Education.* McGraw-Hill: Australia, p. 44.
21. For example, Getzels, J.W. and Jackson, P.W., 1962, *Creativity and Intelligence,* John Wiley & Sons. New York.
22. Blythe, T.C., 1974. 'Creative Writing', in Bassett, G.W., *Primary Education in Australia.* Angus & Robertson: Sydney, p. 178.
23. Langdon, Margaret, 1961. *Let the Children Write.* Longmans Green & Co.: London.
24. Clegg, A.B. (ed.), 1966. *The Excitement of Writing.* Chatto & Windus: London.
25. Schools Commission, *op. cit.,* foreword, p. viii.
26. Start, K.B., 1977. 'Exceptional Children'. *Report of a State Conference,* Australian College of Education, Tasmanian Chapter, p. 14.

8. Evaluation

Guidelines for Evaluation

5.1   *The major use of evaluation in schools should be for diagnostic purposes to assist students' learning. Urgent attention needs to be given to the ill effects of public examinations, particularly at the senior secondary level, and to increasing their diagnostic value for tertiary education and employment.*

5.2   *If the curriculum is planned in the form of activities to be engaged in by students rather than subject matter to be learnt by listening or reading, greater use can be made of functional evaluation and less of formal testing.*

Functional evaluation is an evaluative statement of what students actually are doing, or of what they have achieved. It reduces the need for formal tests; it overcomes the standardising effect of class tests; it is likely to be more accurate in that direct observation of performance is possible; and it lends itself more readily to detailed description for the purpose of reporting students' progress.

5.3   *Self-evaluation is a valuable aid to formative evaluation, in that it heightens the student's awareness of the quality of his own performance, and increases the likelihood of increased insight into the nature of the task. Strengthening a student's capacity for self-evaluation is essentially an educative process, and should be recognised by teachers as an important objective. The goal is to create a habit of self-criticism as well as a knowledge of standards, so that each person develops an approach to learning that enables him to apply his own quality control to his achievements.*

5.4   *Reporting a student's progress to parents is best done orally so that other information can be given about various aspects of his scholastic progress and personal development. Such interviews provide an opportunity for the parent to contribute information regarding the child's home life, and for discussion to take place*

252

about constructive measures to assist the child. The time of reporting could be staggered to avoid too great a concentration at a particular time in the year. Written reports, based on various school records, may be used to supplement interviews, or in place of them when they are not possible. Each school should adopt its own scheme of reporting because of the significant differences from school to school.

Introduction

Procedures used in evaluating students' work should be compatible with those used in planning the curriculum and teaching it, and in organising the school. In particular, when concern for the well-being of each student is the dominant feature of school planning, it should also be expressed in the way the progress of students is evaluated.

The importance of a correct approach to evaluation is apparent not only from the obvious efficiency of keeping objectives, procedures and evaluation in harmony, but also from the serious distorting effect that evaluation can have on the other processes when it is out of tune with them. Of all the elements in the round of events in schools—planning curricula, teaching, organising, and evaluating—it is evaluation that is the most influential in practice, even though it may be planned initially as a subordinate role of checking the effectiveness of the procedures adopted. The reversal of roles, whereby the evaluation determines (or significantly influences) the curriculum and how it is taught, is most apparent when evaluation is undertaken for the purpose of selection (as is the case with public examinations), and when the examinations are conducted by an authority different from the one responsible for the teaching. Under these circumstances it is not uncommon for teaching to become coaching, and the curriculum to be virtually reduced to the domain of expected examination questions.

There are other undesirable side-effects of evaluation, and it may be best to consider these before introducing what are considered to be desirable guidelines, since one obvious purpose in proposing guidelines for the use of evaluation is to avoid the harmful effects that commonly occur. Rowntree has discussed the abuses of evaluation in a comprehensive way,[1] and it will be convenient to summarise briefly his analysis. He lists eight abuses:

1. The use of stereotypes by teachers
2. Students' acceptance of stereotypes
3. Evaluation as a reward for effort
4. The encouragement of competitiveness
5. The bureaucratic aspects of evaluation

6. Over-reliance on particular examination methods
7. The inadequacy of grades in conveying information
8. The problems of reporting assessments

The Use of Stereotypes by Teachers

Teachers often hold stereotyped views of the potential of certain individuals or groups, and these expectations tend to produce a self-fulfilling prophecy. Examples are culturally disadvantaged students (e.g. Aborigines) and lower-stream students. Individual students tend to be identified with the group despite differences.

Students' Acceptance of Stereotypes

Students' own view of their prospects in school may become stereotyped by previous school experiences. The student with an adverse self-image, particularly, may be conditioned to a pattern of low achievement.

Evaluation As a Reward for Effort

The grading of work tends to create the expectation among students that work should be given an extrinsic reward rather than undertaken for its intrinsic satisfaction. Common rewards expected are material in the form of prizes, or psychological in the form of approval. Educational aims such as encouraging inquiry for its own sake, or developing the capabilities of students as a means of self-fulfilment, are distorted by this reward syndrome.

The Encouragement of Competitiveness

Although learning is a commodity available to all, the effect of grading is to bring students into competition with each other, as though one person can get more only if another gets less. Students have been led to believe that they cannot all achieve well. The strong influence of the normal distribution curve on both teachers and students has created the expectation of a pattern of performance in which a few do well, the majority do moderately, and a few do poorly. This pattern seems to hold no matter how hard individual students may work.

In a system in which only the best are chosen for scarce places in a particular school, tertiary course, or job vacancy, competition for grades seems inevitable. Teachers are caught up in it as well as students, either because they want to do the best for their students, or because they want to establish their own reputation as successful teachers.

The Bureaucratic Aspects of Evaluation

Grading makes for impersonality. Examination scripts identified only by number, external markers not known to the students and having no personal interest in them, and standardised procedures are all part of the bureaucracy of external examining. It attempts to achieve fairness by uniformity and anonymity. It makes no allowance for the fact that some students best reveal their powers—for example, of creativity, fluency, imagination, reasoning, drive, persistence, empathy—in *interpersonal* situations for which the typical examination system makes no provision.

Over-reliance on Particular Examination Methods

Over-reliance on particular assessment techniques distorts the assessment process. The dominance of essay-type questions, for example, devalues many other useful skills that children have, such as conversation, acting, etc. Multiple-choice questions, which are also popular in some quarters, encourage students to concentrate on isolated matters of detail rather than on sustained argument.

The Inadequacy of Grades in Conveying Information

Grades convey inadequate information. They are a kind of shorthand or average, smoothing out and concealing irregularities and variability. The fact that two students receive the same grade does not mean that they have performed in the same way. If the task involved is a complex one their individual performance could vary substantially.

The Problems of Reporting Assessments

There are a host of problems about how assessments should be reported to various people who have an interest in them such as parents, other teachers and employers; there is also the problem of whether there is a breach of privacy in reporting them at all. The question of confidential reporting, which is quite common in connection with applications for employment, is also somewhat controversial. Certainly if the need to report to others is accepted, there is an obligation on those responsible to report accurately and fully.

The guidelines that follow do not attempt to solve all the problems of evaluation or to remove its adverse side-effects. In fact, many of these problems lie outside the school's control, and derive from characteristics of the selection procedures for tertiary education, the award of scholarships, the criteria for employment set by external agencies, and parental and other societal groups. These pressures are legitimate in a sense, and there are few obvious alternatives open to those outside bodies; but they can be harmful when they exert an undue influence on the curriculum, the way in which students are taught, the relationships between teachers and students, and competitive attitudes among the students themselves.

But it is not surprising that in the guidelines that follow there is a much greater emphasis on the role of evaluation in making teaching more effective by helping each student to reach his fullest potential than on demonstrating how well (or how poorly) he measures up to an external standard. It is in its role as an adjunct to teaching that the essentially educational role of evaluation is evident. When used to determine the status of a student's school achievement it is fulfilling a social role rather than an educational one, or as a specialised function it meets the needs of educational research which requires measures of the performance of students so that the effects of various treatments or environments can be studied.

The critical emphasis on evaluation as an aid to teaching is examined in the first guideline.

5.1 The Importance of Evaluation As Diagnosis

The distinction was made in an earlier section between *formative* evaluation (whose purpose is to provide diagnostic information about each student) and *summative* evaluation (whose purpose is to establish a person's standing with respect to a body of knowledge or skill). The concepts are useful in distinguishing between the kinds of tests a student might be given during instruction to reveal whether he has mastered the knowledge and skill required (formative evaluation), and the test he would be given to secure a certificate at the completion of his course (summative). An obvious example is a car-driver under instruction (formative), and a car-driver taking his test for a licence (summative).

Nevertheless it should be emphasised that for educational purposes it is formative assessment that is most important, and particularly so when stress is laid on individual differences. In fact, it would not be exaggerating the point to claim that most forms of evaluation in schools should be formative in character, and that many of the examples of evaluation that are usually cited as being summative may be more profitably thought of as formative.

Examples of these are the terminal school examinations (often public examinations) that have been already discussed as leading to serious problems. When a school passes on information about a student to another institution such as a college or university it enables the tertiary institution to make informed decisions about the student, such as whether to accept or reject, which course among a number of the student preferences is most appropriate, whether bridging courses are needed to overcome gaps in the student's knowledge, and so on. This surely is using evaluation formatively. The only difference from the usual sort of example is that both school and tertiary institution are involved, rather than just a single institution. Similarly in giving information to a funding authority considering the award of a scholarship, or to an employer considering the offer of a job, the school is using evaluation formatively. The fact that there is a break between school and work or further study seems to accentuate the terminal character of the final school examination. But in fact they are continuous, and the situation is not different essentially from that in which a test is used within a single institution to inform those concerned of a student's progress.

The summative character of the public examination is made especially apparent by the award of a certificate, the use of grades in the form of letters (*A*, *B*, *C*, etc.) and numbers (7, 6, 5, etc.) the publishing of results, the secrecy in the handling of examination scripts, and other dramatic administrative details. For most students, also, it is the end of formal schooling.

Today there is a significant reappraisal of the place of formal schooling in a person's life, and there is increasing acceptance of the idea that his education is, or should be, continuing or recurring, and that the pattern of formal schooling and employment may take different forms other than the usual end-on one. These trends reduce the significance of summative assessment, and increase the significance of formative assessment, as it becomes more important to know at various stages of a person's life what he should do rather than what he has done.

If, then, these terminal examinations should be functionally more formative than summative it is fair to ask whether they do convey adequate information. The answer must surely be that they do not. They convey what subjects the student has studied, how well he has done in them as denoted by a grade, and little more. Marshall, writing about examinations at the tertiary level, has this to say about grades. It could be equally relevant, with few changes of wording, to terminal school examinations—

> Outwardly, grades are designed more as aids in administration than as factors in teaching. They furnish a shorthand for recorders, a bookkeeping system for units needed for graduation, a basis for admissions, a key to honours, a tool for discipline, and a sort of coin of the academic realm which serves in assorted ways in educational

transitions. Inwardly, grades are definitely something else. They are crumbs for the frustrated inhabitants of the pedagogic ether.[2]

Marshall was writing of a time of serious student unrest, when one of their objections was to the grading system. This egalitarian philosophy still exists, particularly among senior students, in spite of frequent reminders by parents and teachers that life outside the school is competitive.

Grades (whether compiled by schools or by public examinations) are the shortest of shorthand descriptions, and are obviously convenient, particularly for computer processing; but they hide more than they reveal, and their generally low correlation with performance in many kinds of activity engaged in at a later stage is well documented.

Is it practicable to recognise the formative function of these so-called summative tests, and use a more extended diagnostic type of reporting of students' performance for the benefit of tertiary institutions and employers? As suggested earlier, this is predominantly a social question, and it would become almost certainly a political question if pursued. It is also partly an administrative question.

One rather anguished reply could be given by quoting C.J. Morgan, a secondary school teacher, reporting his experience with progressive assessment. He describes his concern to assess and report the achievement of students in relation to their capacity, and not to the same standard, so that less able students working well would have the taste of success (a literal mark of *A* meaning 'excellent' for a particular student). He concludes in this way:

> There is nothing to stop my lowering my correlation between literal and numerical marks still further, so that at least the end of term unit profile continues to reflect effort and achievement *within the limits of academic capacity*. But it is a fantasy world. The real world, as represented by institutions of further education, employers and the body governing the territory's schools is interested only in the standardised numerical mark.[3]

Another reply is that extended descriptive, interpretive and evaluative statements could be supplied about each candidate either in place of, or in addition to grading. If it were done as a substitute for grading it would leave the tertiary institutions unable to rank the candidates and unable to select on a basis that they could defend. If it were done as a supplement to grading it would create fairly severe administrative problems for schools to compile them and post-school authorities to use them, although the value of the procedure would be substantial.

An obvious solution (and probably the only one that would be satisfactory on educational grounds) is for tertiary institutions to have an open entry (or one based on some kind of minimum standards) and to make use of the process of self-selection that would be inherent in the system. Employers basically use this self-selection procedure, employing staff on probation, and seeing how well they perform; although they do attempt also to predict success. This 'solution' would have major implications for the costs of tertiary education, and probably would appear to be wasteful. Predicting success and the control of admissions through quotas are obviously economical measures, and have a strong appeal to governments, particularly when they have to pay the bill.

This question of the character of terminal examinations and the problems associated with prediction of future progress and selection for tertiary education have been pursued at some length, even though somewhat inconclusively. This is merited because of their high ranking among important, but intractable problems in evaluation in schools, particularly at the secondary level.

The question of diagnostic testing for purposes that are clearly practicable can now be pursued more directly.

Trow has used the term *illuminative evaluation* to describe a kind of evaluation that attempts to designate and interpret a complex of events and behaviour comprehensively from all the relevant viewpoints and contextual factors that determine its character.[4] The concept has been developed mainly in connection with the evaluation of curricula or other innovatory projects, and takes account not only of intended effects but also of unexpected effects, including reactions of those involved. This evaluation model does seem to be very appropriate in a situation in which the possibility of experimentation (in the sense of setting up a contrived situation, as would be possible in the physical and biological sciences) is limited, and where it is usually not possible to control variables other than those being studied. It is analogous to stopping a moving film to study more closely the detail of a particular point in its progress.

This type of evaluation can be applied profitably to the evaluation of students' progress. It is formative in that it provides information to the teacher to assist him in helping to plan each student's work. An illuminative evaluation in a particular case might provide information about the level of mastery of particular skills, understanding of particular concepts, or memorisation of required factual knowledge; it might provide evidence of specific misunderstandings or other defects in required performance; it might provide the degree of progress for *that student* in relation to past achievement; it might provide information about the student's attitudes to the work concerned, either favourable or unfavourable; and it might identify sources and types of assistance required (homework, remedial teaching, library work, etc.).

It is thus much more informative than merely a test result, and could be used by a teacher to help guide the student through the curriculum, and to make intelligent judgements about the nature and timing of support services where help is needed. It strengthens and extends his knowledge of each student taught and assists him to plan the classroom effectively so that each student is profitably employed. In short, it is an integral part of teaching strategy.

How many students can be effectively handled in this intimate way is problematic. Clearly the teachers of younger children can do it, whether working in an open-plan school or in a single classroom. Some secondary school-teachers are obliged to handle a great many students for relatively short periods in a week. Obviously their problem in building up this information is greater. Since the use of formative evaluation and the knowledge that it gives about individual children is a basic element in efficient teaching, it would be appropriate for school administrators to try to avoid giving teachers too heavy a load of students rather than to shrug off the treating of students individually as impracticable. Of the alternatives of increasing the teacher's specialised teaching (and thus increasing the number of students taught) and increasing his range of subjects taught (and thus making it possible for his range of students to be decreased), the second is much to be preferred, provided the teacher has the necessary competence.

How is the necessary information to be obtained? Personality characteristics can be inferred from observation, provided the teacher has some understanding of child behaviour, is interested enough in his students to want to find out about them, and gives himself the opportunity to meet them at a personal level. Individualised methods allow him to talk to students during lessons, and he can also make informal contacts with them outside. This homespun approach to personality diagnosis may, of course, be very wide of the mark in particular cases. As pointed out in Chapter 2, the teacher needs to know when to seek help from school counsellors and other specialists.

Information about students' handling of cognitive and psychomotor elements of school tasks can be gained from observation and from tests. The value of treating the curriculum so that students' progress is more open to direct observation without any kind of formal test is substantial. The point is elaborated in *5.2*.

Tests involve some kind of measurement and may be made up by the teacher, or by research groups working on statewide or national samples, and providing norms with which the teacher may compare his students. Both are useful, but for most teachers the *ad hoc* test made up by himself, and closely related to his teaching, is the most commonly used, and probably the best. Specialists such as remedial teachers and counsellors need to have access to more sophisticated diagnostic tests, but for the classroom teacher the occasional use only of standardised tests is merited. It is beyond the scope of this book to deal with the technical aspects of test construction and the handling of test scores. This type of information is available in well-known texts,[5] and there is no need to pursue it here. The point to emphasise is that tests, whatever form they take, should be designed to explore the student's handling of a problem rather than to pronounce judgement on him.

It is important that the teacher understand this, but it is equally important that the student understand it also. Because of the history of testing, which predominantly has been summative in spirit, the typical expectation of students (and parents) is that tests are given in order to demonstrate the students' progress. Students should know why they are doing a test, and what use will be made of it. Where terminal schemes of testing have been replaced by progressive testing and the results are used summatively, an expectation often develops in students that all tests are evaluative in this sense. A corollary of this, which is most unfortunate, is that there may develop an attitude of reluctance on the part of students to do any tests unless some mark is awarded that will count towards their final grade. Under these circumstances progressive assessment can have a stultifying effect on school programmes, turning what should be a stimulating and pleasant experience into a series of petty hurdles undertaken in a pervasive spirit of anxiety.

We conclude this section, then, where we began. Evaluation is educationally desirable if it assists the student to learn; the greatest emphasis, then, should be on formative evaluation.

5.2 Formal versus Functional Evaluation

In an earlier section (*3.3*) the distinction was made between formal and functional modes of curriculum structure. The formal mode was described in terms of the prepositions, generalisations, relationships, defined terminology and structure of the traditional school subjects. The functional mode was described in terms of activities in which students engage in a naturally occurring or contrived setting. These activities might be simple, such as writing a letter, or complex, like exploring the social environment of a village school.

This distinction was expressed also in terms of teaching method (in *4.3*), the formal type of curriculum requiring didactic teaching and relying heavily on impression as the major form of student response (listening, watching, imitating, etc.). The functional mode, by contrast, relies on expression, the student learning by practice, by the application of methods of inquiry, or by various creative activities.

The distinction is carried further in this section, by relating it to evaluation. Formal evaluation involves the setting of a test (written or oral) which requires the student to demonstrate factual knowledge, understanding, or skill. Functional evaluation is a judgement made on the quality of some performance (completed or in progress) without involving any special provision for testing.

Just as it has been argued that a functional approach to curriculum and method is the most appropriate way of involving each student in school tasks, and of relating what each does to his unique pattern of aptitudes and interests, so it would follow consistently that functional evaluation is to be preferred for most purposes over formal evaluation. Whether it is feasible or not depends on how the curriculum is presented and carried out. One can formally test a student's skill or knowledge, however it is acquired; but one can test it functionally only if it is acquired through the student's own activity.

There are obvious advantages in using functional evaluation, although it is acknowledged that some formal testing is useful. These advantages are listed, and subsequently briefly commented on, as follows:

1. It reduces the need for frequent formal tests.
2. It overcomes the standardising effect of class tests.
3. It is likely to be more accurate because of the congruence between teaching and testing.
4. It lends itself to more detailed description for the purpose of reporting.

Reduction of the Need for Frequent Formal Tests

There is no need for tests if the progress of students' work is self-revealing. If they are engaged on tasks that are open to observation it must be clear to a teacher how well they are doing them. What may not be clear can be elicited easily by a few oral questions (a more sophisticated form of this at tertiary level is the *viva voce* test of a thesis).

A few examples may make the point clearer:

1. A child's reading achievement can be effectively judged provided there are adequate opportunities for him to be heard; his interest in reading and his level of sophistication can be judged by the number and type of books read; and his understanding of what

is read can be assessed if reading is functionally related to other tasks, e.g. following instructions in cooking, the care of animals, the construction of objects by the assembling of components, the carrying out of studies in social science, science, and the arts. These are much more realistic assessments than can be secured from the formal tests of reading that are usually used.

2. Writing (calligraphy) can obviously be evaluated by inspection; and writing (composition, style, formal accuracy, etc.) can be similarly evaluated provided the methods of teaching allow scope for the child to write, and for samples of his work to be easily accessible.

3. Mathematics can also be assessed by reference to work covered. If students are working progressively from prepared materials at their own rates, their progress is obvious, and can be reported accurately without a formal test.

4. Achievement in social science and science is open to observation if the student is working on an environmental or laboratory study. His skill in handling equipment (if this were involved), his understanding of the problem and its implications, his capacity for planning the inquiry or co-operating with others, his grasp of appropriate methods, his skill and ingenuity in the modes of reporting, etc., are all directly assessable.

5. The more obviously practical subjects, involving handling of wood, metal, textiles, cooking ingredients, typewriter and other equipment, and the arts such as drama, singing, orchestral work, physical education, dancing, painting, etc., are clearly open to observation, and hence to direct assessment.

This informal mode of assessment reduces the need for the frequent testing which does seem to occur in schools. If tests are used as incentives for study, the substitution of informal evaluation for them, of course, is less likely to work. Informal evaluation assumes that the main dynamic of the curriculum is interest. But to the extent that knowledge of results is a spur to endeavour, the immediate and self-revealing nature of functional evaluation is likely to provide as much motivation as the formal test.

Overcoming the Standardising Effect of Class Tests

Formal tests, whether prepared by the teacher, or by an outside body, are usually set for a whole class, and success is judged by each child's reaction to the standard requirements of the test. Such tests may have some diagnostic power, but the conditions under which they are administered tend rather to accentuate their role of grading and ranking the class. More than anything they measure the inability of some of the students to meet their requirements. The same tests, when used with an individual student, may be quite useful diagnostically, but it is less usual for them to be used in this way by teachers.

Likelihood of Increased Accuracy

When teaching is conceived as input, and testing as output, the chances of disparity between the expectations of the teacher and of the tester are high. This is particularly so when they are different people. But even when the teacher sets his own tests, his understanding of what he has taught that he builds into his tests may differ substantially from what has been taught as interpreted by at least some of his students. If novel features are included in the test with the idea of finding out how well the student can apply what is taught in a new situation, the gap between teaching and testing is even greater. What the student's performance in the test actually means under these circumstances is difficult to say, but he is usually not given the benefit of any doubt about the worth of his answer.

When teaching is done through expressive activities, performance and evaluation are closer together. There may, of course, be a difference in the evaluator's criteria of judgement and the performer's objectives, but in the realistic situation envisaged, when performance and evaluation are virtually contemporaneous it is quite possible for the student and the teacher to exchange ideas about criteria and reach a higher level of mutual understanding. Moreover it is what the student achieves that is evaluated, not his reactions to the limits set by the test. Creative students may complete a task with quite novel and unexpected results, and these may be its most worthwhile features.

Lending Itself to More Detailed Description

Evaluation of work by direct observation lends itself much more readily to illuminative evaluation than does formal testing. Because of its individual character all relevant detail can be noted. This might include such matters as the speed at which it was done, the attitude of the student towards the task (his confidence, satisfaction, regard for standards, etc.), his resourcefulness, and the care taken to seek resources needed for the task. These factors in school achievement are virtually eliminated under the usual test conditions, yet they are the very features which anyone interested in the student, such as a parent or employer, would want to know. Examples of some personal types of evaluation are given in a later section dealing with reporting (5.4).

5.3. Self-Evaluation

Evaluation is usually conceived as an independent act of diagnosis or judgement by one person of another, but it may also be self-evaluation. While, at first glance, the essential quality of objectivity is lost if a person is allowed to be his own assessor, there can be substantial benefits from self-evaluation because of its contribution to formative evaluation.

In a sense all evaluation has its roots in self-evaluation. Through the experience of relating one's achievement to effort and skill, and comparing this experience to that of others (either known personally, or through report) a repertoire of criteria and standards is progressively built up. It is on tnis basis that a person attempts to evaluate the achievement of others.

Strengthening a student's capacity for self-evaluation is essentially an educative process, and should be recognised by teachers as an important objective. The goal is to create a habit of self-criticism, as well as an awareness of standards, so that each person can develop an approach to learning that enables him to apply his own quality-control to his achievements.

This is less likely to be achieved if the responsibility for evaluation always lies with the teacher. The teacher's own standards, and his access to the wider range of standards embodied in formal knowledge, are a rich resource for students, as are books, other media, and other adults, but these are likely to be most useful to students who have grappled with the task of judging their own performance. The desirable process, then, by which self-knowledge grows is one of interaction in which recognition by the student of his own inadequacies, strengths and uncertainties, and constructive criticism by the teacher are both involved. Children do need models of performance, but they are likely to see the point of them when they have a better appreciation of their own standards.

Self-evaluation involves affective as well as cognitive elements. Ideally, it should be objective. A person should be able to assess his own achievements without bias, even though he may lack the knowledge to assess them accurately. Probably such people are rare. One is more likely to find under-confidence or over-confidence among students, and these traits need to be taken into account in helping them in self-evaluation.

The under-confident student, faced with self-evaluation, is likely to be self-effacing, and to react to the task with uncertainty. His sense of inferiority is made explicit by such an exercise. The over-confident student is likely to believe, wrongly, that he is coping with his schoolwork, or to be satisfied with slapdash work. He is likely to work erratically, and generally below his aptitude level. Both need to be handled carefully.

The practical steps that the teacher may take to increase the students' own responsibility for evaluation will depend on his own ingenuity, and on the task involved.

In arithmetic the student might be asked to make an estimate of the answer to a problem and check it with the obtained answer. Those who have little awareness of the appropriateness of the way the problem has been tackled may obtain an answer with an absurd order of magnitude without appearing to notice it.

In written work emphasis could be placed on proof-reading, and a game made of it by using a number of different judges in the search for formal errors. The use of peer evaluation could be associated closely with self-evaluation. Both emphasise the need for the student's alertness to the quality of his work before the judgemental role of the teacher is involved.

Children could be asked to assign a mark to a piece of work, e.g. a painting, and give a verbal statement explaining and justifying it. This provides a basis for discussion with the teacher and eliminates much of the apparent arbitrariness of assessment.

These are intended only as examples. For teachers who see the value of increasing their students' responsibility for judging the value of their own work, there will be many opportunities.

5.4. *Reporting*

> Tanya is a very dreamy child and I am never sure whether she is really concentrating or whether she is dreaming. In spite of this her work is good, especially her reading and written expression. She often falls down badly in word knowledge and spelling but again I feel this is lack of concentration rather than lack of ability or knowledge. She shows very little interest in Mathematics and this is her weakest subject. Tanya mixes well with other children, but I would like to see her assert her individuality a little more and not simply follow someone's lead.[6]

This report on a primary school pupil is quoted as an example of a report to parents that is informative and personal. Its intimate character is very different from the sort of report that looks like a score-card, and treats the child as a statistical entity. Other information of a more formal kind might also be supplied to the parent, but the pen picture of Tanya, with its attention to personality and social development as well as achievement and aptitude, conveys the important message that the teacher and the school care about her as a person.

For Tanya's parents, however, even this report may have its limitations. Can Tanya's concentration be improved? Should some special steps be taken with her Mathematics? (Her difficulty with this subject has been noted at home, but the kind of work she does is unfamiliar to her parents and it has not been easy to help her.) What kind of behaviour did the teacher have in mind in suggesting that she assert her individuality more? (Actually this comment is puzzling, as at home she is rather bossy with the other children.) It is clear that in this case a meeting between teacher and parent is needed. The major reason for a school report to parents is to carry formative evaluation a stage further by enlisting the help of the home, and in an interview the contribution of both teacher and parent can lead to greater insight into the child's behaviour than would be possible otherwise. What the parent can tell the teacher about the child's reaction to school—her personal and social growth as evidenced in the house setting, and special domestic problems that might have influenced her schoolwork—is a necessary complement to what the teacher can tell the parent about her life in school. Both teacher and parent are better informed by such an interview, and the child is the beneficiary.

In individualising reporting a discussion between teacher and parent is the most desirable form of communication. There are, of course, practical difficulties in doing this on a large scale—finding a time suitable to both teacher and parent, the reluctance of some parents to come to school and the reluctance of some teachers to give the extra time needed, working mothers, migrant families with language difficulties, etc.—but none of them is insuperable.

Perhaps the strongest barrier to change is the persistence of the traditional view of the role of reporting which historically has been linked with the grade system of progression. The end-of-year examination and report was an essential part of the administrative machinery of annual promotions. Today, however, these transfer points from year to year, and the transition from primary to secondary school, are much less critical. Even the term *grade* has been officially abandoned by the state education authorities in favour of *year*—a significant indication of greater acceptance of the continuity of progression through school.

In these changed circumstances the end-of-year (term or semester) assessments and reports are less necessary. It should be possible to report to parents at any time, or as the need arises several times in the year. In some cases it would be most appropriate to report early in the year when it is apparent that a student is not reacting well to a new teacher or a new subject. If it is accepted that it is not necessary to report on all the students at the same time, the practical task of reporting in a more informative way, and of conducting interviews is made much easier.

The discussion has centred on reports to parents, but reports are necessary also for other teachers (either in the same school or in another school to which the student has transferred) and for employers. Both of these should attempt to capture the uniqueness of each student in the same spirit as the report to parents, but the details would differ. The teacher-to-teacher report would be a more technical document giving a cumulative record of the student's status in the various subjects, details of any standardised tests given and comments on significant personal qualities, special interests or abilities. The report to employers is most meaningful in terms of the particular kind of work involved. A statement of examination results may tell an employer some of the things he wants to know, but it does little to advise him how well the student may cope with the job in question. Most employers attempt to seek this personal knowledge for themselves in an interview.

In concluding this section the point should be stressed that the problem of reporting is one that each school should approach in its own way. A school with a large migrant population of parents cannot report in the same way as a school in a middle-class suburb; a school for Aboriginal children needs its own methods; a secondary school needs a different approach from a primary school or a school for handicapped children, and so on. Moreover it should be approached in an experimental way—a way that the staff of a particular school thinks is worth trying. The principle is common to all—the need to report *personally*, in a way that is *informative, diagnostic,* and *constructive*; but there is no one best way.

References

1. Rowntree, D. 1977, *Assessing Students: How Shall We Know Them,* Harper & Row: London.
2. Marshall, M.S., 1968, *Teaching Without Grades,* Oregon State University Press: Corvallis, Oreg., p. 97.
3. Morgan, C.J., Pangs of Conscience—My First Year with Continuous Assessment, Unpublished paper.
4. Trow, M.A., 1970, 'Methodological Problems in the Evaluation of Instruction', in Wittrock, M.C. and Wiley, D.E. (eds) *Problems in the Evaluation of Instruction,* Holt, Rinehart & Winston: New York, pp. 289–305.
5. For example, Lindvall, C.M. and Nitko, A.J., 1975, *Measuring Pupil Achievement and Aptitude,* 2nd ed., Harcourt Brace Jovanovich: New York.
6. Wilson, N., 1972. *Assessment in the Primary School,* Research and Planning Branch, Department of Education: South Australia, p. 44.

Conclusion

This conclusion is brief, and is intended only to indicate that the task attempted in this book is now finished. Not that it has given a complete picture of all the subtleties of individual differences, or of the steps that teachers can take to deal with them in their planning. Both of these tasks are encyclopedic in scope. The pedagogical one, moreover, being open to different philosophical interpretations, is complex and controversial.

The outlook that has guided the formulation of the guidelines presented is that differences among students need to be recognised and provided for, both for the increased efficiency that this gives to pedagogy, and also for the enrichment of personal and social life.

If we can trust the evidence of Bloom, the prospects for increased efficiency are good. He claims that, provided the outcomes sought in education are pitched at a realistic level, achieving equality of outcomes for 95 per cent of students is 'a realistic possibility for most teachers who carefully and systematically apply appropriate instructional means to student differences'.[1]

The goal of personal and societal enrichment is not quite so clear cut. To quote Bloom again—

> But, the issue in the long run is not a cost-benefit analysis of school learning and the conditions under which a particular set of results may be obtained. The central issue is what is worth learning in the schools and the means by which the student's motivation and capabilities are fully engaged in the learning process.[2]

The interpretation in earlier chapters of what is 'worth learning' places strong emphasis on what is of value for each person. It thus stresses learning for personal satisfaction as well as for social and vocational efficiency, and creativity as well as conformity.

This stress on individuality is a little out of fashion at present. 'Cost-benefit' and 'accountability' are more in vogue. Individuality tends to be interpreted as eccentricity, or even as social irresponsibility. It is true, of course, that stressing qualitative differences in students is likely

269

to increase diversity of outlook among the population, but any sort of education does this to some degree. Teaching a child to read exposes him to a new world of ideas, for good or ill.

But an emphasis on teaching children individually need not only accelerate cultural pluralism; it can also strengthen respect for disciplined thought and inquiry and sensitiveness to humane values, and these should act as a counterpoise to social division. A society in which individual talent and skill are cultivated to the full, and in which at the same time (and virtually by the same process) a community of significant social values is built is both enriched and stabilised. It is accountability for this that we should strive for in our teaching.

References

1. Bloom, B.S., 1976. *Human Characteristics and School Learning.* McGraw-Hill: p. 216.
2. *Ibid.*, p. 214.

Author Index

271

Index

274

school organisation 14–5, 17, 152–3; evaluation of 18–20; for curriculum, related to school organisation 190–7; self-evaluation as 252, 265–6
educational opportunity 8–11
educational perspective on individual differences 13–26
educational philosophy 1, 13, 129, 191; and individual differences 21–6
educational practice; element of judgement in 2–3
efficiency in education 13–21, 26
ego 42–4
electronic equipment 179
elementary—see primary
emergent values 38–9
emotion 99
emotional; climate 97; control 101; development 75, 115 [of culturally deprived 143–4]; disorder (x), 75ff (chap.) [and learning retardation, disability 75; recognition of 79–80]; freedom, and learning 79; needs 3; privation or trauma 80–1; stability 64
empathic understanding—as teacher attitude 225–7
employers, report to 268
employment 11–2; evaluation for 252, 258
enactive representation 92, 96, 100, 242–3
encouragement 64, 97–8
endogenous variables 42
England (see also Britain) 64, 155, 177, 227
English (language), standard vs. non-standard 108–9, 114
environment 24, 107, 237; and heredity 110–2; and race 112–4; blended with experience, and curriculum 206–8, 210; control of 33; distal 46–61; proximal 61–7
environmental influences in behaviour 3, 16, 30–1, 90–1; origins of personality characteristics in 46–7
equal outcomes 10
equality of opportunity (x), 8–11, 20–1; process of education in 9
equipment 10, 152, 178–81; electronic 179
ethnic groups (see also minorities); and cognitive and linguistic functioning 112–4; determining personality characteristics 47–53
ethnocentric individual 40
Europe 47, 54
evaluation (ix), (x), 14, 19–20, 117, 150; abuses of 253–5; as reward for effort 254; by peers 266; bureaucratic aspects of 255; educational role of 256; external pressures on 255–6; formative 202, 252, 256–61, 265, 266–7; functional 252 [vs. formal 261–4]; guidelines for 252ff

(chap.); illuminative 259–60, 264; internal vs. external 203; of objectives and procedures 196; of teachers 165; related to school organisation 201–4; self- 252, 265–6; studies 2
examination 65, 199, 201–3, 252, 253, 255–61; essay type 255; final public 257; formative vs. summative 202–3, 252, 256–61; multiple choice 255
excursions 195
existential goals of teaching 227
existential knowledge, process 205–8; in curriculum catering for individual differences 218–20
existentialism 7, 24
expectations 16, 30; and parent-child interactions 64–5; and school-student interactions 67; concepts of 41; ethnic variability in 51–2; in classroom 41–2; individual differences in 42; social class variability in 55–6; teacher's, of pupils 98
experience 7, 45–6; blended with environment, and curriculum 206–8
exploratory behaviour 44
expression; teaching methods stimulating 238–42; vs. impression 221, 238–9, 261–2
expression, written 5, 240–1
extended family 49

facilities 2, 3, 146, 152, 178–81; school, use by community 138, 150
failure, fear of 14, 32–3, 35, 41–2, 45, 67, 79, 81, 96, 98, 157, 230–1; due to lack of teacher understanding 109
family (x), 14, 43, 52–3, 61; and child guidance clinic 83–4; and language 107; child's view of 69; 'dope' 81; extended—see extended; grouping 177; nuclear—see nuclear; structure 56–7, 113. 114
fear of failure—see failure
federal government 9; influence in education (Australia) 136
field independence-dependence 100, 242
film 17
five-year-old 44
'Follow Through' 142
foreign cultures 211
formal modes of curriculum structure; vs. functional 213–8
formal operations period of intelligence 92–4
formative examination 202, 252, 256–61
foster home 82
free society 12
freedom, need for 7, 25, 26, 56
friendliness 39
frustration-tolerance 69